Television and the News

7

TELEVISION AND THE NEWS

A CRITICAL APPRAISAL

HARRY J. SKORNIA

PACIFIC BOOKS, PUBLISHERS   Palo Alto, California

First Pacific Books Paperbound edition, 1974.
International Standard Book Number 0-87015-209-2.
Library of Congress Catalog Card Number 68-8629.
Printed and bound in the United States of America.

PACIFIC BOOKS, PUBLISHERS
P. O. Box 558
Palo Alto, California 94302

*To the late Edward R. Murrow
and the many fine and dedicated newsmen of America,
whose lot this book seeks to make easier,
so the people of America may be better informed.*

Acknowledgments

The author is indebted to the several hundred individuals and organizations, credited in footnotes, who generously provided the abundance of materials used in this book.

For their cooperation, generosity, confidence, and permissions to use materials they controlled, sincere thanks are hereby acknowledged.

Contents

1

Introduction

This book is dedicated to broadcasting's newsmen, and to the news and public affairs service essential to democracy.

Speaking to alumni December 29, 1965, Dean Edward Barrett of Columbia's Graduate School of Journalism, while recognizing that "our journalism is at a higher level than ever in history," nevertheless noted that there is "in and out of the profession, a widespread uneasiness about the state of journalism. The School shares this uneasiness, not over any supposed deterioration, but over the probability that journalism is not yet a match for the complications of our age."

While this concern includes the print media, as we shall soon note, many of the most serious problems exist in broadcast journalism. "Rip-and-read" reporting, plagiarism from other media, selection of the visual over the significant, over-emphasis on firstness or fastness, preference for the obvious, conflict, or violence, sponsor and industry censorship or taboos, and similar problems, illustrate some of the most dangerous of the practices which peculiarly affect the broadcast media.

In an address August 26, 1963, Judge Lee Loevinger, later a member of the Federal Communications Commission, said: "Since it is the journalistic function which gives the principal social value to broadcasting, I would measure performance principally by the degree to which it performs this function."

We too rarely realize the real value and importance of news and information in our daily lives. We vaguely understand that information is essential to citizen decision-making, which is the life-blood of democracy. Erwin Canham of the *Christian Science Monitor* has said: "Without information, people cannot rise to the grave decisions they face in this crisis-laden period, nor take them with sufficient wisdom."[1] And these decisions are made on the basis of what Walter

Lippmann has called the pictures in our heads, which we think constitute reality.

Too little realized, however, is the fact that news, or orientation to reality, is essential to the happiness and emotional balance of democratic man. "Disorientation" is one of the things we have most to fear. John De Mott has said:

> Every newsman is practicing psychiatry without a license. He's manipulating the mental state of thousands of his fellow citizens every day, with or without any knowledge of mental hygiene and its principles.

He goes on:

> When newsmen talk about the public's need to know, they're usually talking, it appears, about the need for political news. . . .
> Regardless of a man's personality, his politics, his economics, his religion, or his sociology, he has a psychological need to know. And that need can be frustrated only with serious consequences.[2]

Undoubtedly news and public affairs programs represent what U.S. television and radio do best. Millions of dollars and thousands of people are devoted to them. U.S. networks have many correspondents abroad. Over half of these correspondents, disturbingly, were until recently* in Europe, with less than half in all the rest of the world together: Asia, Australia, Africa, and Latin America. Is that proper distribution and orientation?

There is increasing evidence that Americans are still not receiving from TV and radio the diversity and depth of news, clarification and interpretation of the right type, from the right places, that they need for responsible decision-making. This book examines the causes of certain weaknesses and failures of this nature and proposes some possible improvements for public and industry consideration.

Unless they live abroad, or have access to foreign publications or broadcasts, few Americans have any standards against which to measure or compare the service we now receive. Nor do they have any way of knowing how many happenings in the nation or world are never reported, and therefore never reach the status of "news" because of various industrial, government, or human policies or prob-

---

* A report at press time estimated that there were approximately two hundred correspondents for U.S. media (not all U.S. citizens) in Viet Nam covering that conflict.

lems. Many of these are not intentional and many are unconsciously practiced. They are nonetheless real.

The reconcilability of news and advertising, as they co-exist uniquely in radio and TV under sponsorship systems, is still one of our greatest and most difficult problems. John de J. Pemberton, Jr., Executive Director of the American Civil Liberties Union, has raised the question of their compatibility. "An idea's capacity to win acceptance in the market place of ideas is simply not the same quality as that which will enable it to sell hair spray."[3] Pemberton is disturbed lest "private-sector control will not alone suffice to assure free speech." Disturbing as it is to raise such questions about present practices, it would appear desirable to begin "no-holds-barred" discussions of all kinds of changes, if our political and broadcasting systems are to be flexible enough and dynamic enough to keep us abreast of the imperative questions that confront us nationally and internationally.

In his article for *Life* magazine's National Purpose series in 1960, Albert Wohlstetter, who was then National Defense Specialist for the Rand Corporation, declared: "I doubt that the public of this country was ever less informed on matters directly affecting its life and death."[4] Surely, in an age of television, such a situation, if true, is intolerable. Three years later, in 1963, Ralph Ingersoll, former editor of *PM,* declared, regarding the press generally in America: ". . . its record to date has been a sorry one—at least if judged by results. Clearly there has been something basically the matter with our source material that, using it, we have come up with so many, and so consistently, wrong answers."[5]

Broadcast leaders, of course, can justly point out that broadcasting is only one of the press media, and therefore cannot be blamed for all or even most of the press failures alluded to. However, since broadcasters frequently claim that their media are the primary ones in keeping America informed, they cannot escape a large share of responsibility for the present situation. For example, the Television Information Office, the public relations arm of the National Association of Broadcasters, reported in January, 1964, the result of a study it had employed Elmo Roper and Associates to conduct. According to this study, 55 per cent of the people consulted reported that they got most of their news from television; 53 per cent credited newspapers and 29 per cent, radio, as primary sources of news. When asked which source they considered the most believable, 36 per cent chose television, 24 per cent listed newspapers, and 12 per cent listed radio. In the "least believable" category, 30 per cent listed newspapers, 26 per cent mentioned magazines, 10 per cent radio, and 7 per cent television.

Although these figures have been questioned by various research and newspaper studies since then, apparently the American public, or at least those Americans queried by Elmo Roper and Associates, believe that they *are* getting the news, and that television and radio are providing it, as the industry says it is doing.

A sounder situation than that in which the various media argue over which is the primary, dominant, or major source of news, would be one in which we recognize the importance of all: TV, radio, newspapers, magazines, and so on—all for different reasons and different kinds of understanding, and with different types of limitations. Since the collective total of information of all the networks' output of a single day would fill only a few columns of the front page of the average daily newspaper, if "the people" are relying on anything as incomplete and over-simplified as that, alone, even the distinguished Walter Cronkite warns us that we are likely to be dangerously uninformed. The world is full of many significant happenings every day (other than the crime, violence, and accident news now likely to predominate)—vastly more than can be contained in so limited a time or space. Certainly television and radio together constitute potentially if not actually powerful instruments of communication. Since TV and radio have captured the time and attention of the public, keeping Americans informed is an inescapable responsibility of broadcasting if it is to serve the public interest.

As unique instruments of instantaneous communication, in fact, radio and television, properly used, should bridge the gulfs that separate peoples and nations. If television and radio are to function as democratic instruments of two-way communication rather than one-way or totalitarian instruments of indoctrination, they must provide channels for, and constantly stimulate, dialogue not only between nations but also between generations, and among the many social, racial, religious, and economic groups within the nation, and between the Establishment and those citizen groups whose watchfulness and criticism are essential to keeping the total national body itching and healthy. This dialogue, however disturbing it may be to the Establishment which controls broadcasting, must be kept free and uncensored. Democracy's very life depends on this. No nation can long survive on a regimen of self-deception, misinformation, or "facts" from which unpalatable truths—by any criteria whatever—are withheld.

The First Amendment, forbidding censorship, was designed to guarantee the freedom to unlock all kinds of ideas for argument, debate, and free circulation. It was intended to prevent not only government interference with free discourse, but *any* interference with the free flow of the new ideas that democracy needs to survive.

There is increasing evidence, however, that this function of broadcasting, as press, has broken down under various kinds of pressures. The reasons for this failure need to be openly recognized, identified, and corrected. There is increasing and alarming evidence regarding many of the nation's most urgent problems, that too often there is no real dialogue between people and government or people and industry —only monologue or "pronouncements," or handouts. Although some of these obstacles to the great dialogue are traceable to government, as we shall note presently, and these, like others, must be removed, some of the most dangerous appear to come not from government but from broadcast media controllers and their sponsors. Can journalism, press, or news functions in the "pure" form needed survive at all, surrounded, interrupted, and interpenetrated with advertising and public relations elements and pressures, as they are in the broadcast media under current practices?

At his address for the Elmer Davis Memorial in 1966, David Brinkley mentions one of the problems which plague broadcast news.

> We have no models to follow, no traditions to accept or reject, and so we have haltingly and fitfully taken what flimsy traditions there were in the media that gave us birth—from the marriage that may have been illegal and certainly was immoral.
>
> From its dubious parentage, television has inherited both the dominant and recessive genes of such movie and radio ancestors as Sam Goldwyn and the A. and P. Gypsies. Of Clark Gable and Amos 'n Andy. Of Cecil B. deMille and the Fitch Bandwagon. Of Fox Movietone Newsreels covering beauty contests and radio commentary by such diverse personalities as Raymond Swing and Fulton Lewis, as Ed Murrow and Gabriel Heatter, and as Elmer Davis and Father Coughlin.
>
> In about 15 years, we have come from nothing to news programs that are a pretty good summary of the biggest of the news, fair and factual, reasonably imaginative, and all in color. But there is far more to be done and done better. . . .

Instead of the open market place of ideas, broadcasting has too often become a controlled arena in which only certain kinds of problems are presented under the spotlight of public attention. Indeed there is some evidence that the proprietors of the electronic media and their corporate friends and sponsors, whenever possible, would prefer to present only facts that will not adversely disturb their status quo—those facts which they find it profitable to present. What would profit their competitors, or competing social or economic groups—such as labor, education, small business, agriculture, and so on—is too often "censored."

A broadcast system operated largely by firms with huge defense contracts which find the cold war, the space race, and high preparedness and armament budgets profitable, for example, can hardly be expected to be favorable to the promotion of peace, or peace groups, even in an age when war is madness. How many readers, in fact, would find it possible to be this altruistic in a similar situation? No implication or accusation of villainy is intended here. But there is a problem. No wonder the image of peace-marchers and demonstrators is so frequently a negative one in so much television and radio reporting.

Unfortunately many critics have lost sight of the fact that when industry itself fights off government dictation, and then sets up its own so-called codes, this is not *resistance* to censorship; it is censorship itself; it is merely the assumption of the function of censorship by private rather than public agencies. Numerous illustrations of this practice will be noted in a later chapter.

Repeatedly, as we look back on the reporting of news from Communist China, Viet Nam, and in the areas of economics and national resources, television and radio seem to have broadcast much wishful thinking rather than facts. This is less disruptive of the buying and spending habits of Americans. Broadcasting's failure to report the strength and growth of enemies, or the storm signals from many areas, however, has left Americans unprepared time after time for the crises and realities to come: the bitter resentment of the Japanese to our atomic tests and fall-out in the 1950's; the solid growth of Soviet science and education, later dramatized by Sputnik; the withholding of many kinds of desegregation news by Southern stations, which thereby fail to help promote the slow adjustments and maturation needed in their coverage areas; the implication for years that Red China was on the verge of collapse; the continued optimistic reporting for years of a deteriorating situation in Viet Nam; concealment generally of alarming depletion of the mineral, water, and other resources of the United

States, resulting from wasteful industrial practices—these illustrate the withholding from Americans of facts they need to have if they are to make the correct decisions and face the national and international facts of life.

These facts have not always been *deliberately* withheld, of course, although later sections will illustrate many instances of deliberate withholding of information under the rubrics of censorship, taboos, or black-listing. In more typical cases, however, inadequate performance is traceable less to deliberate policy than to short-sighted and often well-intentioned vetoes or blockages based on ignorance or poor judgment, lack of reportorial freedom, training, experience, or independence, and the lack of adequately trained professional personnel with the professional courage or opportunity to refuse to do or say certain things.

Lest readers believe that only outsiders are concerned over the dangerous failures of TV and radio as news media, it is well to note, before proceeding further, the declarations and warnings of some of our most respected broadcast newsmen themselves, as well as David Brinkley, quoted earlier. In each case, it is significant to note, these declarations were not nationally *broadcast,* but were delivered to smaller groups, in person, a fact which in itself graphically illustrates broadcasting's problem as a censor, and its sensitivity to self-criticism on the air.

When he was still with CBS, the late Edward R. Murrow, speaking to his news colleagues in Chicago in 1958, said:

> . . . If there are any historians about fifty or a hundred years from now, and there should be preserved the kinescopes for one week of all three networks, they will there find recorded in black-and-white or color, evidence of decadence, escapism, and insulation from the realities of the world in which we live. . . . Surely we shall pay for using this most powerful instrument of communication to insulate the citizenry from the hard and demanding realities which must be faced if we are to survive. I mean the word—survive—literally.[6]

NBC's Chet Huntley, in his Dean A. L. Stone Address at Montana State University in 1959, expressed a similar concern. "I wish I could say to you that American journalism today provides little justification for deploring," he said. "But such is not the case."[7] He told of listening to radio news as he drove across the country at the time of the

Geneva conference and critical congressional sessions. He wanted and needed to know what the big developments were. He heard reported instead, as he said, "local murders, local thievery, assorted cussedness, even baseball scores" as news. But little of what he as a newsman considered the world's big developments at that moment was to be found. The implication that all is well in international and national affairs, Huntley warned, is both false and dangerous. *Life* magazine's Shana Alexander gave the A. L. Stone Address in 1966. She complained of similar practices, from a slightly different angle:

> . . . I am bothered by the appalling number of what Prof. Daniel Boorstin called pseudo-events—events staged solely to be covered. . . . But speaking as a consumer of news—. . . . My complaint is that I'm being Over-Communicated-At. I hesitate to use such a wildly ungrammatical term. . . .
>
> . . . Being Over-Communicated-At means being hit over the head, blinded and deafened by news, information, entertainment, self-help advice and more news that pours out of the radio and the TV set and the mailbox in a truly terrifying Niagara of communication. While it is possible to shut off this Niagara—just become a hermit or move to a desert island—it is far more difficult to sort it out.[8]

Foreign broadcasters and journalists have also warned us of dangerous tendencies they observe in broadcast news as practiced in the United States.

Sir Gerald Beadle, former President of the British Broadcasting Corporation's Television Service, has described in a very readable book his reaction to scores of hours of careful viewing of U.S. television news programs:

> I found the national and international news almost impossible to follow because it was so heavily larded with irrelevant information about cigarettes, soap flakes, shoes and so on. . . . I reached the end of the bulletin little wiser about what was going on in the world. If the Americans want an informed public opinion I think they will have to do something about this. Advertising is setting up an almost impenetrable barrier between the viewer and the information.[9]

Another friend of America, who has dared to warn us that all is not well, is the foreign news editor of the Japanese newspaper, *Tokyo Shimbun,* Yuji Isobe. Speaking at the United Nations Seminar on

Freedom of Information in New Delhi, India, in February, 1962, Mr. Isobe declared: ". . . the news regarding Red China is a blind point that can be said to be a fatal weakness of the news reporting of American news organizations." He noted: "This undesirable tendency of American news agencies is also found in their news concerning Laos and South Vietnam. We wonder why American news agencies take a preconceived idea towards the news concerning Red China even though they are (now) comparatively cautious and fair in handling news regarding Soviet Russia."[10]

Over ten years ago, when the writer was head of the National Association of Educational Broadcasters, the Association's radio network did a series of programs on Communist China, by a distinguished British journalist. Many protests were received. It is our position now, as it was then, that our nation's survival as a democracy depends on accurate, blunt facts about enemies or dangers, whether they are palatable or not. We should know everything possible about Communist China. To close our eyes, or to let well-intentioned gatekeepers of the media protect us from bad news, is equally unacceptable. We need the truth, and we need it straight.

Professor John R. Rider, speaking of Edward R. Murrow, wrote in *The Quill* of August 1965: "In his memory I call upon newsmen to re-examine themselves as gatekeepers of society . . . and I call upon management . . . to re-examine and re-assess their motives. . . ."[11] It is in this framework that, in the following pages, journalists conscious of their responsibility are invited to make such a re-assessment and plan new directions for broadcast journalism. In this volume, symptoms are examined which tell us that the citizens of America and the world are too often *not* getting the news they need, and that all is not well in the areas of broadcast news, public affairs, and related practices. From these diagnostic essays, it is hoped, improvements can be found to help correct this dangerous situation. Some modest proposals in this direction are therefore offered for consideration.

NOTES

1. Quoted by Robert Colby Nelson, "How They Got Started," *The Quill,* November 1964, p. 55.

2. John De Mott, "Every Newsman Practices Psychiatry Without a License," *The Quill,* January 1965, pp. 12-13.

3. Address of John de J. Pemberton, Jr., to National Conference on Broadcasting and Election Campaigns, October 13-14, 1965.

4. Albert Wohlstetter, "A Purpose Hammered Out of Reflection and Choice," *Life,* June 20, 1960, p. 134.

5. Ralph McA. Ingersoll, "Postscript to *PM*," *Nieman Reports,* September 1963, p. 23.

6. Edward R. Murrow, Address to the Radio and Television News Directors Association, Chicago, Ill., October 15, 1958.

7. Chet Huntley, Dean A. L. Stone Address: "News Coverage in 1959," *Journalism Review,* School of Journalism, Montana State University, Spring 1959, p. 4.

8. Shana Alexander, Dean A. L. Stone Address: "On Being Nothinged to Death," *Journalism Review,* School of Journalism, Montana State University, Spring 1966, p. 3.

9. Sir Gerald Beadle, *Television: A Critical Review* (London: George Allen and Unwin, Ltd., 1963), p. 85.

10. Yuji Isobe, Working Paper, No. 16, United Nations Seminar on Freedom of Information, New Delhi, 20 February—5 March, 1962. (English text kindly provided the author by Mr. Isobe.)

11. John R. Rider, "Oh, the Humanity!" *The Quill,* August 1965, p. 19.

2

Some Trouble Spots

CBS Board Chairman William S. Paley's statement: "at no period in our history has the function of news and public affairs broadcasting been so critical and important to our national life"[1] has been quoted often. So has former CBS News Director Fred W. Friendly's: ". . . every day there is more for the people of the world to know and every day what we don't know can kill us."[2] Probably few readers or critics could be found who would disagree with either statement. Friendly left CBS in dissatisfaction over his freedom to do what he believed necessary and important.

At a time of population explosion, the birth of new nations, crucial shortage in water, mineral, and food resources, and proliferating atomic activity and radioactivity, there are many indeed who wonder whether we really are getting all the news and information we need. Many of those who ask are representatives of new nations, looking to the United States as the leader of Western democracy as a way of life. Expecting a steady flow of special efforts of the most courageous type, many of them report that instead they find business as usual. What they see is far more advertising and entertainment than news. British writer Norman Swallow has observed: ". . . latecomers to television seem to be recognising that education, like medicine, is inadequately served when it takes second place to commercial interest."[3]

We, too, need to ask: Is the job of informing and arousing that needs to be done really one that can be crammed between records and commercials, or restricted to so-called 5-, 15-, or 30-minute newscasts as now conceived, or a few documentaries or specials? An industry management tradition that believes that the news and public affairs that the nation needs can be squeezed into such limitations of time and budget appears analogous to a hospital management that would decree that no surgical operation may take more than thirty or sixty minutes or cost more than a specified amount.

Norman Swallow, the British writer and TV news producer quoted earlier, has said: ". . . Television matters because so many millions of people watch it. Therefore it also matters in whose hands television is controlled, and the hands which control factual television matter most of all."[4]

When basic questions are raised about the management controls under which newsmen and news departments operate, management usually resents and denounces such questions as unfair. Television is a *mass* medium, they say. It must give the people what they want. Its problems are special and difficult. Yet, as Swallow says further in his book, *Factual Television:*

> . . . You cannot be committed to a mass medium and then spend your time dodging its implications, running away from size, excusing it because it is broad and coarse and unsubtle.[5]

> . . . If this book helps in any way to correct the quite extraordinary illusion which our American friends and colleagues seem to hold about their pre-eminence in factual television, it will be a splendid victory. They are really unbearably complacent, especially and surprisingly, I regret to say, in academic circles, about a comparatively minor contribution to what old John Grierson called the "enrichment of observation," minor in the sense that it is neither as consistent, nor as widespread, nor as deep, nor commanding anything like the regular proportion of the audience as what we do over here in our genuinely competitive situation, which with all its faults does give us the best television in the world.[6]

The news function of broadcasting in America is peculiarly hampered by a "but first" tradition which puts profits and commercials first, and causes news reports to be cut off when it is time for a commercial or a station break, or shortened to fit into the proper commercial pattern. How many readers have failed to note the increasing frequency with which commercials run over into program time and stations cut back in, having missed a play (in sports), part or all of a news item (in news), or a joke or musical passage (in entertainment)? The hope for adequate news and information is doomed to frustration as long as sponsors and other friends of broadcasting management can buy or bribe their way into newscasts through devious advertising or public relations channels, or can purchase immunity to exposure of anti-trust, anti-labor, and other anti-social practices by being sponsors or friends of networks and stations.[7] Adequate news is impossible under a sponsorship system, until and unless this system guarantees freedom of news departments from public relations "plants," managerial or sales pressures, or orders to use or not use certain items, and until it outlaws other practices now common in the industry.

The press and mass media create the intellectual, emotional, and political climate in which the nation lives. Walter Lippmann was one of the first who warned that people make their decisions on the basis of what they *think* are facts. If the pictures in their heads are wrong, their decisions will be wrong. The faults and errors of any medium that claims to be press have therefore ceased to be private vagaries. If broadcasting claims for itself the freedom of the press, it must assume not only the usual press responsibilities, but also those growing out of the peculiar, unique dangers and powers characteristic of TV and radio but not the print media. Neither broadcasting nor any other instrument of the press can be left free to be ineffective, deceitful, partisan, or inaccurate if the public's right and freedom to know are to mean anything.

Certainly Americans can be grateful for the many things they know from television and radio, and for the many fine newsmen, in radio and television, who devote their best efforts, often under tragically inadequate conditions, to keeping our nation informed. A brief glance backward at some of the programs of which U.S. networks may justifiably be proud might be worth while at this point.

Although the budget, the limited time available, and the times of the week and day when they have been presented have frequently been less than desirable, a considerable number of documentaries and specials have suggested what could be done on a regular basis in the United States, if the effort were made.

Following *See It Now,* which was started by Fred W. Friendly and Edward R. Murrow in 1951 and ran until 1958, and a number of such specials as the Army-McCarthy hearings and the CBS special on McCarthy, the Kefauver crime hearings, the McClellan labor-rackets inquiries, the Ed Murrow program on J. Robert Oppenheimer, etc., *CBS Reports,* first narrated by Edward R. Murrow, covered many important problems from the time it began with *Biography of a Missile* on October 29, 1959. Among the most promising areas explored, and deserving continuing efforts, were *Harvest of Shame,* on migratory workers; *Biography of a Bookie Joint,* on gambling; *Thunder on the Right,* on right-wing political groups; and programs on Viet Nam, the Ku Klux Klan, racial discrimination, education, teen-age smoking, the population explosion, and so on. More recently CBS specials of the audience participation type—on voting, automobile safety, physical fitness, and similar problems—have won deserved praise and recognition, as have several NBC programs of similar types on similar topics.

NBC's *White Paper* series with Irving Gitlin and Albert Wasserman have likewise revealed a trace of TV's great potential in programs dating from *The U-2 Story* in early 1960, through documentaries on local welfare scandals (*The Battle of Newburgh*), gambling (*The Business of Gambling*), and similar problems. At the end of the 1965-66 season, four White Paper programs were broadcast for a total of six and one-half hours of viewing time, on such subjects as *U.S. Foreign Policy, The Age of Kennedy,* and missile flights. By late 1965, NBC's Chet Hagan had produced some four hundred news specials, giving NBC an enviable position in the United States in this field. CBS's *Who Speaks for Birmingham?* and NBC's *Sit-In* represent two of the finest programs yet done in the United States on the segregation problem.

For the most part, NBC has seemed to schedule its prestige news and documentary programs on a less regular and more "special events" basis than CBS. As of late March 1966, NBC reported that it would have broadcast thirty-eight specials (excluding reruns) for the season for a total of 40½ hours of broadcast time. As noted in our earlier reference to second-quality time for such programs, it is important to note that only thirteen of these were to be broadcast in prime time (7 to 10 P.M. in the Midwest). The fact that a fairly large proportion of these "news" specials seem to have no valid connection with news, being on education, the Spanish Armada, Michelangelo, the Reformation, etc., or testing, public participation programs, should also be noted here. The question of the appropriateness of having a variety of cultural, science, education, history, and other non-news programs done by the *news* department will be discussed more fully later on. The practice of having (eight out of twenty-one NBC) newscasts named after the commentator, a "star system" practice growing out of show business rather than journalism, and seriously questioned by newsmen like David Brinkley himself, is also examined more fully later in this book.

To return to specific news program records, however, on the basis of a careful inventory and analysis made in early 1966 by a student of the author's, NBC easily led the networks in its accomplishments in this area. (Since ABC did not provide the complete and excellent data graciously provided by the news departments of both CBS and NBC, its performance could not be assessed as adequately as those of the other two networks). On the basis of TV schedules and reports at that time from CBS and NBC themselves, NBC was pre-empting eighteen hours and twenty minutes a week for news, while CBS was broadcasting only eight hours and twenty minutes. CBS, for example, carried two daily five-minute news reports while NBC carried eight. This, of course, does not take into account possible qualitative differences between the two networks, which are not examined here, but which make generalization from mere quantitative comparisons premature.

Although ABC did not provide comparable data for the study mentioned above, to meet the competition of CBS and NBC, ABC began to allocate more resources to national and international problems, with its series: *Close-Up,* begun in the fall of 1963, to run for three years. *Walk in My Shoes,* on "being a Negro," introduced new subjective documentary techniques later used by Gregory Shuker in *Crisis: Behind A Presidential Commitment,* showing the late President John F. Kennedy and Robert Kennedy in the anguish of decision-making at the time Governor George Wallace was pledged to ban Negroes from the University of Alabama.

One of the great accomplishments of *Close-Up's* producer, John Secondari, was to bring to TV one of the most original minds in the documentary field, Richard Leacock. It is to be regretted that he has not been given greater leeway, and has had to find much of his recognition abroad.

Besides these sample series, to the credit of network news in the United States it must be noted that NBC's *Outlook,* with Chet Huntley and Reuven Frank, CBS's *Eyewitness to History,* ABC's weekly Thursday *News Report,* plus such specials as the NBC-Xerox program on *The Kremlin,* and ABC-Philco's on *The Soviet Woman* also provide samples of what might be done regularly to meet national needs, if adequate resources and prime time were allocated to this problem.

During 1967 and 1968, under the pressure of tragic events in our nation, and about it, the news and documentary efforts of all three commercial networks were stepped up still further. This increase deserves recognition, commendation, and encouragement.

Besides several more audience-participation shows exemplified by its *National Driver's Test,* CBS did several significant special one-shot programs and series like its three-part series, *The Cities,* programs on the Viet Nam war and its participants and causes, specials on Red China (such as Morley Safer's *Red China Diary*), and a number of general documentaries on developments like *The Computer Revolution.* These seemed to more than close the gap between CBS and NBC. One of the most powerful, perhaps, was CBS's *Hunger in America.* However, to use this program as an illustration of a fairly usual trend, there was a tendency to over-simplify, and to find scapegoats for the problem presented. After tracing a complex and tragic problem in superb pictures and words, the principal "finger" was pointed at Secretary Orville Freeman and the Department of Agriculture for alleged mishandling of food stamp programs. Most problems of America do not lend themselves to quite such simple "solutions," or identification of "villains" as TV, in news or other programs, seems to assume. With greater opportunity, it is hoped that the level of responsibility of such programs will rise, and ways will be found to handle complex issues more adequately.

NET and PBL, over the nation's educational TV stations, provided examples of rare (in the U.S.) courage in political, racial, urban, and consumer fields. Though some of these programs may well have left room for improvement, great promise has been demonstrated in this first year. One of the principal effects of such programs has been to lead the commercial networks to do likewise. Aroused by their courage, and their underfinanced but imaginative efforts, like NET's special *Color Us Black* and its regularly scheduled new weekly *Black Journal,* CBS came up with plans for *Of Black America* and ABC produced *Time for Americans,* in which it examined *Bias in the Mass Media* and racial prejudice in other institutions, in brief series.

John Secondari's commendable *Saga of Western Man* on ABC came up with at least one outstanding success: *In the Name of God,* and NBC, though apparently yielding its lead to the other networks during this period, when its list of specials seemed both shorter and different from what might have been suggested by its earlier record, also produced several news specials of high quality.

Its news special entitled *Discover America with José Jiménez,* however, seemed to signal a trend which should be questioned for documentary approaches. Are "personalities" from "show-biz" now to be imposed on news departments as "leads" or "talent" for serious documentary efforts? Is CBS' announced plans for using Washington lampoonist Art Buchwald, perceptive though he is, on CBS News' *60 Minutes,* another step in the same direction, and therefore an indication that news and comedy are now to be tried as a new combination?

Despite the strides made by TV news in 1967 and 1968, a number of developments and trends are still disturbing:

1) Fred Friendly's resignation from CBS, and the reasons for it, indicate that the situation is not yet entirely happy in the CBS News Department. For an exposition of the reasons, readers are referred to his *Due to Circumstances Beyond Our Control,* published by Random House in 1967 as a solid contribution to the cause of TV news in America.

2) As late as January 1968, when the opposite might have been expected, after a year of several superb and sustained efforts, the morale of the ABC news staff was shattered by a reported twenty per cent cut in its already inadequate $35 million annual budget. This is reminiscent of the late Edward R. Murrow's claim that, however high network profits are, cuts always hit the news department first.

3) The Emmy Awards, on May 19, 1968, while finding plenty of time for recognition and adulation of all kinds of song-and-dance and show business acts and personalities, relegated America's most talented and courageous news programs and news personalities to an almost insultingly inferior position on the program. In a year when, if ever, news programs stood out and deserved praise, it was nothing less than tragic to see news relegated in Emmy presentations to the same secondary position that allotting non-prime time for news illustrates in national network and station schedules. The status of news in the Establishment still has far to go before it receives the honor and recognition it deserves.

4) Network coverage of the aftermaths of the tragic assassinations of the Reverend Dr. Martin Luther King, Jr. and Senator Robert F. Kennedy revealed the usually superb way in which individual newsmen and departments have reacted to crisis and tragedy. The floundering and repetitious way in which the networks had to feel their way, hour after hour on an *ad hoc* basis, however sincerely, in un-

accustomed prime time, also revealed how desperately TV news, as a profession and a regular service, needs definition of function, clarification of goals, operational standards, and adequate staff and equipment of its own.

Each time news departments have been so "released" and told to do the job, or "take over," they have done their best. But soon the thin red line becomes depleted and exhausted. Reporters, on duty around the clock without sleep, begin to falter and err. The total news department, as an independent institution within the network structure, is neither large enough nor independent enough to handle such crises and overloads without taking a heavy toll of the health and quality of the dedicated reporters on whom the burden falls.

5) This year provided repeated examples of greatly improved and more responsible coverage of riots, demonstrations, and other violence. At many individual networks and stations, the record is good. But still lacking on an industry-wide basis are carefully designed, professional policy and procedure manuals (drawn up by the networks, stations, the NAB, and educational broadcasters alike) for the guidance of journalists, particularly the younger ones, often pressed into service.

6) And finally, in an age when so many challenges and opportunities exist for news and public affairs departments to do significant programs on crucial issues and problems, why must network news departments be saddled with doing (News?) specials on Frank Sinatra, a collection of female singer-personality-beauties, and other subjects in the entertainment or even historical field, far removed from the kind of thing which professional journalistic training qualifies them to do. Must network news departments have their meager staffs and resources sapped to do programs on popular music, art, science, history, education and other fields which should have departments of their own in the network structure? This problem is not a simple one. But it must be confronted, if American TV is to hold its own with that of other nations.

However commendable the news, documentary, and public affairs record traced above is in comparison with that of earlier years in which news was sinfully neglected, the uncomfortable fact remains that United States television networks devote a far smaller proportion of prime time, staff, and budget to this service than do their counterparts in England, Japan, Germany, or any of a dozen other nations.

In England Richard Cawston, Anthony de Lotbiniere, Peter

Morely, Cyril Bennett, Tom Hewat, James Hill, and a generation of others have joined earlier documentary film essayists like Denis Mitchell, Philip Donnellan, Ken Russell, and John Schlesinger, providing in prime time a regular diet of great documentaries and what the British call actuality essays, which are timely documentaries on everything from capital punishment, venereal disease, birth control, and homosexuality to communism and pacifism. *Panorama, This Week, Tonight, Gallery,* and a host of other award-winning series illustrate some of these efforts.

France, Western Germany, Italy, Japan, Australia, and Canada have also, in recent years, devoted to news, public affairs, and problems of domestic and world significance several times the proportion of resources and prime time that U.S. television management has seen fit to allocate to this type of program.

As this is written, promising efforts by educational television's PBL and NET, with the cooperation of Westinghouse, the Australian Broadcasting System, and several other national systems, are beginning to be noted. Surely the age of the satellite would suggest the need for internationally collective and cooperative efforts if some of the world's most pressing problems are to be solved. The leadership of U.S. networks in this area is sporadic. Courageous efforts of a wholly new dimension, less conspicuously dominated by profit considerations, are needed if U.S. news and television are to win the respect the nation as a whole deserves.

Impressive as the list of American TV network achievements is, when viewed in this way, many writers, particularly newsmen themselves, are far from satisfied. There is enough evidence that network programming is falling short of the full potential of radio and television for news, either unintentionally or deliberately, to justify both the deep concern and the careful examination urged here. In an age when the instruments and the people are available to make Americans unquestionably and absolutely the best-informed people in the world, anything less cannot be tolerated.

Are Television and Radio Really "Press"? In recent years the broadcast media have claimed and justified their various freedoms and privileges on the basis of those provisions of the Constitution which guarantee freedom of the press, freedom of speech, and freedom from censorship. In other words it has been widely assumed that the broadcast media deserve *all* the immunities which newspapers and journalism have earned over a period of several centuries. A closer look would seem to be in order, however, in view of the fact that broadcast leaders repeatedly remind critics who ask for more TV news that "television is show business." The problem which broadcast journalists encounter in attempting to do their job adequately, when their bosses take this position, is central to our discussion. To what extent can journalism survive in this kind of an environment? Can the First Amendment really be stretched to cover advertising, public relations, and entertainment as well as press functions? If television and radio are to deserve treatment as *press,* should news (i.e., press functions) not make up at least as large a percentage of their time and budget as entertainment or advertising? Should newsmen not be paid more, not less, than salesmen? Does news not deserve prime time?

Bernard Kilgore, President of the *Wall Street Journal,* considerably disturbed many broadcasters in his November 9, 1961, Lovejoy Convocation address at Colby College when he observed: "We are going to get the idea of freedom of the press dangerously obscured if we try to stretch it to fit radio and television."[8] This point has been touched on by others, including broadcasters. Appearing on a panel in his home town in February 1964, Dean Alexander, news director of Station KDWB in Minneapolis, declared:

> I believe it is time for a number of "rank and file" broadcasters to either put up or shut up. They should either start handling news with professionalism or stop bragging about what they are doing with news departments they don't have. No one would dream of opening a newspaper without hiring at least one competent journalist, yet some broadcasters have the audacity to open a station and pompously lay claim to all sorts of journalistic achievements without a single newsman on its staff.[9]

Robert Lindsay, former Chairman of the Council on Radio and Television Journalism, speaking of some of the shortcomings of broadcast journalism, declared: "I rank first the continued widespread prevalence among far too many radio and television stations of the broadcasting of non-news by non-journalists." The disc jockeys and adolescents hired by many stations have reduced the quality of radio news to dangerous levels. As Lindsay described it: "Rip-and-read is too polite a term to describe their concept of news programming; it is more like yank-and-yell." As for television, he warns:

> Television news, too, still needs to mature, to appreciate that relent-
> less coverage by sound film of police run news isn't at all the same
> thing as informing viewers about the important issues and trends affect-
> ing them and their community. . . . People are getting tired of hearing
> ma and pa tell how the robber ordered them to stick 'em up, and of
> watching those stretcher cases being stuffed into ambulances.[10]

At this point, one of the most basic and dangerous characteristics
of television needs to be identified and understood. Time and again
people confuse the so-called "reality," which news is intended to por-
tray, with "shoot-'em-up" scenes in television *drama*. As will be noted
later, there are scores of instances in police records of people beaten
or murdered while bystanders watched entranced, "unable" to do anything, as if they were watching TV.

Framed with fantasy materials, and operated under show business-
oriented executives, the relatively little news which television presents
(perhaps the equivalent of two or three newspaper columns of words
per day at most, for the average station) is pressed into molds to
make it fit the same pattern as fantasy or fiction. Are television and
radio really "press"? They seem to be so only to a very small extent.
And they can and should justifiably be covered by press immunities
only to the extent that they meet the criteria and definitions which
news media must meet as reality rather than fantasy media. Some of
the problems involved in this achievement will become clearer as they
are illustrated more specifically below.

Television as a News-Maker. One obvious respect in which television has effects different from those of the print-based press is observ-
able in the great difficulty it has in restricting itself to *reporting* the
news rather than in becoming a news-*maker* or a part of the event
reported. The appearance of a television camera and crew on the
scene causes people to "act" as they would not otherwise. Instead of
an independent event, the occurrence becomes partially or wholly a
television "production," irrespective of the intentions of the producers
involved. The nature of TV itself is what presents the problem.

Eric Sevareid and other top-flight reporters, following the first Kennedy assassination and the death of Oswald, noted with concern the
inability of TV to *fail* to transform the events it covers. Alexander
Kendrick has explained the problem particularly well:

What often worries me about reporting by television is not so much that it distorts whatever it chooses to cover, but that it has a way of changing its essential nature. . . . Instead of spontaneous truth we get a public performance. . . . A Presidential press conference takes on a new form by the very fact of being televised. The words of the President are true words, but if television had not been there he might never have said them. . . .

We have reached a point in human history when political decisions might well be taken for the sake of the television audience, when the tactics of wars might be modified to suit the convenience of television technicians, and when riots and demonstrations might be so timed that they can be sure of full TV coverage. . . . Television, partly because it is so conspicuous a thing, and partly because its audience is so enormous, has got itself in the position of being able to change the very nature of the events which, in theory, it is there merely to record.[11]

Discussions in the fall of 1966 recognized the fact that live coverage of the Viet Nam war is now possible. The only question was whether it was desirable. *Newsweek* already a year earlier had noted: "Government troops have been known to hold up operations until television crews arrive on the scene."[12]

This power or characteristic of television seems generally not to have been admitted or appreciated by television management, the superiors of the Sevareids, Cronkites, Brinkleys, and Huntleys. In an editorial over CBS radio August 26, 1954, Dr. Frank Stanton declared that "after all, radio and television hear and see exactly what happens. They don't create spectacles or circuses." This explanation needs to be challenged on the basis of the nature of the medium itself. Day after day television magnifies small, even microscopic objects until they fill the entire home screen as completely as the largest objects. Television daily makes unequals equal, and equals unequal, as it pleases. As individuals who have tried to put over school bond or fluoridation campaigns well know, TV can magnify minorities of opposition, or phoney authorities, so enormously as to make them appear equal or superior to *authentic* authorities or democratic majorities. The flimsiest evidence or proof can be made to appear conclusive or significant by TV. And with the corruption of the meaning of the words "evidence" and "proof" as used daily in commercials adjacent to and within newscasts, truth and false claims become most difficult to identify.

But Dr. Stanton's statement must be challenged on the basis of TV reportorial and editorial practices as well. Early in 1960, Governor Buford Ellington of Tennessee accused the CBS television crew sent to Nashville of instigating a racial demonstration.[13] Apparently the cameramen, and those to whom they were accountable, wearied of having nothing to report. The crew and trip were costing CBS money. To liven things up, a few local citizens were enlisted as actors. Before long, the situation was no longer peaceful or quiet. Television had *created* news, so it could report it. However, what they reported was in a sense a lie. Instead of the news or the truth, which was that all was quiet in Nashville, CBS-TV had action to report—action which television itself had instigated.

The *New Republic* of October 14, 1957 reports an earlier, similar event at Central High School in Little Rock. Quoting from the *New York Times* dispatch of Homer Bigart, the *New Republic* story explained how, "egged on by one television crew," students were soon "hooting derisively" in what quickly became a scene of violence, hate, and effigy-burning—one more of all too many examples where television *causes* or *becomes part of* news events instead of merely reporting them.[14]

In 1948, television cameras showed Southern delegates to the Democratic National Convention apparently splitting their party in two; many took off their badges and angrily threw them on a table. This was drama, but it was hardly honest reporting; for it did not show these delegates putting the badges back on a few minutes later, as soon as the television cameras turned away. People attending the convention in person saw no such serious threat of a party split.

In 1960, Robert Mason, who monitored the CBS coverage of the Democratic Convention for the Associated Press, observed that the network, in an apparent effort to build up showmanship suspense, held out the possibility that John F. Kennedy's candidacy might be challenged. The Associated Press, however, flatly declared that Kennedy was certain of the nomination. Most other reporters supported the AP position. Those who saw CBS coverage, according to these other news sources, apparently saw a threat, or "drama," which never existed. The showmanship ingredients of suspense or conflict were added to make "news" a better "show."

One of the most conspicuous examples of television as a newsmaker, or distorter, is found in the reporting of the 1959 visit of

Khrushchev to the United States. A visit which needed to be reported coolly and soberly became a circus. As two young reporters described it:

> CBS alone used 65 cameras and 375 cameramen and technicians. . . . Paul Levitan, Director of Special Events for CBS News, estimated the total production cost for the three major networks at over two million dollars. . . . James Reston, Washington bureau chief of the New York *Times* . . . said . . . 'There were so many newsmen reporting the trip that they changed the course of events. . . . They [the reporters] were not the obscure witnesses of history but the principal characters in the drama.'[15]

The London Sunday *Times* Washington correspondent called the coverage a chaos, principally because of television's presence and pressures. Peter Trueman of the *Montreal Star* placed the blame for distortion of the meaning of the visit on television personnel and equipment. Instead of seeing Khrushchev greeted by restrained, polite, small crowds, as he traveled about America, television audiences saw him constantly surrounded by hundreds of individuals, milling about excitedly. The fact that these individuals were principally television personnel was difficult for viewers, or foreign observers, to know. For they clearly saw "eager throngs," supporting Moscow propaganda claims that "thousands" turned out to greet Khrushchev wherever he went.

Whereas television may come only to report, it usually seems to end up running the show. When it reported the Republican Convention in San Francisco in late 1959, it was soon cueing "spontaneous" demonstrations which could not fail to change the nature of the convention. Soon, because of television, speeches were displacing the dinner hour on the West Coast, so prime-time viewers in the rest of the country could see the "show" at a convenient after-dinner viewing time. And the long speeches of yore began to be replaced by short TV-style remarks, cued by television producers, and assisted by television make-up artists. These shorter speeches may well have been an improvement; the fact is, however, that the nation's political operations are being run and shaped—not merely reported—by television more and more.

In the 1964 convention, CBS's Bill Leonard's appeal to Lyndon Johnson: "Will you wave to Mr. Trout and Mr. Mudd, sir?", and the President's obliging wave, illustrates not only the unintentional but deliberate way as well in which television· makes and shapes "news," which it then, or simultaneously, "reports."

Former President Eisenhower has firmly stated that TV cameras should be barred from the floor of national conventions. The picture the public comes away with—of noisy confusion and improper deportment—he believes is bound to breed disrespect rather than respect for political process. Many TV journalists have been somewhat surprised to find Mr. Eisenhower's proposal supported by Walter Cronkite, whose proposal to ban TV from the convention floor would, if adopted, be effective in 1968. Excellent newsmen like Cronkite certainly recognize the problems described here. The business pressures on them, however, make it unlikely that their decisions will prevail.

Researchers who studied the behavior of people lining the streets at the MacArthur Day celebration in Chicago some years ago were considerably less impressed with the enthusiasm of the crowd than were television viewers. The networks, in their effort to get the unusual rather than the typical crowd reactions, selected shots and used other "editorializing" techniques which showed principally enthusiastic, dramatic reactions, rather than typical or negative ones. This provided not *a picture of what was happening,* except in a very selective sense, but an impression which was heavily slanted. Control over the *description* of events in effect gives television a large measure of control over what appears to have happened. By what it fails to show, television prevents an *occurrence,* however real, from becoming *news.* By what it promotes, or shows, it *creates* both news and history. What TV shows *becomes* news, however un-news-*worthy* it might be by more reflective standards.

Discussions and panel shows on television often become news-makers or news events rather than merely news reporting or explorations of problems. Interviewees are goaded into anger, frustration, or conflict. Panelists become contestants. What is the effect on the relations between people scheduled on programs together, as well as on the public or the course of politics, of the *provoking* role of television in such instances? How many political and personal estrangements has television thus caused, and what is their effect on history? Is this television as only a reporter? Or is it television as something vastly more, requiring the greatest of care and control in its use?

The Reverend Bruce Hilton has described both press and TV effects on the civil rights demonstrations and meetings:

> The press plays a strong, almost over-powering role in the march. It not only reports but participates. . . . And the press is a major reason for the march.

> The presence of the press has a powerful influence on the content of the speeches too. At dimly-lit open-air rallies each night, the speaker's face lights up in the glare of photofloods during those passages a camera-man thinks most likely to win ten seconds of network time. The lights go off abruptly when the cameraman's interest flags, leaving the speaker blinking in the dark, and undoubtedly fishing for another and even more startling statement to bring the lights back on.[16]

The story of an accident, as reported by good journalists, often must now include a description, or film, of the interruptions and adverse impressions on police and bystanders of individuals sent by radio and television stations, pushing microphones into sobbing faces and asking rescue squads to "hold it" till they can get a picture. Such "reporters" are usually not qualified newsmen but rather "personalities" or the untrained, immature individuals stations so often hire as newsmen. They tend to get in the way of police and rescue workers, and become a part of the picture and story later reported. This situation could be corrected by insistence on the employment of only professionally trained journalists with both the ethics and maturity which character-ize reporting at its best. But with "showmanship" values as criteria, these are not the types of individuals whom television management normally employs.

To the extent that television, as so far operated, has proven itself unable or unwilling to prevent shaping, changing, or distorting nearly everything it touches, it is far different from press. To expect tradi-tions and freedoms designed for this concept of *press* to suffice for television, therefore, is to expect the impossible. Some new ap-proaches and standards, unique to television, are obviously needed here.

Although television presents far greater dangers as a news-maker than radio, the latter deserves some of the same concern, being part of the same network structures, and the same management practices and traditions as television. Because of its greater pervasiveness, in fact, radio also presents other little-noticed dangers.

Dispatches throughout Illinois on May 24, 1964 reported that East-ern Illinois University and the Coles County, Illinois, sheriff had charged Chicago clear-channel Station WLS, with being "largely responsible" for student demonstrations and general disturbance of the peace in Charleston, Illinois. They also accused it of jeopardizing public safety by creating an unmanageable traffic jam. The crowds which converged on Charleston were allegedly attracted by a WLS report of rumors that a water fight was to take place between the students of Eastern and another university. The airing of such rumors, without checking, attracted hundreds of outsiders to the expected trouble area and at the same time caused many students to try to make the predicted "show" a reality.

Paul Smith, Coles County sheriff, reported that on the basis of monitor reports of WLS's so-called news items on the subject, "We feel that this station was the responsible party in this affair." Quincy Doudna, President of the University, stated: "I note that no other news media reported the fact that a water fight was expected on campus."

Until broadcasting establishes controls to insure against its being a news-*maker,* and confines its activity to reporting, far from deserving *more* freedoms than the print-based press, it would seem to require special and far more rigid controls—either of its own devising or, failing this, by public agencies representing the public interest.

After noting how television has already become "more important than the House of Commons or the White House" in the extent to which political democracy has been changed, British writer Norman Swallow reminds us that there is no escape.

> . . . That it might sometimes change those events, or even alter those decisions, is a price that we have to pay. All we can hope for is to minimise the danger, by appointing television reporters of integrity and then encouraging them to seek the truth before their own popularity.[17]

It would seem that certain safeguards, perhaps devised by such newsmen themselves, might also be indispensable. For, even with honest reporters, the situation does not seem to be improving as much as one would wish—if at all.

Television's Redefinition of News

Since radio and television have the ability—and often do not hesitate to use it—to "stimulate" or create news, are such "staged" or pseudo events as burning in effigy, water fights, and so on really "news" as Daniel J. Boorstin has asked in his book: *The Image?* Is thus defining news not a very dangerous game? To what extent, in a nation that thinks of news as normally independent of the media which report them, can news be *created* by television and radio at will? Certainly it is obvious that under the pressure of television and radio, in which showmen and salesmen are the superiors of journalists, the definition of news has changed. And this change has not affected only broadcasting. The new definitions also begin to apply to newspapers and magazines, as it is discovered how profitable this new entertainment concept of news is.

The *Speaker's Guide for Television Broadcasters,* published by the National Association of Broadcasters in 1959, states that television *advertising* itself is a news medium. To quote from the suggested points to be covered by speakers, under the heading, "Advertising and the General Welfare," ". . . What you learn is news to you."[18] Information about new products is "news"; in other words, news is whatever people are told by broadcasting, whether as advertising, public relations, or journalism. With such elastic definitions, it is no wonder the distinction between what used to be called news and what used to be called advertising, public relations, promotion, and salesmanship disappears. This distortion of the definition of news is not merely the result of erosion, or of the different nature of the television medium. It is a result of deliberate extensions of the definition of news which perhaps no professional journalist would agree to, but which non-journalistic management imposes. Of course, broadcasters wish to immunize advertising, promotional spots, and all their other activities against regulation. They seek to do this by crowding them all, indiscriminately, under the tent of the First Amendment, which was erected to protect "press" or news. This practice must be challenged if real news, rather than feigned news or non-news, is to be protected. Soon, even in other media, news comes to be defined as what is published and *called* news. In broadcasting, people can tell what is news, under this deterioration of definitions, simply by whether or not it appears in a so-called newscast. What is excluded, then, becomes non-news.

Since television is a visual medium in which *action* and motion attract so powerfully, it is natural for it to prefer news of action, and *gross* action over less conspicuous or more subtle action. In news sequences as in television drama, the more figures that cross the screen with action and noise, the greater the attraction value. In the news land of television, where the showman is king, news is expected to entertain rather than primarily to inform. Soon it comes to be seen as similar to most other television programs in its function. It helps kill time pleasantly. What might be disturbing in any long-term sense is kept out as long as possible. So is the non-visual or non-dramatic, no matter how important to the nation it may be. Fallout cannot be seen. It is therefore non-news. This role for news, so frequently promoting action, the personality, the celebrity, and the human interest story in preference to the inconspicuous but significant idea, tendency, movement, or world event, is frightening in an age when hundreds of events are occurring daily which may seal our fate unless the people are told, so they may personally and through government take the proper steps to avert calamity.

Other considerations and commitments, wholly unrelated to news values, also prevail. Events which have had film shot of them are likely to be what we hear and see as today's news. If a station has spent several hundred dollars on film sequences of an event, it is unlikely to leave the film unused, however much more important other less visual events or developments of the day may be. This problem —of television's choice of the visual over the significant—is a difficult one. One of the best statements of it appeared in a recent *Saturday Review:*

> That is the common dilemma: whether to play the news for its importance, or for its visual value. . . . If two airliners collide over New York the television newscast has it made. . . .
>
> Suppose instead that one day, shortly before air time, Britain devalues the pound, or on another day the Pope decrees that, after all, he finds artificial birth control acceptable.
>
> . . . does he perform the duty that any serious newspaper would perform, explaining and interpreting the pound devaluation, the papal pronouncement? Through conditioning he is obsessed by picture values.
>
> So whatever he does, the TV newsman cannot really win. He is tempted to let the non-visual news slide.[19]

Because violence attracts crowds for barkers, and hence for television and radio advertising, violence and conflict predominate as news items. Television viewers become so conditioned to believing that this is really news that they rarely question whether the most significant events of the day really are fires, wrecks, crimes, or scandals. Yet what is kept off the air by such police blotter recitals is in many cases of fateful importance to the United States. There is little room for these omens of tomorrow, among the quarrels, crashes, and crimes which litter the television and radio air. Not only is the abnormal stressed, which is basically a problem and function for all news media, but the most gruesome versions of abnormality are presented. In view of the far greater impact and power of television, some special precautions should prevail, which may not be necessary for other, less powerful media. By dint of presenting the violent and abnormal as news, television and radio reinforce in *news* the same effects and impressions they convey with their Westerns and private detective series. What is extreme is presented so often each day that it comes to be considered normal. Violence is viewed as the *normal* way in which people solve problems, both in dramatic and news programs. That many people and nations have peaceful relations, that love reigns in many families, that mercy is not forgotten in daily life—these are largely ignored. The depressing, pessimistic news picture of so-called "reality" prevailing in our nation, added to the picture of a nation afflicted with hundreds of ills (described in patent medicine commercials) needs to be challenged.

At international conferences of journalists, foreign writers from both friendly and Communist countries have asked us why, in news as well as in other programs, we seem to promote war over peace, conflict over cooperation, the abnormal and sordid over the harmonious and beautiful. Jerome Aumente, reporting on one such recent conference wrote:

> The seminar . . . approved a resolution which touches on the subject. It urged journalists to use language that would add to and not diminish peace and understanding. In effect, the journalists were called on to avoid applying partisan formulae to political situations and to reject pejorative or offensive words in describing countries, religions, social groups or individuals.[20]

From October 5 to 10, 1964, the Eighth International Session of the International Center for the Teaching of Journalism, at the University of Strasbourg, heard several speakers address themselves to many common problems. Especially relevant were the remarks of Jean Bikanda of the Federal Republic of the Cameroons, who warned:

> . . . the hunt for shock-pictures, the search for the sensational at all costs, for its own public, that often frivolous public to which everything must be bent, all these efforts I say, mean that it often does us a disservice more than it helps people to understand our problems; thus it does not make mutual understanding between our two worlds any easier.

Mr. Bikanda noted how, from reports of Cameroon independence celebrations in 1960:

> . . . the uninformed reader quickly acquired a false view of the event and of the situation of the nation in consideration.[21]

Pierre Archambault, President of the French Press Confederation and a Board Member of French Radio and Television, asked:

> . . . How many events, situations, hidden motives should be known to the public and are not? . . . And for each unpleasant act, each clumsy word which creates upheaval amongst the masses, how many noble words, good intentions, brotherly gestures are there, which remain unknown, although they are likely to soothe, console and engender understanding between peoples?[22]

The instigational role of TV news, in contrast to its apparently neglected pacifying one, deserves the most searching consideration.

If reports and illustrations of violence served any useful purpose in foreign relations, or even in crime control or traffic safety, leading to significant efforts to eliminate their causes, such emphasis might be fully justified. But such is rarely the case. Television and radio have broken the concept of "news" down to the point where it does not principally inform; it more often provides thrills and excitement in the same way that "other" entertainment programs do.

When news begins to feature the same kinds of violence, abnormality, and conflict that fictional programs do, a serious situation arises. Fantasy and reality begin to be confused with each other. All the world is now a stage and people view events as drama, from which they are safely insulated or removed, rather than as something affecting or involving them. Whatever is seen on television, including news, comes to be thought of by viewers as being *on the other side of the tube,* beyond their power to affect. More and more, people give up trying. Moreover, does concentration on the violence and woes of the world in news, added to the violence already found in our non-news programs, not subject the viewer and listener to more sordidness and morbidity than is good for him? In such a situation don't viewers simply have to treat news and reality as escapism if they are to preserve their sanity? And if television and radio news are treated as escapism or entertainment, when and where will people hear what they *must* hear and *take action* about? Have such possible dangers been given the careful consideration they deserve by those who make broadcast news policy?

Making an individual feel insignificant and unable to do anything about conditions and events he sees is what totalitarian governments do intentionally. It is the opposite of the principles on which *democracy* is based. The subject of a totalitarian regime gives up, as a result of his sense of *helplessness.* The type of spectatoritis created leads to the attitude which prevailed in Nazi Germany during the war; next-door neighbors disappeared during the night while people protested that there was nothing *they* could do about it. American behavior in many events is becoming dangerously reminiscent of such patterns. Often the citizens of our nation remain disturbingly silent in the face of injustice, cruelty, or other outrage, as if there were nothing they could do or say that would make a difference. This posture of defeatism and totalitarianism needs to be replaced by a more positive one. More responsible news practices can contribute enormously to the creation of more positive, active, and constructive patterns of behavior.

The redefinition or mis-definition of news which television has unwittingly imposed upon the nation, as a result of its many unique and unsuspected powers as a visual medium in which action and motion attract most powerfully, is one of the least clearly perceived effects of television. The criteria of news significance which have emerged have changed greatly from pre-television days. Some of these criteria, and non-news practices resulting from them, deserve separate identification:

1. Emphasis on the superficial. On October 12, 1960, Russian Premier Khrushchev addressed the United Nations. He banged the podium

with his shoe to punctuate what he said. This punctuation was reported by the news media. How many Americans can recall what he said, or what was being debated at the time? How well did television, which showed this scene several times, report the dramatic effect that what Khrushchev *said* (on the subject of colonialism) had on the representatives of new African nations? Before the days of television, would newspapers, too, have magnified this shoe-thumping to such a point that it displaced what Khrushchev *said,* or would pre-television reporters not have had different reportorial standards for reporting this event? While most American correspondents, under the pressure of television competition, were reporting only Khrushchev's shoe-thumping, African and Asian delegates, who in a few years would not even remember whether Khrushchev wore shoes or not, would recall what he *said* about how communism meant more rice, milk, steel, electricity, and education. As long as shoe-thumping makes more news than the pronouncements it punctuates, as it does so generally on television under present conditions, history will continue to take Americans by surprise again and again.

U.S. networks have often boasted of their programs on the Near East, Korea, and other parts of the world. We would hope such programs may increase more in quality than in quantity. For in many instances, such as ABC's program on Korea a month before students rebelled against President Rhee, no suggestion of the latent and explosive omens of things to come was provided. Visual aspects of Korea, a strange troubled land, were reported with little depth. In what respect such programs are greatly useful for genuine understanding, excellent as they may be in production standards, is not clear. Certainly they still have far to go. The same was true of ABC and CBS programs on the Middle East, which seemed to see little danger of trouble only a few weeks before violence burst forth. The scenery, parades, and mug shots were splendid. But substance was thin. Are such superficial reports, which lull rather than awaken or warn, not more a disservice than a national public service?

Perhaps the most urgent danger concerning the foreign news situation is that while Americans are ill served, they *believe* they are well-informed. For this is what they are told. Network and trade association "studies" every few months "prove" how well-informed television keeps its viewers. TV management and public relations departments, particularly, promote this view. But it is contrary to the warnings of the newsmen themselves who know better. Walter Cronkite, among others, has said that if, as surveys show, 55 per cent of the American people get most of their news from TV, then

> . . . fifty-five per cent of the public is inadequately informed. . . . It is impossible by the spoken word to communicate all the information that the individual citizen needs. . . . We are charged with a responsibility which in all honesty and candor we cannot discharge. . . . We do such a slick job that we have deluded the public into thinking they get all they need to know from us.[23]

The temptation to glance at a problem, comment briefly on it, and consider that "coverage," leaves much to be desired. Problems cannot be grasped when given such brief review. The impression that they have been covered is conducive not to action but to smugness or passivity on the part of American viewers. More seriously, since an adequate analysis of cause and background would take too much time by management standards, the news is usually simplified by finding scapegoats for events. The fact that the delinquent may have been partially created by slums, unemployment, poor schools or no schools, racial or religious persecution, or drunken parents is assumed to be of no interest. A news service characterized by these types of blindness, exclusions, discontinuities, astigmatisms and by such superficial coverage, however visually exciting or entertaining, does not provide adequate news.

2. Editorial avoidance of anti-sponsor, anti-business orientation. Distinguished journalists like Eric Sevareid, Gunnar Back, Howard K. Smith, and the late Edward R. Murrow have repeatedly pointed out that the conditions under which they must work give a one-dimensional view of news, and give the lie the same prominence as the truth. What is needed is analysis, and the time to explain and discuss. But most networks forbid such analysis or allow too little time for it. There is, of course, much disguised editorializing on behalf of business, sponsors, and commercial values. One commentator has said that analysis is acceptable to the extent that it agrees with the viewpoint of television managers and sponsors. When it differs from what they want, it is called editorializing and is banned.

The peculiar and intimate nature of the electronic media and the way in which news and non-news are intermingled, make non-news as well as news programs editorial. Many so-called institutional advertising programs provide examples of non-news, but editorial, uses of television.

The very selection and balance of programs generally, of course, reflect a kind of editorial judgment. Commercials, with their loaded words and psychological implications, are editorial in effect. The way announcers speak, as well as the words they utter, constitutes editorial comment. Pictures selected, and those rejected, depend on editorial judgment.

In a few cases, such as New York's radio station WMCA, proud traditions of fair broadcast editorializing *have* been established. So far, however, networks seem to have editorialized mostly on behalf of matters affecting their own profits, rather than on broad public issues. Speaking to the National Press Club Conference July 2, 1957, Dr. Frank Stanton of CBS told how CBS fought to get the FCC's 1949 ban on editorializing reversed. "CBS fought hard for this right," he said.

> Having won it, we have not used it very much. For editorializing over the air involves a whole cluster of problems that call for much wiser solutions than we now have, and not until they are found do we at CBS feel that we can exercise this significant right fully and in the public interest.

The most important CBS editorials, for example, as Dr. Stanton knew, were directed against subscription television, equal-time broadcast requirements, and other problems in which CBS itself had a vested interest. An examination of the extent to which the editorial privilege has been exercised overtly by the networks, and in whose behalf, as opposed to hidden editorialization, is a project awaiting the attention of young doctoral students in search of interesting subjects. It should be fruitful. If newspapers followed the lead of the television networks, they would use their editorial space principally for opposition to proposed postal rate increases, increased paper costs, or other threats to their own profits and interests rather than giving their considered views on *broad* issues of the day.

Meanwhile, although what is *called* editorializing by individual stations has begun to be practiced increasingly, its negative effects frequently appear to outweigh its positive ones. Editorials predominantly on behalf of motherhood, the community chest, good schools, good highways, honesty, and so on seem something less than the editorial *analysis* needed. And at broadcasting conventions, broadcasters "sell" each other on editorializing and suggest gimmicks to use, justifying them on the basis of the fact that such programs bring high ratings. Thus approached, editorials cannot fail to suffer from the same afflictions which plague news generally, as discussed in this chapter. Attention-getting, profits, or ratings are hardly valid criteria of significance for editorials. The subject of overt editorializing, however, will be more fully discussed in a later section of this book.

3. Firstness and recency as news criteria. Among the principal criteria of news which have come to predominate in a television age is that of being first—of scooping the competition. By these standards, "fast news is better news." Recency comes to have a value of its own. In this system of values the second phase of a crisis in a given country is likely never to be heard because "something new" or totally different and unrelated has happened more recently somewhere else. Continuity and relevance are replaced by other values. Emphasis on firstness results in both discontinuity and lack of planning or coherence in news handling and understanding.

In his address to the International Conference of Journalists in 1964, referred to earlier, the U.S. representative, Robert Manning, noted:

> . . . the all too-common phenomenon of important developments being "authoritatively" reported and analysed for a curious public and officialdom before the developments have emerged from their cocoons and sat in the daylight long enough even to be properly classified. . . .
> . . . more interest in what is *going* to happen than what in fact *has* happened. . . .[24]

Commenting on the problem raised by Manning, Jerome Aumente observed: "The rush and superficial fullness of news reporting (which) leaves the modern man with hardly time to notice the day's vital developments before a new flood of fragments overwhelms him the next day. . . ."[25]

This emphasis on speed often leads to dangerous irresponsibility. A few illustrations might be useful:

Item: On August 23, 1944, Charles Collingwood and CBS reported Paris liberated by French troops; this, however, we later learned, did not occur until August 25. This episode is described by Collins and Lapierre in *Is Paris Burning?* (Simon and Schuster, 1965).

Item: The Watts riots in 1965 were covered by direct reports by helicopter by station KTLA. Writing in the *New Republic,* John Gregory Dunne declared:

> Not only did television exacerbate an already inflammatory situation, but also, by turning the riots into a Happening, may even have helped prolong them. One channel went so far as to score its riot footage with movie "chase" music.

> No rumor, however unsubstantiated, went unreported. Hovering over the riot scene in a helicopter, a reporter for KTLA suddenly announced, "There's a report that one or two policemen are surrounded, so we're going for a look." The report was unfounded, but by the time that was established, there were other unconfirmed stories on the air. The Shrine Auditorium was on fire, the Minute Men were invading Watts, a contingent of Hell's Angels was even now careening down the Harbor Freeway toward the riot area; all were false alarms. . . . quite isolated events blurred into holocaust and a riot became a massacre.

> Watts is a vast sprawling ghetto, fifty miles square. Normally the dweller in such a peculiarly horizontal slum, in such an immense area, would hear of an incident with the police only the next day, if at all, when he read it in the newspaper. With 24-hour on-the-spot news coverage, however, reality for the viewer in the eye of the storm became not the quiet outside his own bungalow, but the place, often miles away, where the action was. . . .

> Since only high points are reported, an incident soon becomes a skirmish, a skirmish a full-scale war. . . .

> . . . By virtue of the microphone in his hand, an electronic journalist is automatically a participant in any story he covers, particularly in one as volatile and fluctuating as a riot. There is no rewrite man to temper his immediate emotions, no time to reflect before a typewriter upon what he has seen. He is forced to shoot from the lip, as are those he interviews.[26]

Item: An imminent invasion of Laos by Communists was featured in United States news broadcasts in 1960. United Nations observers, Reuters, and other *foreign* news-service reporters found no evidence to support this report. It proved to be a fabrication, broadcast without being checked. The United States press and broadcast media were apparently the only ones which carried it. When it was found to be false, no retraction, correction, or apology appears to have been made. Yet one such false report some day may trigger global holocaust.

Item: A UPI reporter, concentrating on speed, reported UN Secretary General Dag Hammerskjold safely landed in Africa in September 1961. U.S. stations carried this story. Actually the plane had crashed September 17, there were no survivors, and the Secretary General was already dead at the very moment his safe arrival was being announced.

Item: A report that Jacqueline Kennedy, when First Lady, was doing the twist in a certain Florida night club was proven false, *after* it had been released by AP. The dancer, it was later learned, was another person. But thousands of broadcast listeners and viewers heard this "scoop."

Item: The texts of speeches not yet delivered are being broadcast as if already given. In 1964 an Illinois political leader wrote a speech for delivery in Chicago, but found that, owing to a misunderstanding, he had been invited only to attend, not address, a given function. He returned with his speech still in his pocket. The never-delivered "speech" was *reported* as given before it was learned that it would not be delivered.

This list could be expanded with scores of other examples. It is thanks largely to television and radio that pressure for ever more speed is transferred to the news services, with results such as those noted above. More valid values than firstness, or scooping others, need to be found. Certainly reports which affect the life, death, and reputations of individuals and nations should *not* be broadcast until they have been absolutely confirmed. The speed and vividness with which television and radio can report world happenings or alleged world happenings represents a hazard as well as an advantage. It requires, as never before, coolness, mature judgment, and restraint. There is too little evidence of either today.

Unlike the leaders of American networks, who are usually businessmen by background and who emphasize speed and competition, Lord Reith, first Director of the British Broadcasting Corporation, sometimes used to broadcast the news himself in the early days of the BBC. He was in the midst of a newscast when a bulletin was passed to him stating that the British general strike was over. He paused, scrawled on the slip, "Get this confirmed by 10 Downing Street," gave it back, and concluded reading his prepared newscast with no reference to the bulletin. When he read the bulletin announcing the strike settlement on the air a few moments later, it had been confirmed and checked. The BBC had not scooped anyone. But neither had it risked broadcasting a report until it had been confirmed.

The motto of a Swiss news agency in Zurich is "Better to be second to publish a piece of news than the first to publish false." Such an approach is highly recommended to American broadcasters. This is especially relevant since many of the millions of dollars spent in rushing news to television and radio viewers and listeners is spent on relaying "news" of the latest accidents, divorces, and scandals. Certainly such news would not be harmed if slightly delayed until it could be checked. Such procedure would greatly reduce the tragic and dangerous cases of mistaken identity and other errors which result from present practices. It would also reduce costs considerably.

Part of the problem involved here is traceable to lack of clarity regarding the respective roles of television and radio as news reporters and interpreters. Can the sort of division of labor that distinguishes newspapers from magazines not be developed between them? Certainly television cannot compete with radio in the speed with which it reports, if its peculiar visual qualities are to be utilized. Should it try? Or should it not, rather, aim at adding its special qualities of reliability and understanding to all it broadcasts?

Newsreels for many years served a worthwhile function for moviegoers. They were usually a week or so late. To what extent did this reduce their value for understanding? Can TV not afford to be late in order to be considered, like reliable news magazines, definitive, interpretive, and careful, with the added advantages of personal and intimate impact? In view of the explosive potential for demonstration, investigation, suggestion, and news-making which television peculiarly possesses, should accuracy and care not be to it what virtue is to a woman, as Joseph Pulitzer used to say of great newspapers?

4. Preoccupation with gadgetry and celebrities. In his Elmer Davis Memorial Lecture February 15, 1966, David Brinkley urged an end to the "star" system for news reporters. Several passages from this address are admirable statements of television's problems as a news medium:

> Journalism, well-practiced, requires time for reading, thought, reflection and study. It requires time to get about, to see, to listen, to talk to people, and then to reflect on what has been said and heard.

It cannot successfully be combined with the time-consuming, taxing and fatiguing trappings of the star system.

It may be that Huntley and Cronkite and I and a few others are the last of a type. . . . The world and the news of it grow more complex. . . . And the time when one man can give it to them is coming to an end. . . . Television's ancestor, the movies, promoted stars because they were selling romance and sex and adventure. . . . Television . . . ought to be developing an identity of its own, a coherence, a clear sense of itself and its place. Not what stars it can offer, but what it itself is. . . .

When it does . . . it will have its own institutional, or corporate, status of integrity and stability, free of the artifice of show business. And it will then have grown up.[27]

Meanwhile, however, the star system goes on, and emphasis on celebrities rather than historically significant events is preserved.

As might be expected in a medium which is admittedly show business, as Brinkley and other newsmen have ruefully noted, there is a heavy preoccupation with gadgetry. This view of TV and radio news leads to the use of a wide range of sound effects, whistles, echo chambers, space sounds, vibrations, buzz saws, oscillators, predictions, alleged exclusives, recordings of news tickers, opinions of ignorant celebrities and members of the public on the most specialized subjects, and other similar habits. Trained by such practices, television viewers, it appears, have come to judge newscasts by excitement and other *entertainment* standards, rather than by substantive news criteria. The impression which foreign visitors receive of what is considered "news" on American television or radio has been criticized often, as noted earlier in this chapter.

E. B. White, in his classic story, "The Crack of Doom,"[28] recreates a typical network coverage of a hospitalized scientist. Coverage is achieved by placing reporters at various places in the hospital while others are in planes, diving at and passing by the hospital window behind which he lies. A heroic newsman is killed when his plane crashes. This calls for other planes to cover the crash, as a simple story is escalated by broadcast practices and is blown up out of proportion.

With control of newsmen, procedures, and policy in the hands of the kind of individuals who are likely to label as "good show" the type of coverage E. B. White describes, we come very close to what might be termed Hollywood news standards, instead of journalism. In such an environment, it is not too surprising that the falling of government or tragedies in which millions may be involved, are left unreported if Frank Sinatra decides to take a swing at someone, or take a young bride, or if Elizabeth Taylor and Richard Burton appear in any conspicuous public spot. Television and radio news media then cease to report news; they become tools for the indulgence of the public in the entertainment sense.

In a speech to the American Society of Newspaper Editors a few years ago, the late Adlai Stevenson recalled a period of great crisis for the United States. Krushchev was in India; Mikoyan was in Cuba; the French had just exploded an atomic bomb; the United States had just discovered the missile gap. What was most of the "news" on TV about? Baseball; Jack Paar's flight to Hong Kong; the family problems of several Hollywood stars; and political accusations and counter-accusations of American politicians. Is preoccupation with show business and celebrity values not a dangerous practice for a news medium?

5. Quantity and expense as criteria of excellence. Since the superiors of most news directors are not journalists, the effectiveness of the news job being done by television and radio is usually "proved" by quoting quantitative criteria which are their stock in trade: costs, ratings, number of personnel engaged, number of pieces or tons of equipment used, what a "great show" it was, how much income the networks sacrificed, value of time "given," and so on. Quoting how many millions of dollars coverage cost, or how many hundreds of people are used, however, is not necessarily a valid way to measure television's news effectiveness. Sometimes a single man speaking simply may communicate more than the most expensive documentary or team production. Few great reporting successes, in fact, are traceable to the efforts of crowds of so-called newsmen. Most, instead, are the results of the efforts of single fine journalists, left free to do their jobs without being hampered by the taboos, orders, or requirements of salesmen, advertisers, or business magnates.

In the field of international news, especially, television and radio network executives would have the people of America believe a remarkable job is being done. This job is "proved" in terms of how many correspondents they have overseas, how many "direct reports" are used, and so on. Equating the job done in terms of dollars, bustle, and numbers, a quantification of quality, is characteristic of present network leadership. But it seems to deserve to be challenged as valid criteria. As a result of emphasis on quantity, distance, numbers, and expense, broadcast news becomes a flood of occurrences, reports, and stories. Many people are busily hurrying back and forth. Correspondents rush back and forth by jet. Cars crash, rushing films to planes. Thousands of feet of film are being used. Hundreds of people are being interviewed. Huge expense accounts are approved. Hundreds of news personnel are pushing each other aside to scoop each other daily. But is this the way news should be measured? I think not.

6. Giving people what they want. One of the attitudes of station management which seems to this writer to violate the meaning of news most flagrantly is the philosophy that broadcasting should give people what they want, in news as well as in other programs. This concept requires closer examination if its full implications are to be understood.

The Communications Act speaks of "the public interest, convenience and necessity." A person's needs are often quite different from his desires. There is a vast difference between reporting the truth, which may or may not be pleasant, and telling the people what they want to know, or know about, which may or may not be the truth or the whole truth. There is also a great difference between what is to a person's interest and what is to his liking, just as there is a difference between the real *need* which the word *hunger* describes and the *desire* for something, possibly harmful, which the word *appetite* describes. Most critics acknowledge that people do not know what to expect of broadcasting as a news source except as broadcasting itself has instructed them in what is news, what they have a right to expect, and what the electronic media are capable of providing.

Information or news about any subject, by the very act of being broadcast, generates interest in the topic involved. Supply is not merely shaped by demand; demand is equally created by what the media supply, and by the latent appetites awakened. Likes and interests can no longer be considered as innate. They are bred and developed by the media. What will result in highest profits rather than in the greatest good has recently come all too often to dominate value judgments about what to broadcast. This can be as dangerous in the news field as it is in nutrition or medicine. For an editor or publisher to follow majority appetites in news selection is to reduce to meaninglessness the profession of journalism. Men and societies must be told when their houses are on fire, or their children dying of malnutrition, whether or not that is what they wish to hear. John Q. Public, given a choice, of course would certainly rather not hear about the growing power of Communist China. But to fail to tell him is neither responsible journalism nor operation in the public interest; it is a violation and evasion of both.

Several responsible newsmen and editors have indicated what use they think should be made of ratings. If the people know little about *international news,* such editors say, they consider low ratings, or low readership, a challenge to do *more,* and work *harder* to make international news vital and interesting—not to *give up covering* international news. Such is the kind of guidance that "what the people want," as compared to what they need, would seem to offer responsible journalists. In TV, low ratings are generally used either to cause or to rationalize dropping or de-emphasizing whatever is rated. This practice, surely, should not be applicable to news.

Democracy must place certain needs ahead of appetites. To select news on the basis of "what the people want," or ratings, or any extraneous values is to destroy the meaning of news. If news meant no more than this, a long line of distinguished American journalists would not have dedicated their lives to it.

7. Misleading or neutralizing by other techniques. There are several practices in the handling of certain kinds of facts, evidence, and statistics which seem to have developed peculiarly in broadcast journalism. This should not be surprising since in commercial TV and radio, claims and counterclaims, "evidence" and contrary evidence, so dominate the environment in which news is placed. One such practice is the "leveling" of values or evidence in such a way that the trivial and the great, the urgent and the unimportant, are presented as of equal weight. This perhaps grows out of desire to avoid favoring one sponsor over another. The lie and the truth are given the same prominence. A few "antis" or fabricated authorities, with the help of public relations agents, can be amplified by TV or radio to sound as numerous and qualified as thousands of scholars and such specialists as chemists, dentists, doctors, or lawyers. On almost any subject someone who "thinks otherwise" can be found and cited to equal or neutralize the expert or specialist. By what clues can the listener or viewer tell which is the real expert? A sort of objectivity which equates quantity with quality, as if any fifty words were equal to any

fifty others, or any speaker were as good as any other, prevails not only in broadcasting but also in other media which must compete with it today more and more. This appears to have dangerous consequences in the production of confusion or indifference of public opinion, whether deliberate or unintentional. How many citizens are restrained from legitimate action as a result of being neutralized by "evidence" presented in the media as if it were valid, rather than merely intended to preserve the status quo, or to confuse the opposition? What are the social and political effects of such practices? Certainly great care should be taken to insure against such practices becoming more widespread, consciously or deliberately. The consequences for decision-making are too great.

8. Fragmentation and discontinuity. Some of the consequences of firstness and emphasis on speed were noted earlier. Left until now, however, is an analysis of the extent to which these practices lead to fragmentation and discontinuity as characteristics of broadcast news as a whole.

If an item started yesterday, and was mentioned then, it usually is considered as having been "covered." Fewer listeners and viewers than one would wish write to stations to ask: "Whatever happened to ——?" There is simply not time enough under present practices, nor are records generally kept (in TV or radio, in contrast to newspaper morgue practices and "tickler" files) of *continuing* developments, to be sure the whole story about any one item mentioned is ever heard. Consequently, historical processes are too often lost sight of, and treated as of no interest. Instead of keeping us up to date on what is happening, however slowly and gradually, in all fields of human endeavor such as politics, commerce, science, education, religion, aviation, medicine, law, labor, conservation, communication, transportation, and so on, television and radio news seems to have become rather a fragmented listing of isolated accidents and acts of violence and abnormality without apparent causes or explanation, hanging in space. One of the dangers of this approach is that reporting events without background or cause gives an impression of fatalism to history. That slums or poor educational facilities or unemployment, or the use of alcohol or certain drugs may be the causes of the crime or accident reported is all too rarely examined. Snippets of discontinuity proliferate in a plethora of confusion.

9. Rigging. Another all too common characteristic of news presentation as now practiced is *rigging,* not too dissimilar to that used on quiz programs. In world news roundups, networks go through the motion of a direct report, whether it is needed or not. If the "direct report" from Hong Kong fails, however, the anchor man can generally report as much and as adequately as the man-on-the-spot, or perhaps more. As in quiz shows, he "has the answer" all the time. The "remotes" are often rigged up and staged largely for show. To view news as something to be "rehearsed" and then "put on" in this sense is not a news but a showmanship practice.

Television and radio practices, by their power, then come to be copied in other media as well. A young reporter at New York University, who did a biography of Kim Novak, tells how she got Miss Novak on the phone and had her describe the room from which she was speaking. The reporter then wrote the story as if *she* herself had actually been there. This is, of course, a technique used for years by TV and radio newsmen in "You Are There" type re-creations and documentaries. In the co-existence of reality and fantasy within news departments many dangers arise which have so far had too little attention. Whether space shot coverage is real or by "animation" comes to be irrelevant. Whether programs are live or pre-recorded, actual or "enacted," all come to have effects—and dangers, when labeled "news" or said to be the product of a news department. When such news standards and criteria begin to be adopted by the other news media in order to compete with television and radio and the new pressures they bring with them, the need for adoption by the latter of criteria which take into account and clearly identify significance, truth, and other real values, becomes obvious. Present criteria of television news selection and presentation, thus viewed, seem overdue for revision.

One aspect of *rigging,* less within than *about* news, arouses special concern. In statements of networks and stations regarding the amount of news broadcast as compared to the amount of entertainment presented, we read repeatedly that 25 per cent or more of a network's time is devoted to news department offerings. Besides overlooking the fact that most of these broadcasts contain advertising often taking up to 10 or more per cent of this time, several other essential facts are concealed by such claims. A quick review of the principal problems involved would be useful at this point.

Because television and radio are evanescent media, it is difficult for the public to check on them or to tell how *much* news, if equated in terms of newspaper column inches, for example, our vaunted "complete newscasts" contain. As much as three thousand words (or picture and film equivalents) of solid news appears to be considerably above the average available daily from most stations, if we exclude repetitions on successive newscasts, and non-news items.

Any reader or observer who cares to use a stop watch and pencil can himself check to see how many minutes of a newscast on TV or radio are really devoted to news; how many to commercials; and how many to what may be considered pseudo events or public relations releases which are sometimes difficult to identify. Once openers, closers, commercials, and other extraneous elements are timed and noted, the complaints of the best newsmen in the country that they do not have enough time, in uninterrupted segments, to do the news job the nation requires, can be more fully appreciated.

When human interest, sports, and weather stories (which are often duplicated elsewhere), fashion and celebrity notes, and so on are deducted, many 30-minute newscasts are found to average not over ten to fifteen minutes of solid local, national, and world news. At average reading rates this is perhaps two thousand words, which would take very little space, if seen in print. Martin Agronsky once estimated that the average 15-minute newscast did not contain more than two minutes of Washington news. Only rarely is there any more international news than that on many stations, as has been found by stop-watch monitoring of news programs each year by university students in radio and television courses.

Another kind of rigging is found in trade association brochures and ads which list the total hours of news available on all networks or stations. The rigging lies in the implication that the viewer can watch or hear this much news, whereas nearly all these programs are scheduled within the same few hours, and thus overlap. There may be six hours of news, additively computed, on six stations in a given area, but since the viewer must miss the other five if he selects one, he can watch the number of hours of these different newscasts for a given day as listed in the ads only if he has several television receivers and several sets of ears, eyes, and attention. If one wishes television news between 7:00 P.M. and 10:00 P.M. in most sections of the Midwest (or 8:00 and 11:00 in the East), one finds *none,* no matter how many hours of news a day the published figures seem to indicate as "available." If you are unable to watch at 10:00 P.M. on weekdays or 10:30 P.M. on Saturdays in a given area, you miss not one but *all* the evening news broadcasts. The long list of programs missed is impressive but of little consolation or help to the viewer unable to view at those hours. Furthermore, viewers are often scolded for "missing" a larger number of hours of good programs than it is physically possible to view because such programs are scheduled simultaneously. This is of course an entertainment practice. (Many viewers would like to have supported both the *Danny Kaye Show* and ABC's *Stage 67* in the fall of 1966. But to choose one meant to "vote against" the other, although many *other* hours of the week offered these same viewers nothing of interest, or a choice only of one of several game shows, Westerns, comedies, or fine news or documentary programs.) Some opportunity for listening to more than one news program and documentary, and comparing them, using one to complement the other, should be found.

Contrary to the claims of certain defenders of present practices, the Department of Justice appears to favor this practice (alternating and staggering program types) as "integration" rather than opposing it as "collusion." Besides claims regarding the *number* of hours devoted to news and public affairs, which would seem to deserve more careful scrutiny and greater honesty than they usually receive, two other facts regarding news on the air deserve to be identified and corrected.

One of these is the fact, noted earlier in this chapter, that few newscasts, or even news specials, are seen in prime time. If prime time is, depending on time zones, approximately 7 to 10 or 8 to 11 in the evening, very few regular news programs or specials appear to be scheduled then. In a famous instance in Philadelphia a few years ago, one network boasted of an exceptionally large number of hours devoted to educational, documentary, public affairs, and other such programs. More careful examination revealed that most of these were broadcast after midnight. Neither prime time nor prime importance seem yet to characterize network or station news in the United States.

In his carefully documented study of news practices in various countries, Norman Swallow found that:

> . . . The BBC not only produces more regular current affairs programmes than any other single organization but, significantly, it shows them at a more popular time . . . The record of the British commercial

network was less glorious; *This Week,* lasting thirty minutes, was the only regular programme of comment placed during the "peak" period, though *World in Action* missed it by only five minutes. In the USA the position was as bad; of the three main national networks only one, CBS, allowed a major public affairs series to be seen at peak times. *CBS Reports* was accurately described in 1964 by its producers as "network television's only regularly scheduled public affairs programme in prime evening time."[29]

He notes later:

. . . To place them at ten or eleven o'clock at night, or perhaps in the barren wastes of a (British) Sunday afternoon, is merely to ensure a continuation of the very state of affairs which is supposed to cause so much concern.[30]

Perhaps even more questionable is the network practice of having news departments produce every conceivable type of non-news as well as news program. A casual glance at the organizational charts of broadcast networks in other nations usually reveals departments of science, education, health, music, drama, and numerous others. In the United States, all such programs, which usually have in common only the fact that they may lose money and are of a "prestige" type, are by some strange quirk produced by the "News Department." A journalist's judgment and training certainly qualify him to say the last word without being over-ruled by sales and management superiors in news matters. Here he should be supreme. But to expect him to be qualified also to do programs on art, music, and so on, as in documentaries on the Louvre or Pablo Casals, seems to be giving trained newsmen increasingly non-news responsibilities. And they have already repeatedly complained that they have neither the staff, budget, or time even to do the *news* adequately.

The National Driver's Test, presented by the CBS News Department on CBS-TV, was a fine program, and swept three of sixteen Sloan Awards in 1966. We can all be grateful for it. But why "news"? Or how did the CBS News documentary *Sinatra* require the efforts of CBS News instead of a special entertainment, variety, or musical documentary unit? In this case especially, the tactics used in the promotion of the program (threatened lawsuits against CBS by Sinatra and other performers) were hardly the kind that would seem in the best news tradition. They illustrate what happens when news and entertainment values and functions become mixed. How many non-news chores can the staffs and personnel of news departments be stretched to cover without causing real news to suffer—and without creating confusion regarding what real news is? Does assigning such a program as *Casals at 88* on CBS to the news department for production not invite having such a program distorted in order to give it news or political relevance when *artistic* excellence and criteria are the only ones which should be relevant? Or in what respect was *The Stately Ghosts of England,* an hour-long NBC news color special, a news program? Is the long list of "show you the place" programs (Louvre, Kremlin, White House, etc.) now to take up more of the time and energy of news departments? Can news departments really be expected to be also the education, science, history, music, and other departments of the networks? Can networks really not afford separate departments for these functions, although the networks of other great nations can? If they could, then perhaps news departments could once again concentrate on news.

Unobtrusively, then, a great many things have happened to the definition and selection of news, and the role and function of news departments, which need more careful consideration. Let us look now at some of the values, and motives and practices, however honestly conceived, which have brought about these distortions and displaced values.

MANAGEMENT AND SALES VALUES, VETOING NEWS VALUES

In a speech November 21, 1963, Herbert Brucker, Editor of the Hartford *Courant,* described the fatal effects which follow in any news medium when non-professionals begin to control professional newsmen. He quoted Ben Hibbs, when Hibbs was still editor of *Saturday Evening Post,* in his description of the reasons for the demise of *Collier's* magazine. Hibbs had said:

> Editorial independence went down the drain at the house of Crowell long years before the final collapse of the publications themselves. During the last ten years of their existence, as financial troubles deepened, the *editors* were given less and less freedom of action. Someone from the business office was always looking over their shoulders.

This, Hibbs had said, was "one of the tragic stories of publishing, and it should be known." Brucker added: "You cannot have survival in journalism, let alone excellence, if editorial decisions are made on business grounds."[31]

This warning is relevant here, because of the increasing evidence that broadcast news departments and employees at the networks—the houses of Sarnoff, Paley, and Goldenson—are constantly hampered and over-ruled by non-journalistic, non-professional bosses or supervisors, who put "business grounds," as Brucker calls them, ahead of news values and professional standards. This is natural, of course, since most broadcast empires, unlike newspaper properties, were not founded by journalists but by entrepreneurs who entered the broadcast field, attracted principally by profits rather than the desire to "publish the truth." But it is perhaps the most serious flaw in the structure of broadcasting as a news medium and as press. A principal requirement for a free press is that the professional journalists who comprise it must be kept free from inhibitions, pressures, and interferences which might reduce the integrity of their work. There is considerable evidence that government interference has been better held at bay than commercial and management interference.

The extent to which qualified newsmen have been prevented from doing the job they know needs to be done, in fact, is too little known by the public. Former network newsmen have explained the pressures often brought to bear on them while they were in network news operations. Since newsmen, like other human beings, have families, and are interested in promotions, they are likely to "go along" with the wishes of the top executives of their enterprises, on whom their promotions and security depend. Messrs. Paley, Sarnoff, Stanton, and Goldenson, in the last analysis, with men they have picked on the basis of business credentials, determine what shall be considered news by their hiring or firing at will of the Hagertys, Brinkleys, Huntleys, Smiths, and others whose choices then become decisive. In addressing his colleagues in 1958 in Chicago, Edward R. Murrow referred to the constant need to consider radio and television news as salable, packageable, and selected so as not to antagonize a sponsor. He said: "I don't care what you call it. I say it isn't news."[32]

Television and radio are business enterprises. They are controlled by individuals who see eye-to-eye with other business men. They are opposed to labor and to any other antagonistic interests likely to be disruptive of their profitable status quo. Their sense of values and their definition of news therefore let certain things through the channels they control and withhold others. This is not to say that these business-oriented executives intentionally distort anything. They may well reall*y* believe that *their* judgments and general policy directives *are* the best ones possible for the public interest. Since these leaders are business and corporation men, salesmen and showmen, not political scientists, economists, or journalists either by training or orientation, their beliefs should not be surprising. But they are not necessarily views which are in the over-all national interest. In fact, they are likely to be extremely atypical and they can be fatal if left unchecked.

Judged by the values of such network and station owners and executives, the time and emphasis provided for news now are undoubtedly adequate or even generous. This judgment says more about their sense of values than it does about the nation's needs for better news services. Their criteria must be challenged. To treat news as something to be sandwiched between music, commercials, pistol shots, guffaws, and celebrities, and framed in music and sound effects, is to misunderstand not only the role of our electronic media but also the omens of tomorrow, the many cracks and strains in our society which may be distressing but which demand attention. These demand to be seen, recognized, and interpreted in a way that only trained observers, i.e., journalists, left free from all extraneous pressures—the kinds of pressures which now seem to prevail—can provide.

In addition to the general corporate and show-business orientation of the network chiefs, other characteristics are discernible. These include militaristic as opposed to pacifistic orientation; conservative and anti-labor attitudes; increasingly monopolistic control of news media in fewer hands; and inordinate preoccupation with higher and higher profits. A closer look at each of these tendencies is overdue. Although not all these characteristics apply uniformly to all managements, enough would seem to apply universally to justify consideration.

Militaristic Orientation. A critic of United States journalism, Harold Innis, once said that "world peace would be bad for the pulp and paper industry."[33] Today, a glance at the proportion of the incomes of RCA and CBS, particularly, which comes from defense contracts raises questions about the likely effects of world peace, or relaxation of tension, on *their* profits and corporate positions. Is it good to have news, as well as entertainment, controlled by a complex for which military interests, orientations, and contracts are so profitable?

The position of pacifists under present controls is significant. They seem generally to be depicted, if at all, as misfits in society. Conditioned by abundant public relations from the military, the bias with which we view pacifistic and other "impractical" activities and individuals seems not even to be noticed. News of the Japanese man who walked throughout Japan, collecting over half a million signatures on a petition begging the United States to rain no more atomic fallout on his nation, after Pacific atomic tests, did not find its way to the United States people via television and radio. Yet it and similar events would have helped explain anti-American student demonstrations in Japan a few years later, when President Eisenhower planned to visit Japan—better than the simplified explanation broadcast, which was that the students were "Communists" or leftists.

The military orientation of broadcast leaders is not surprising. It has prevailed from the first. Both Brigadier General David Sarnoff and William S. Paley, who has carried out SHAEF and other assignments with distinction, as a colonel, have had close connections with military traditions and military thinking. Since a large part of the income of both firms comes from defense contracts, their daily close contacts with and admiration and respect for military leaders are natural. At both the top and second echelons in the dominant networks, two generations of leaders who have fought two wars and become accustomed to secrecy and the tradition of regimentation and discipline down the line in both the military and corporate sense, supervise those responsible for news operations. They are accustomed to exercising authority, and expecting obedience. If reporters get too hot on the scent of secret contracts between AT and T and the Pentagon, or RCA and the Defense Department, or CBS and the Air Force, some high-ranking executive is likely to suggest tactfully that the disclosure of such information is not in the nation's interest. The combination of Madison Avenue, Wall Street, and the Pentagon as forces which have shaped those who control television and radio as news media is a difficult one to overcome. Surely it is not tolerable in broadcast *news*. This militaristic bias of broadcast leadership, however honestly come by, is a factor which needs to be considered in any evaluation of television news.

Anti-Labor Tendencies. The conservative and anti-labor orientation of the networks, briefly alluded to earlier, is serious enough to deserve further attention. Early in his career in the tobacco business, young William S. Paley and other members of his family found labor problems troublesome. Labor problems in Chicago were cited as a principal reason for moving the base of operations of the family-owned cigar interests to Philadelphia.[34]

In discussing the problem of covering labor news, Louis Lyons in 1959 pointed out that "the publisher is a big employer himself." The same is true of broadcast station owners and networks. The fact that they represent the attitude of business rather than of labor is natural. However, the double standard between the news coverage of unions and of business is more flagrant and conspicuous than one would expect. Over 90 per cent of the news of labor on television and radio, as in newspapers, has been reported to be unfavorable.[35] Newspaper and broadcast station network management, being the antagonists of labor, seem prone to denounce the "public be damned" attitude of labor. They also all too often seek out news of strikes, violence, or other unfavorable news if any news of labor is to be reported at all. A. J. Liebling found that the most usual picture of labor in the news media of the nation is an adverse one. "It is still stubborn, selfish, unreasonable, overpaid, grasping, domineering, un-American, irreverent, blind to its own interests and living in an unreal world. It is also inefficient, undemocratic and gangster-ridden. . . ."[36]

In connection with press coverage of railroad and steel strikes, there seems to be much reference to labor's high wages and featherbedding but little reference to industry's frequently very high profits, the number of officials added to the administrative salary payroll, and increased benefits for the executives.

Televised summaries of the Kohler Company strike hearings in Washington, to be discussed later, covered management's presentation, but did not carry summaries of labor's side of the hearings. The significance of this kind of coverage, as an example of television's ability to provide balance, in case of access to court trials, or the Congress, should not be overlooked.

The difference in the coverage of anti-trust violations by RCA, General Electric, and other firms, which own stations, and the coverage given to suits against labor unions, and union leaders like Hoffa, is also conspicuous. Professor Harvey J. Levin, in his study of some of the dangerous practices resulting from joint ownership of newspapers and broadcast stations, has reported how Hearst newspaper and radio officials cooperated to secure the cancellation of CIO programs over station KYA in San Francisco. CIO Director Allan Haywood testified before the FCC regarding the inability of the Transport Workers Union to secure any time, day or night, free or paid, over Hearst's station WINS and station WNEW, then owned also by a newspaper.[37]

The respects in which labor has been fought, opposed, and discredited both in and by newspapers and the broadcast media generally are hardly a secret. However natural or understandable this prejudice is, in editorial or negotiation contexts, it would seem to be a dangerous situation when the public can no longer count on receiving from broadcasting the full truth about labor or any other segment of American life and society. The problems of America should be seen in a perspective which puts the interests and forces of labor, business, education, and all other *parts* of the public interest in proper perspective. A news service which is *controlled* by one of these rival interests not only does not but probably *cannot* see or reveal the total economy and culture as a balanced whole, made up of these many parts.

Network policy-makers, like the membership of such trade associations as the National Association of Broadcasters (NAB) or the American Newspaper Publishers Association (ANPA), are business executives rather than journalists or professionals. Again and again, network newsmen and others have been found quietly applauding and identifying with former FCC Chairman Newton Minow or E. William Henry, or other critics, rather than with their superiors. They do not dare publish their feelings, of course, because they still must work for and obey the latter. It is interesting to note how often the thinking of critics and government regulators is closer to the thinking of those whose freedoms free speech is intended to protect, viz., the journalists and newsmen themselves, than it is to the views of management.

On problems of medical care or the more stringent regulation of food drugs, or advertising, too, it is not surprising to find the attitudes of the networks consistent with those of big business generally. Readers are invited to check the position which the networks and the National Association of Broadcasters take on laws affecting cigarettes, cosmetics, the Securities and Exchange Act, child labor laws, higher second-class postal rates, fair labor standards legislation, truth in labeling and packaging, and virtually all subsidies except those provided to the newspapers and larger magazines by postal rates. Like the American Medical Association and the National Association of Manufacturers, they naturally favor the status quo. This is obvious both in the news and in the public pronouncements and the testimony of industry leaders. (This is natural, since the top executives of television and radio have not changed, as national political leadership has, with the Hoovers, Roosevelts, Trumans, Eisenhowers, Kennedys, and Johnsons; the Sarnoff and Paley families are in control today just as they were during the Hoover administration. Many of the economic and social theories and perspectives of the late 1920's are still in the saddle.) Whatever news reaches the public must do so through the kind of filter which the known orientations of the chief executives of the parent corporations provide to all employees.

Whereas the citizen needs access to all possible points of view on important problems, and perhaps thinks this is what he has, the market place of ideas is actually controlled by similar kinds of individuals, with similar interests. It is preposterous to maintain that the present business-oriented broadcast service, which reduces labor, education, art, and religion to an infinitesimal status, as if they were minor or non-essential parts of our political and cultural system, adequately serves our nation's news and public affairs needs.

Supremacy of Profit Considerations. Another characteristic of broadcast leadership, which greatly hampers the adequacy of the job broadcasting is doing in the field of news, is its emphasis on profits. In 1963, Leonard Lavin, President of the Alberto-Culver Corporation, told broadcast and advertising executives: "To be frank with you, gentlemen, I think you are getting greedy."[38]

The study of Illinois television stations in 1963 by Gregory Liptak[39] indicated the preponderance of stations in which, in the judgment of newsmen, profits ranked ahead of news. This study also revealed that stations employ more salesmen than newsmen and pay them more. The stringent limitations placed on news departments are illustrated in one news director's statement that the station manager has imposed a limit on the number of long-distance calls the news department may make. "This makes the gathering of a story difficult," he said, in a revealing statement about management values. In a majority of the stations, management, on various occasions, has influenced news decisions. In some cases, newsmen had to "lay off" friends of the boss. Scandals or accidents in the family of the boss, or indictments of his firm or those of friends, are very unlikely to be disclosed in the boss-dominated complex that broadcast news, especially at the local station level, appears to be.

The networks and larger station groups often boast of the number of dollars, or millions of dollars, they *lose* on news each year. Yet these stations are licensed only on the condition that they provide adequate service in the public interest, convenience, and necessity. Since news is perhaps the crucial item in such service, what broadcasting does in news and public affairs does not represent any *gift* to the public. It does represent a debt and obligation to the public. And the kind of payment the public is now receiving is overdue for review. To protest that television cannot do an adequate job of the news because it has only 5 or 15 or 30 minutes to give to newscasts needs to be challenged. There is no reason why as much time cannot and should not be given to news and public affairs as to Westerns. And for television and radio to claim they would go broke if they provided this kind of news service also needs to be challenged. They are likely to find the American public more responsive to responsible leadership than they suspect.

To boast of the time given to news, or of other *free* time *given,* is no more characteristic of good leadership than for a newspaper editor or publisher to boast that today he gave his readers 100 column inches of "news," instead of cutting it down to 50 inches to make room for more advertising.

Mark Ethridge was once asked how much the cost of the *news* function of the Louisville *Courier-Journal* amounted to. He said he had no idea. News coverage is taken as a principal part of what newspapers exist to do; they are expected to do this as a primary responsibility, without separately counting their costs. Television executives, however, are likely to report these costs as "losses," carefully computed, and displayed as a badge of generosity. Certainly, an adequate job in news and public affairs cannot be done with present typical news staffs, salaries, and budgets. But there is no reason, as one notes the magnitude of network and large station profits, why all these news services cannot be tripled or multiplied tenfold.

Edward R. Murrow once observed how each rumor of a slight budget stringency in the network seemed to result in an immediate cutback in bodies, not in the sales or entertainment departments, but in the news and public affairs department, even at times when network profits were at all-time highs. Yet he could find nothing in the Bill of Rights or the Communications Act "which says that they must increase their net profits each year, lest the Republic collapse."[40] News departments, being less popular with management than others which are more profitable, are usually the first to feel the axe in economy drives. Murrow found it difficult to believe that the decisions of network executives were made by men who love, respect, or understand news. They seemed to him to love the highest possible profits more.

Admittedly, there has been an increase in the length of one or two newscasts each day per network from 15 minutes to a half-hour. This has resulted in proportional increases in the advertising they contain as well as in solid news, however, so this is less of a news gain than it first appears, as listeners are invited to see for themselves, watch in hand.

These increases do not reveal either increased generosity on the part of network management or even increased enthusiasm for news or recognition of its importance. Rather, they generally are grudging concessions made to head off threatened regulation or other kinds of outside pressure. Extorted from industry by former FCC Chairman Minow and others, such changes as have been made in recent years indicate only changes of degree. The pattern remains the same. What are needed are *basic* changes in approach.

Louis Lyons, the distinguished Curator of the Nieman Fellowships at Harvard, asked Edward R. Murrow several years ago, on a program broadcast over educational but not commercial stations, if a half-hour in-depth program from Moscow or Berlin instead of the usual two- or three-minute reports was beyond the economics of television. Murrow replied that he was not sure it was, but that this was a question for the management of CBS. Management's reply by now seems obvious, both from profits reported each year and the amount of news available.

Multiple Ownership as a Problem. In his 1959 study of joint ownership of the media,[41] Professor Harvey J. Levin reported a disturbing trend. In 1956, multiple owners in the 100 leading markets not only controlled 153 of 168 television stations, but were also joint owners of 22 newspapers, 53 radio stations, 6 magazines, and 3 motion picture enterprises. In 1959, group owners controlled 90 of the 181 newspaper-affiliated television stations. Group owners also held 160 of the 431 newspaper-affiliated standard (AM) radio stations. In all these figures, group and newspaper chain control is considerably more serious than the numbers indicate, since the *largest* stations in the highest population centers are usually involved. One large group-owned station often has more coverage, power, influence, and profits than a dozen or more independent stations.

Since 1959, when Dr. Levin's study was published, a greatly intensified trend toward more and more mergers has been observed. Of the nearly 1,000 broadcast stations identified with newspaper or magazine ownership in early 1963, there were 34 in California, 44 in Illinois, 29 in Indiana, 50 in New York, 47 in Ohio, 50 in Pennsylvania, and 30 in Texas alone. Press interests most conspicuously represented were *Time-Life,* McClatchy, Meredith, Triangle, Newhouse, Hearst, Scripps-Howard, Whitney (former *New York Herald Tribune*), and the *Chicago Tribune.*

When to these group controls are added those of electrical manufacturers, show people, and a dozen such family corporations as Storer, which are diversifying by moving into electronics manufacturing, the rapidly diminishing diversity of ownership and control becomes more obvious. Such combines represent tremendous control over what the people of the nation shall be allowed to know as news. Certainly little news which would reflect discredit on the practices of the stations, their owners, and their sponsors and friends, is likely to pour forth from such stations. This immunity protects from criticism and public examination many of the practices of the most powerful social and economic mechanisms in the nation. Are such management values, practices, and immunities in the public interest?

Advertising as a Base and Determinant for News. News, at least, of all program services, should be brought to the American people by a broadcast system it pays good money to support structurally—not by any specific product or sponsor, who is described as "bringing the news," or "making possible" certain coverage. The industry itself should make all coverage possible. News is a job for broadcasters, not for salesmen, merchandisers, or manufacturers. United States broadcasting stations—not sponsors—were licensed to serve the public interest. The sponsorship system, applied to news, contains so many taboos, blockages, and obstacles to the free flow of information, as analyzed in the next chapter, that it must be challenged.

Before he became President of the National Association of Broadcasters, even the late Judge Justin Miller vigorously opposed the inclusion of commercials in newscasts. What has happened since the early days of broadcasting is a revelation of the trends of management. At first a few commercials were self-consciously allowed, as a concession to a desire for higher and higher profits. Newsmen almost unanimously opposed them. But news practices in the networks are not decided by journalists; they are decided by management, which sometimes even decides not to hire journalists as newsmen. And many so-called newsmen are consoled by a payola-type practice which enables them to share in the spoils by collecting fees themselves as talent for doing commercials on non-news as well as news shows.

CBS President Dr. Frank Stanton has categorically denied that any

CBS news or public affairs programs have been affected by sponsor interference, control, or influence. There is beginning to be some doubt on this score, since evidence to the contrary seems to be increasing. But even if it is true, it conceals much of the problem. It may be true that the news departments of CBS and NBC allow no meddling by sponsors or other outsiders directly, as they declare. As long as the news service of a network or station is largely supported by sponsorship, however, certain newsmen become either acceptable or unacceptable as talent, both on the basis of what they do or do not report, and on the basis of how attractive to audiences they are as personalities or showmen. Certain networks' acceptability to sponsors depends on how advantageous to a given sponsor's interests their policy or "line" seems to be. Sponsors may not often dictate what network newsmen will do or say. But they can and do affect who is hired in the first place. Once hired because he is "safe," a newsman is unlikely to change his orientation or "spots." And once a network finds a kind of operation that is profitable, it is unlikely to change it.

In *Broadcasting and Government Regulation in a Free Society,* former Federal Communications Commission member Clifford J. Durr relates:

> A fellow came in and said: "I have a program of an hour of good music at dinner time . . . no spots, no interruptions . . . and the people love it. Now the advertising agency has said 'We want a spot right here for Ex-Lax or whatever it might be.' I said, 'I can't give it to you.' And so the agency says, 'Well, we not only control this account, but that account . . . and if you don't want to do business with us. . . .' "[42]

In most cases, the pressures on newsmen are exerted by managers or sales managers, rather than directly by sponsors. Liptak's 1963 study of more than 100 Illinois and Indiana broadcast news departments stated: "In approximately 33 per cent of the stations studied, management, on occasion, exercises influence which is detrimental to proper news judgment. This is an alarmingly high percentage."[43] The type of interference mentioned included the order not to report in the news legal suits involving the station's advertisers, refusing to carry as a news item the opening of new stores and shopping centers unless they purchased advertising, and the order to include in newscasts films of the opening of stores, however insignificant, which *were* sponsors of the station. In such an environment, advertising and news become dangerously confused, and even so-called newsmen can no longer tell which is which.

Public Relations Pressures. In many cases, particularly with regard to broadcasting, advertising ceases to be called (overt) advertising, and becomes what is called public relations. With the weak resistance offered by television and radio management to press releases of friends and sponsors, public opinion begins to be molded by publicity rather than by those channels of democracy which we think prevail. Today, in our national and state capitals, there are several times as many public relations men and lobbyists as there are newsmen. More tragically, both cross the line between these two fields to take jobs in the opposite camp. Even United Press International, a news service, offers public relations services. The difference between handouts and news begins to fade under such practices.

In an address November 29, 1937, entitled, "The American System of Broadcasting," William S. Paley said: "We sell time to sponsors solely for the advertising of their goods and services. We do not sell time for propaganda."[44] This policy appears to be violated daily over virtually all networks and stations. The institutional commercials of the automobile, steel, oil, electrical, and chemical companies and the public utilities are illustrations of precisely the type of public relations or propaganda message which Paley said broadcasting would not carry. The press releases of large firms regarding strikes, and their replies to government anti-trust actions, are frequently carried both as news and in commercials by television and radio. Often one cannot be distinguished from the other. Networks, which are big business, obviously cannot be expected to be unbiased in reporting controversy involving their parent firms, and sponsors, which are big business. Television and radio thereby come to play a large, though hidden and biased, role in "government by publicity," which is beginning to be increasingly characteristic of decision-making and legislator-manipulation in the United States.

Public relations firms in the United States are hired by foreign powers, for example, to secure favorable reports in news media. *The Reporter* magazine of December 22, 1960, listed several film companies, public relations agents, and other United States publicity men who, for a price, seek to color and control the news from and about whatever country hires them. On March 25, 1963, frightening practices came to light in the hearings conducted by Senator J. William Fulbright.[45] For example, one veteran publicity agent estimated that he placed between one and two hundred stories a month in the United States media on behalf of his Asian client; often they were used verbatim, without crediting their source. The use by NBC and others of films of Formosa, for example, was not accompanied by any statement of the fact that these films were produced by firms on the Nationalist Chinese payroll, paid not to tell the truth but to influence American and world public opinion in favor of continued subsidies to Nationalist China. Across the nation, television and radio stations use hundreds of "free" films and recordings, whose axe-grinding sources are not fully revealed to the station's audience. Since viewers think they are bona fide news, such films and recordings have tremendous impacts. Besides the newscasts which are contaminated by such materials, non-news programs are also infiltrated by them. In the average small television or radio station, the news department often is not even informed, to say nothing of being consulted, about such materials before they are broadcast as "films" or "entertainment," or as "educational" or "instructional" features. News departments would seem to be more obligated and qualified in this area than in that of producing programs about art or music.

When stations and networks begin to accept film and other materials without fully checking on their objectivity, it is not surprising that many false items will be broadcast. In 1959 when former Mutual network officials Alexander Guterma and Hal Roach were concluding a $750,000 contract with Dominican dictator Trujillo, his representatives asked to be shown what he would receive for his money. It was decided to invent a sample item and broadcast it. The network executives decided it would do no harm for Walter Winchell to say that negotiations were under way for Hal Roach to make a picture in the Dominican Republic, even though, of course, this was all an invention. Listeners to Walter Winchell heard this make-believe, "exclusive" false news item broadcast the following Sunday.[46] The "harmless" fabrication proved it could be done. What it revealed about the sacredness of United States broadcast "news" is, of course, equally significant.

A press association stringer in Cuba, it was learned after the Castro revolution, was on Batista's payroll. A Miami newspaper columnist whose stories, like those of the press association, were used on television and radio, was drawing $2,300 a month from the Dominican Republic to do favorable stories on Trujillo. How well can democracy work under conditions such as these, where broadcasters will do anything, including broadcasting false information, as news, for money? How much freedom to perform this kind of service should broadcasting enjoy?

It is time to ask whether, under present broadcast news practices, our nation is not being "operated" more as a "reportocracy" than as a democracy. Reporters and public relations men increasingly shape the image of reality. Once broadcast, this becomes the "reality" on which we proceed. Quoted on the floor of Congress as fact, the statements, releases, and opinions of such reporters and agents become part of the policy-making process. Their activities should be known, and their qualifications and biases should be checked, at the very least, before their word is taken in matters affecting our nation's activities both at home and abroad. That broadcasting has not itself taken the steps necessary to prevent such manipulation of public opinion is an indictment of its leadership and an indication of the need for public agencies to do so. Under such practices Americans begin to be the most deliberately misinformed citizens in the world. This is an intolerable situation in the greatest democracy on earth.

Conclusion. In a democracy, whose lifeblood is the free flow of information, the most treasonable act imaginable is to block or obstruct freedom of information. This is no less an offense when it is done by *private* gatekeepers than when it is done by government. It is disquieting to see so many violations of basic press freedoms coming from broadcasters who ask for *more* freedom, and claim the status of press. Are television and radio, mixed as they are with entertainment, really press? Their management continues to say that television and radio are "show business." Can they really be both?

Thanks to the pressure of television and radio and what they have come to call news, hundreds of newspapers have perished. What the rest must do to survive has changed. To meet television competition, Sunday papers have gone to more features and less serious editorial material. The financial pressures on newspapers caused by the competition of television for the same dollars, have also forced them to devote a higher proportion of space to advertising copy than they used to. For television leadership to point to these practices in justification of their own excesses is to overlook broadcasting's role in bringing this condition about. For such a small proportion of space and time in all media to be devoted to news as compared to advertising and entertainment at a time when both the population and the complexity of the news demand more, is one of the disquieting signs of our time.

Editorial and analytical content seem to be increasingly inadequate. This shortage, of course, trains viewers and readers not to expect such material; this leads to still further contraction of the supply, as broadcasters quote "what the people want." In their struggle to survive, newspapers and magazines are forced to counter television practices with competitive tactics of their own, but in the end many are bought out by broadcast combines and in the process professional publishers are replaced by profit-oriented entrepreneurs. Until recently it seemed shocking to hear publishers attempt to justify the increased emphasis on violence, celebrities, and vulgarity by saying that this is what sells newspapers. Today, matching television, it is the rule.

The concern expressed here is not therefore only with television and radio news per se; it is also with what their news role has done and is doing indirectly as well as directly to our nation as a community of citizens entrusted with the making of fateful and historic decisions. This is everyone's business and only secondarily television's or radio's. Each time another newspaper closes, or another qualified newsman leaves television or radio in disgust, or makes one more compromise with his conscience, a little more of democracy dies. Where citizens of democracy do not know the full facts, they are no less helpless and ineffectual than are the subjects of a totalitarian nation.

If the power of television and radio as news media were not so great, we could take violations of their role more lightly. But their performance virtually determines the course of future events. Broadcast journalism not only reports but shapes. When news is viewed in this light, its importance becomes crucial. When it is seen as a necessity rather than merely as a convenience, or entertainment, or as a source of "plugs" for friends, or what the people want, the freedom to be careless, to choose either personnel or news items lightly, or to interfere with its sacred flow can only be condemned as rank irresponsibility. Broadcast "press" should have no right to suppress news or voices or viewpoints it doesn't like. Broadcasting is a public, not a private resource, and it is a part of the very framework of democracy. Termites in such a structure are a *public* menace, no matter who is responsible for them. The lifeblood of democracy itself flows or fails to flow through these public channels, no matter how jealously private broadcasters may consider them their own. If television and radio wish to enjoy the freedom of the press, they should earn press freedoms in the same way newspapers have won *their* freedoms: by the excellence of their staffs and the freedoms from management pressure with which these staffs are encouraged to seek and report the *truth;* by dedication to higher goals than profits.

If the withholding of news, and the blockage of the free flow of information, were undertaken by a foreign power or by the United States Government, the people of this nation would be aroused. When these practices are traceable to the controllers of these media themselves, we hear little of them. But democracy is equally jeopardized, regardless of who constricts its freedoms. Thomas Macaulay years ago declared that nothing could be more fatal than to give the people of a nation power and then to withhold from them, in any way, the full and free information they need if they are to wield this power wisely. In all too many instances, television and radio have used *their* freedoms to reveal only their side of the nation's problem, and to conceal that which would discredit or challenge them and their practices, legal or illegal.

In our democratic tradition, Americans have been taught that any restraint upon the people's access to *all* the information needed for their decision-making is bad. It is easy to forget how crucial are the qualifications and standards which must be demanded of the gatekeepers of these media, and how far above their own selfish interests and affiliations these people must rise if they are to perform the crucial and sacred function which they have voluntarily assumed: that of keeping America informed. Since they determine what will be heard and seen, their qualifications, and the criteria which their employees are allowed or forced to use in news selection and presentation are most important. Many newsmen who have sought to make television the courageous and truthful medium they thought it could be, have been dismissed. Others have resigned themselves to present conditions. Putting some muscle and courage back into the concept of news for television and radio is both possible and desirable. The personnel, the knowledge, and the courage are available. But it will mean that broadcasting, especially broadcast news, must be freed from the advertising, public relations, and other chains which now bind it.

The potentials of these great media are greatest precisely in such fields as news. For radio and television are unique in their gifts of immediacy. These potentials cannot be realized as long as news is offered only through sponsorship. To advertisers who wish regularity in scheduling, the unexpected developments and needs of news are both irritating and disruptive. They prefer to ignore them, "regularize" them, or reduce them to non-disturbing proportions. For sponsors to decide, however indirectly, who shall be newsmen, and what shall be considered news, is intolerable. That is what, in effect, they now do by their sponsorship or non-sponsorship of certain talent and certain kinds of news programs. The fullest pressure on television and radio leaders must therefore be maintained, on behalf of the qualified journalists available, who are only hoping for the freedom and resources to do the job needed. Only thus freed can these instruments realize their full potentials, as many fine journalists wish them to do. Only then will the nation's television and radio news service become what a great democratic nation has a right to expect of it.

In ways which newspapers or magazines cannot match, these instruments *can* give Americans an understanding of world events and their citizen role in shaping them. With this understanding can come a new sense of purpose, a new optimism, and a new faith and strength.

But before this can happen, leadership's fear of controversy, of antagonizing sponsors, of arousing people to anger and action, must be replaced by courage and by rigid protection of news professionals from the pressures of sales, management, and public relations.

NOTES

1. Quoted in Giraud Chester, Garnet Garrison, and Edward Willis, *Television and Radio* (New York: Appleton-Century-Crofts, 1963), p. 393.

2. Fred Friendly, *CBS Reports,* New York, CBS-TV Network press information release, October 1963.

3. Norman Swallow, *Factual Television* (New York: Hastings House, 1966), p. 171.

4. *Ibid.,* p. 215.

5. *Ibid.,* p. 220-21

6. *Ibid.,* p. 221.

7. Although such practices have generally been denied by the industry (as quiz-rigging, blacklisting, payola, plugola, etc. were for years), a number of studies have documented this practice. Though this will be discussed in another connection in Chapter 3, the following studies and articles may be of interest at this point:

a. A 1963 questionnaire study made by a student of the author's, Gregory Liptak, and later used as the basis of his master's thesis at the University of Illinois, revealed that 33 per cent of the news directors at Illinois, Indiana, Wisconsin, Iowa, and Missouri TV and radio stations reported being told by their management to:

  (1) "Play down" certain stories (lawsuits involving advertisers; stories involving "friends of the manager"; news of unions).

  (2) Cover otherwise insignificant stories (opening of new supermarket if management a sponsor, though it would *not* be covered otherwise), etc. Over three-fourths of some 100 news directors replying reported being "requested" by management to use as news certain stories, and

many others found themselves asked to emphasize certain stories already scheduled for broadcast.

Over 65 per cent reported sales department pressures. Nineteen of some 100 news directors reported that they could not ignore such sales department requests and had to comply with them. Involved was the "killing" of such items as lawsuits involving local businessmen.

b. Per Holting, reporting on "An Investigation of Influence of Sponsors on the Content of Local News Shows of 118 TV Stations in the U.S. and Canada," stated in a *Journalism Quarterly* article: "Where Does Friction Develop for TV News Directors?" (34, No. 3 [Summer 1957], 344-59) that a disturbingly large number of sales representatives, speaking for their "accounts," force news department changes in news coverage and emphasis.

c. As long ago as 1931, H. V. Kaltenborn reported such pressures on him. See "Radio: Dollars and Nonsense," *Scribner's Magazine*, LXXXIX, No. 5 (May 1931), p. 496. Reprinted in Harry J. Skornia and Jack William Kitson, *Problems and Controversies in Television and Radio*, (Palo Alto, Calif.: Pacific Books, 1968).

d. Charles Winick, in *Taste and the Censor in Television*, an occasional paper on the role of the mass media in the free society (Fund for the Republic, 1959), also reports a large number of sponsor pressures, mostly exerted via sales departments or management.

8. Quoted in *Static*, III, No. 1 (December 15, 1961), p. 14. Published by the Council on Radio-Television Journalism of the Association for Education in Journalism (AEJ).

9. *Static*, February 15, 1964, p. 9.

10. *Ibid.*

11. Quoted in Swallow, *op. cit.,* pp. 105-7.

12. "Big Show: American White Paper, U.S. Foreign Policy on NBC," *Newsweek*, September 20, 1965, p. 90.

13. *Broadcasting*, LVIII, No. 15 (April 11, 1960), reports the accusations of Governor Ellington, the denial of CBS, and Governor Ellington's reiteration of the charge.

14. Several other examples of television as an instigator of violence, and as a news-maker, are reported in Stan Opotowsky, *TV: The Big Picture* (New York: E. P. Dutton and Co., 1961), pp. 181-83.

15. Robert Feit and Fran Elkin, "The Khrushchev Visit: Thirteen Days That Shook the World," *News Workshop* (New York University), XI, No. 1 (January 1960).

16. Rev. Bruce Hilton, "An Interim Report . . . The March to Jackson," *Presbyterian Life*, July 15, 1966, p. 30.

17. Swallow, *op. cit.*, p. 107

18. National Association of Broadcasters, *Speaker's Guide for Television Broadcasters: Where the Industry Stands:* Part 1: Advertising and the General Welfare (Washington, D.C.: The Association, 1959).

19. Jack Kinkel, "When the Tail Wags the Dog," *Saturday Review*, March 12, 1966, p. 140.

20. Jerome Aumente, "A Critical Look at Journalism's International Responsibilities," *The Quill*, May 1965, p. 25.

21. Jean Bikanda, "International Fund for the Development of Mass Media," *Journalism* (University of Strasbourg), 22 (Fall 1964), 45-46.

22. Pierre Archambault, "A French Point of View," *Journalism* (University of Strasbourg), 22 (Fall 1964), 21.

23. Quoted in *Newsweek,* October 11, 1965, p. 96.

24. Robert Manning, "An American Point of View," *Journalism* (University of Strasbourg), 22 (Fall 1964), 12.

25. Aumente, *op. cit.,* p. 24.

26. John Gregory Dunne, "TV's Riot Squad," *New Republic,* September 11, 1965, pp. 27-29.

27. From the typed text of Mr. Brinkley's remarks February 15, 1966 at the Elmer Davis memorial observance. (Text kindly provided the author by Mr. Brinkley).

28. E. B. White, "The Crack of Doom," in *Quo Vadimus* (New York: Grosset and Dunlap, 1938), pp. 53-57.

29. Swallow, *op. cit.,* pp. 25-26.

30. *Ibid.,* p. 157.

31. Herbert Brucker, "Distinction in Journalism," Remarks at Dedication Dinner, Academy of New England Journalists, Colby College, Waterville, Maine, November 11, 1963. (Manuscript)

32. Edward R. Murrow, Address to Radio and Television News Directors Association, October 15, 1958. (Later published in *The Reporter,* November 13, 1958, under the title: "A Broadcaster Talks to His Colleagues," and in the author's *Television and Society* (New York: McGraw-Hill, 1965)).

33. Harold Innis, "Great Britain, the U.S. and Canada," in *Changing Concepts of Time* (Toronto: University of Toronto Press, 1952), p. 111.

34. Mr. Paley's entry in *Current Biography: Who's Who and Why 1940* (New York: H. W. Wilson Co., 1941), p. 627, reads: ". . . His father and his uncle, Jacob Paley, had a cigar factory in Chicago. When they had labor troubles they decided to open a branch in Philadelphia, and Samuel Paley went there, taking his son with him. . . ." The 1951 edition reads ". . . labor troubles prompted Samuel and Jay Paley to start a branch factory for their Congress Cigar Company in Philadelphia . . ." (p. 469).

35. See "Labor and the Press," a discussion program in the series, *The Press and the People* (Fund for the Republic, 1959). Participants were Sam Romer, labor editor of the *Minneapolis Tribune* and Gordon Cole, editor of union publications, with Louis Lyons as moderator. Cole declared "in terms of the attention newspapers gave our activities, 97 per cent of the attention . . . went to strikes and lockouts, and probably less than 3 per cent to our peaceful activities" (p. 3).

36. A. J. Liebling, *The Press* (New York: Ballantine Books, 1961), p. 107.

37. Harvey J. Levin, *Broadcast Regulation and Joint Ownership of Media* (New York: New York University Press, 1960), pp. 79-80.

38. Leonard H. Lavin, "The Solid Gold Egg," Address before Television Bureau of Advertising, November 20, 1963, p. 10. (Mimeographed)

39. Gregory James Liptak, "Influences on News Broadcasting in the State of Illinois," University of Illinois, Urbana, December 1963. (See also Footnote 7a.) (Mimeographed)

40. Murrow, *op. cit.*

41. Levin, *op. cit.,* pp. 6-7.

42. *Broadcasting and Government Regulation in a Free Society,* An Occasional Paper, Center for the Study of Democratic Institutions (New York: Fund for the Republic, 1959), p. 10.

43. Liptak, *op. cit.,* p. 15.

44. William S. Paley, "The American System of Broadcasting," Address to Second National Conference on Educational Broadcasting, Chicago, Illinois,

November 29, 1937. (This address was later published in brochure form and distributed by CBS.)

45. United States Senate, "Activities of Nondiplomatic Representatives of Foreign Principals in the United States," Hearings Before the Committee on Foreign Relations, 88th Congress, First Session (Washington, D.C.: Government Printing Office, 1963).

46. Douglass Cater and Walter Pincus, "The Foreign Legion of U.S. Public Relations," *The Reporter,* 23, No. 11 (December 22, 1960), 15-22.

3

News Blockage and Suppression
in American Broadcasting

Section 326 of the Communications Act, which controls broadcasting, reads: "Nothing in this Act shall be understood or construed to give the Commission the power of censorship over the radio communication, or signals transmitted by any radio station, and no regulation or condition shall be promulgated or fixed by the Commission which shall interfere with the right of free speech by means of radio communications."[1] Thus the regulatory commission primarily responsible for broadcasting, the Federal Communications Commission, is effectively prevented by law from exercising censorship over broadcasting.

Yet censorship seems to exist. The *New York Herald Tribune*'s television critic, John Crosby, wrote in 1959: ". . . there is censorship of the air waves so complete, so blinding, so choking—that no government body can make it much worse."[2] Stan Opotowsky in *TV: The Big Picture,* bluntly states that "television is the nation's most censored mass medium."[3] In the report to former President Eisenhower, by the President's Commission on National Goals, submitted on November 16, 1960, we read:

> For the most part television has not even come within hailing distance of the press as a device by which Americans can communicate sensibly with each other. . . . Sooner or later we are going to have to face up to the harsh fact that the democratic dialogue is in real danger of being smothered . . ."[4]

Many symptoms are beginning to appear which justify concern about the freedom with which news and other essential information flow, or fail to flow, through the broadcast veins and arteries of the United States.

In news and information, as in nature, there is no vacuum. If one agency is disbarred from exercising the selection function, other agencies must perform it, for daily decisions must be made. Who then performs this function?

Through the years, history has seen various wielders of this function come and go. Two principal controllers have been the church, through the Middle Ages, and government, from the years of Milton up to the Industrial Revolution. With the development of large corporations as principal controllers of the broadcast media, in the triple role of owner-operators, sponsors, and pressure groups, there is considerable evidence that business itself, protected by legislation against government regulatory agency interference, now exercises this role to a surprising degree.

Sir Ian Jacob, former Director General of the British Broadcasting Corporation, and later President of the European Broadcasting Union, has cautioned that today ". . . Independence for broadcasting means freedom from two kinds of pressure, the political and the economic. The nature of political pressure is obvious. Economic pressure is, however, more subtle. . . ."[5] The repressive influences, taboos, and other blockages which *economic* pressures bring result in unfreedoms which may not be *called* censorship but which, no less effectively than government censorship, determine what can be said and learned through the broadcast media.

Since the controllers of the broadcast media, generally, represent corporate and business orientations, and find the present broadcasting and economic systems profitable, they have a special stake in the continuation of the present situation. They therefore view as disruptive, radical, subversive, or even unpatriotic, forces, materials, and programs which might, however indirectly, disrupt the present arrangement. It is natural that the voices of these media should speak the language of business, for their masters are big business, and there are many things about which they would prefer to keep the people of America quiet and uncritical. The consequent slanting and censorship are probably less a result of deliberate decision than they are the natural and perhaps inevitable way anyone in a similar position would see things, and describe them, for the general public. The truth yes, but not necessarily the whole truth.

The protections on which the nation relies for free speech and free press are traceable to the Bill of Rights and the First and Fourteenth Amendments. These provisions were designed when most discussion took place either in town-hall-type meetings or small, independently owned newspapers. Section 326 of the Communications Act, quoted above, was written when most stations were individual operations, like the hometown newspapers of that time, each responsible for its own program output, rather than acting principally as an outlet or pipeline for centrally produced network programs. The conditions which prevail, and the situation of the people who need protecting, are quite different today.

In the nearly one hundred years since these safeguards were last reviewed, the corporation, which hardly existed at that time, has become a dominant controller of communications. One of the obvious consequences of this situation is that business applies to programs and information the same practices it applied, and still applies, to goods.

It has long been standard industry practice, for example, to hold back certain products until the moment when it is most profitable to introduce them. Nylon and dacron were held off the market until the market could be prepared. Some products are withheld permanently, because they would be unprofitable, or disruptive of one's monopoly or profit position or for other reasons. Is it any wonder then that industry should find it reasonable to hold off the market *facts* or *ideas* also, which might similarly jeopardize their profit or monopoly position? These are some of the types of questions suggested by the web of developments, controls, and taboos to which attention is now directed.

Censorship Redefined. Censorship is the process of examining literature, art, news, etc. in order to prevent distribution of anything which might be considered by the censor or those in authority to be unsuitable for the intended audience. The courts have agreed that censorship involves "previous restraint." The motives for censorship may vary from sincere efforts by democratic society to prevent the corruption of children, to the efforts of totalitarians to prevent the dissemination of material which might endanger their position.

Safeguards against censorship are supposed to protect primarily the rights of the citizen to hear and read a variety of viewpoints rather than the rights of the speaker, writer, or other disseminator of the materials. Herbert Hoover, for example, in 1925, made clear whose freedom he was interested in: ". . . There are two parties to freedom of the air; and to freedom of speech, for that matter. There is the speechmaker and the listener. Certainly in radio I believe in freedom for the listener."[6]

Kent Cooper, longtime President of the Associated Press, used to point out that freedom of the press was not designed to protect the disseminators of materials, but the rights of the public to access to all kinds of information. He said he would like to ". . . amend the First Amendment to include the *right* to *know*."[7] Newton Minow told the National Association of Broadcasters in 1962: "I am not so much concerned about the right of everyone to *say* anything he pleases as I am about our need as a self-governing people to *hear* everything relevant."[8] Another former Chairman of the Federal Communications Commission, James L. Fly, has said:

> It's of no great concern to me whether I get the emotional catharsis of being able to say my piece. . . . What is important is the diffusion of information and of opinion to the electorate. . . . Whether or not any given speaker is permitted to talk has a major impact, not on the speaker, but on the public. The public is the one that is injured.[9]

Safeguards against censorship, it therefore appears, were designed to insure the free exchange of the views and ideas of citizens, however radical, so the citizenry might know of them, weigh them, and decide what to do about them. Unfortunately, as broadcasting became increasingly a medium of advertising and entertainment, safeguards which had been designed to protect *press* and political functions were stretched to cover these two other more profitable functions of broadcasting: advertising and entertainment.

Since broadcasting *did* perform *some* of the functions of the press, broadcasters succeeded in convincing legislators and the public that broadcasting is *truly* "press." They then concluded that if they as broadcasters were press, *anything* they did, including advertising, entertainment, sports, drama, or public relations, was protected by press immunities. It is not surprising that, in the stretching of the definition necessary to cover *all* of broadcasting's functions, many confusions arose.

It used to be assumed that the purpose of regulations and standards was to guarantee a good or pure product or service. The regulation of the food or drug industry would be meaningless if the government were forbidden to concern itself with the *product,* i.e., the foods and drugs involved. Regulation of transportation would be equally meaningless unless the regulatory agency could check and judge the *service* rendered the public. Yet in broadcasting, the government has no control over the product, only over processes, traffic, and other peripheral aspects. In broadcasting, "censorship" has been so ambiguously defined that it now is used by broadcasters to refer to virtually anything that government does through its regulatory efforts. An editorial in *Broadcasting* magazine clearly exemplified the industry position in 1960, when Attorney General William P. Rogers, in his report following the quiz scandals, suggested to President Eisenhower that the television industry was not serving the public interest as fully as it should. "The real danger lies in any step, however slight, towards program control," *Broadcasting* wrote. "*That* constitutes censorship."[10] The previous year the industry position had been clearly stated by the National Association of Broadcasters: "Any tendency on the part of government to censor or dictate program content would be a deadly threat to basic freedoms."[11]

Court decisions through the years, however, have stated that the FCC "must control the *nature* of the traffic" of broadcasting, for programs are the essence of broadcasting. Louis L. Jaffe, the distinguished communications attorney, has asked: "How does telling a broadcaster to put on some news programs or to have a little agriculture, or to make some weather reports contravene this function of free speech?"[12] Even one of the National Association of Broadcasters' own spokesmen realized that to forbid the FCC to do *anything* about programs was going too far. "Collecting information is not censorship. Nor, I submit, is asking broadcasters to make a reasonable effort to determine community needs and requiring a broadcaster reasonably to match up promise and performance."[13]

Yet the opposite view has begun to prevail more and more. At the network hearings before the FCC, in February 1962, Robert Sarnoff declared that ". . . the FCC is going beyond its authority when it outlines program standards or indicates the types of programs it favors or disfavors." He added: "The power to license stations does not give a government agency the responsibility of raising viewers' tastes or broadening their interests to conform to its own views."[14] And communications attorney W. Theodore Pierson has gone so far as to say that ". . . perhaps it is better that television remain ineffectual than make this concession to censorship and conformity."[15]

Under the steady pressure of a powerful industry lobby on Congressmen, who count on the facilities of friendly broadcasters for election or re-election, several other things have also happened to confuse the issue of censorship and weaken the authority of the FCC to regulate even the traffic of broadcasting. The provision which authorized the FCC to forbid and punish the use of obscene language was taken out of the Communications Act and put in the U.S. Criminal Code; this helped to limit the FCC's rights to prescribe or proscribe *anything* in the program area. A bill (H.R. 8316) was introduced by Representative Walter Rogers in 1963 to prevent the FCC from limiting the number or length or nature of commercials in broadcasting. It promptly passed the House. This was enough to warn the FCC to desist.

Asking the industry to *give,* rather than withhold, certain kinds of information—which at first glance would seem to be the opposite of censorship—ends up itself being labeled censorship. Suggestions that programs, like drugs, that are unsuitable for children should be so labeled, are condemned as censorship. Efforts by the FCC to *prevent* the muzzling or censoring of certain groups by broadcasters are labeled censorship. The effort by the FCC to prevent or correct any "condition—which shall interfere with the right of free speech," as Section 326 of the Communication Act states, has itself been denounced as censorship.

Some of the statements regarding what constitutes censorship are so inconsistent as to defy logic. In an address May 15, 1962, at Southern Illinois University, Gene Wilkey, Vice President of the CBS-TV Stations Division and General Manager of Station KMOX-TV, St. Louis, declared: "Governmental controls of programming, no matter in what form or how beneficent the purpose is made out to be, will still be censorship of communications."[16] Thus censorship comes to be defined in terms of *who,* instead of *what.* It is defined by who wields it, rather than what is done, or to what purpose.

When Dr. Frank Stanton was asked whether it would be censorship for the FCC even to ask network stations why they had not carried the network news programs or documentaries offered them, he replied: "Yes, sir."[17]

When proposals were made that industry's profits should be made a matter of public record, these proposals were denounced as censorship. Commenting on the so-called Jones Report of 1955, *Broadcasting* magazine wrote:

> The biggest threat we see in the Jones document is the hammering away at a "uniform accounting procedure," the results of which would be thrown open to all competitive eyes. . . . Economic data . . . has never been disclosed except in aggregate . . . to protect their confidentiality. This Mr. Jones would confiscate."[18]

Gradually, any effort on the part of government to *prevent* or *remove* censorship, in the sense of preventing the withholding of information the public should have, has come to be called censorship.

The definition of the term censorship has deteriorated in other respects as well. A producer, speaking of a program that was later cancelled, declared: "Whether or not the network allows me to put it on, they will never tell me what to put in it. It will not be censored nor will any of the network heads interfere with it in any way."[19] Keeping a whole program off the air, by this implied definition, is not considered or called censorship, whereas making smaller changes in it *is* considered censorship.

The networks maintain that agencies and sponsors have no voice in newscasts and documentaries, although naturally they view such programs before deciding whether or not to sponsor them. The objections of sponsors which keep a great number of programs off the air or their decisions to sponsor other programs instead (*censorship by displacement*), represent conditions which are considered quite different from censorship. They are, however, a form of blockage which must arouse some concern in a study such as this. For if whole programs, instead of merely certain program elements, are vetoed or otherwise kept off the air, surely something less than free access to all kinds of controversial material is available to the public.

Beginning in 1935, various bills were introduced into Congress which would have required stations to devote a certain number of hours to unrestricted and "uncensored" discussions of public issues. These bills were defeated as "censorship" in spite of the fact that the Supreme Court declared in the Associated Press case:

> It would be strange indeed if the grave concern for freedom of the press which prompted the first amendment should be read as a command that the Government was without power to *protect* that freedom. . . . Freedom to publish is guaranteed by the Constitution but freedom to combine to keep others from publishing is not.[20]

As more and more examples are found of blockage of the free flow of information in broadcasting, whatever term is used to describe them, it must be asked whether legislative efforts designed to insure the preservation of freedom of access by the public to all kinds of information, rather than to reduce or destroy it, are not acts of *liberation* rather than censorship, whether their source be private industry or government. And it is liberation, or *freedom* from restraints, that must be our goal, if freedom of speech and information are to prevail. The question of who blocks the national circulation is of little interest if the patient succumbs and democracy dies. Let us therefore look at some of the principal sources of blockage of information which limit broadcasting's information function as a communications medium.

Official Government Censorship. Much of the information needed by the American public for decision-making, voting, and understanding is owned by the government and is either released or withheld at the government's discretion.

In previous pages, we have described censorship by such regulatory agencies as the FCC, rather than government censorship generally, as having been held at bay by industry. There *are* numerous sources of very effective government censorship or news management which are still a problem in broadcasting. In many cases, news-gatherers may justifiably complain of managed news, or concealments and distortions which make the job of news reporting most difficult. This type of censorship or blockage, it should be noted, affects principally *news* programs. The other types of blockages noted here permeate other programs as well, and need to be noted, because of their subtle nature.

In his remarkable study for the American Civil Liberties Union in 1955, Allen Raymond tells us:

> . . . an incident occurred in 1950 which should have rung a note of alarm like a tocsin in the night to every person in America. . . . That was the invasion of the premises of *The Scientific American* by Federal agents to see that an article by Hans Bethe, widely respected scientist who had helped build the A-bomb, was not printed and that all type set for the presses was destroyed.[21]

Raymond documents a score or so of other instances of blockage by government departments of news which the people might otherwise have received. Contracts of the Defense Department with AT and T, details regarding Internal Revenue Service enforcement and non-enforcement of the laws, and numerous other instances of government secrecy are discussed in Raymond's study. He suggests two steps to improve the situation:

The establishment within the Federal government of an independent agency to represent the public interest in the declassification of records hitherto kept secret . . . and the extension of the act, which now requires registration of lobbyists in Congress, to cover lobbyists in the Executive agencies of government. . . .[22]

Whether the law signed by President Johnson on July 4, 1966, will meet the need for more ready access to government sources remains to be seen. Informed observers are inclined to believe it will not.

In the April 5, 1958, issue of *Saturday Review,* a southern publisher, Thomas Braden, describes "Why My Newspaper Lied." He tells of printing a headline: "Russ Not Ahead in Missile Race, Wilson Declares." Then he asks:

What is a reporter to do when the Secretary of Defense, nearly three months after Washington had certain knowledge that the Russians had tested a missile of intercontinental range, says that he doesn't think they have such a missile and that the United States is still ahead?

To some extent, the press of the United States, like the press of Russia, becomes a vast sounding board, reverberating to the beat of the official drumstick. . . . Few Government officials will consciously and deliberately lie, either to newspaper men or to the public. But a tailored version of the truth . . . a part of the truth . . . can in the net impression it conveys be a lie. . . . My readers, and other readers . . . had been deprived of their right to know.[23]

Fernand Gigon, a French writer, describes other disturbing types of censorship by the United States. In *The Bomb,* he tells the story of the raining of atomic fall-out on Japan during the 1950's from United States atomic tests, and of the bitter resentment built up toward the United States by the Japanese.

So long as the American occupation of Japan continued, no newspaper could even publish the word "atom" without obtaining the permission of the censorship first. For example, Tamiki Hara's beautiful book, *Summer Flowers,* was banned. This banning of his book, combined with the outbreak of the Korean War, led Hara to commit suicide.[24]

Censored for Americans were the stories of Setsu Mukodani's "one-man march" through Japan, collecting over half a million signatures pleading for an end to United States atomic testing in the Japanese area of the Pacific. Censored too were the accounts of the inability of another Japanese, a Mrs. Kouboyama to get a passport to come to the United States to place her appeal, and that of other millions of Japanese, before President Eisenhower. Not heard in the United States were accounts of the dilemma of Japan, "crushed, from a geographical point of view [between the U.S. and Russia], in a vise of atom-bomb and hydrogen bomb tests," as Gigon described it, of the refusal of the United States to accept delivery of Japanese tuna and mackerel, made radioactive by our own tests, and of the need for the Japanese, if they were not to starve, to eat the heavily radioactive rice, their only recourse against starvation. Americans heard little of this. "Neither are they aware of the increasing wave of anti-American feeling which is rising all around . . . a pacifist agitation which is costing the Americans dear."[25] However, when anti-American demonstrations and outbreaks later occurred, and President Eisenhower was forced to cancel his trip to Japan, Americans were told that the fault lay with pro-Communist student groups and other radical elements. The background facts were not available to Americans any more than were details of reasons for growing anti-Americanism which preceded the stoning of Richard Nixon in South America.

Numerous committees, like the Gaither Committee, presented studies and reports during the Eisenhower administration, expressing deep concern about many facets of foreign and defense aspects of our national policy. Many of these studies were excellent. But they were disturbing, and raised serious questions. Where they conflicted with ongoing military or defense policy, they were apparently promptly shelved.

When the American U-2 plane crashed in Russia, the American press and television were given pictures "proving" that Soviet photographs were fakes; that a U-2 could not survive a 65,000-foot fall. Later admissions that it was our plane after all greatly damaged the credibility of U.S. official releases abroad. For many nations, believing that our government speaks the truth, had already broadcast and published our denials.

One would have hoped that the number of such incidents might have been reduced during the following ten years. Such does not appear to be the case. Both the Cuban crisis and the Viet Nam war presented many more instances of government management of news. Morley Safer's CBS report on the burning of the South Viet Nam village of Cam Ne was at first denied, then admitted and justified on the grounds that it contained Viet Cong tunnels. When the State Department asked former CBS News President Fred Friendly to air a retraction, he fortunately and courageously refused.

In his last address as President, delivered and broadcast January 17, 1961, Dwight D. Eisenhower warned of the ". . . conjunction of an immense military establishment and a large arms industry." He went on: ". . . We must not fail to comprehend its grave implications. . . . In the councils of government, we must guard against the acquisition of unwarranted influence, whether sought or unsought, by the military-industrial complex."

The House Freedom of Information Committee, chaired by Representative John Moss, has protested against news management of many kinds by the Department of Defense, the Atomic Energy Commission, and other government agencies. How both the Truman and Eisenhower administrations covered up information unfavorable to them in the Dixon-Yates, Adams-Goldfine, and other cases has been described in Clark Mollenhoff's book, *Washington Cover-up* (New York: Doubleday, 1962). Later evidences of governmental control of news, as in the Billie Sol Estes, Bobby Baker, and other cases, are not difficult to find.

The Atomic Energy Commission, which had earlier withheld information on fall-out dangers, in 1964 was finally pressed into disclosing how it had quietly buried Project Pluto, a program to build a low-flying atomic-powered missile.

The National Aeronautics and Space Administration was the object of a House sub-committee investigation into the withholding of news regarding Soviet space efforts. Such reports, it appeared, would in no way have endangered our national security. As a civilian agency, Congressmen asked, should NASA not protect and promote the public's right to know, rather than seek to hamper that right?

William Lederer in *A Nation of Sheep*[26] discusses reporting of a Matsu invasion that never took place. Reporters were told of a big sea battle. Though they were unable to confirm the incident, they filed the story and it was broadcast and published. The incident was later revealed to have involved a firing on a lone fisherman lost in the area of the Chinese off-shore islands.

The Defense Department's refusal to divulge defense agreements with Spain in effect since 1953, although the Spanish public was told even by the totalitarian Spanish press, is disturbing. Following the repeated suppression of bad news from Viet Nam, in which the press was used to promote a "basic policy of optimism," Wes Gallagher, AP General Manager, questioned how far the press should go in cooperating with the Defense and State Departments in spreading the view that all was well in Viet Nam.

During and following the Cuban crisis, the position declared by Assistant Secretary of Defense for Public Affairs, Arthur Sylvester, that managed news is "a part of the weaponry that a President has" drew bitter criticism from Sigma Delta Chi and other news organizations and groups.

While certain news is withheld, other items are "leaked" to support defense and other policies. Is it the duty of the press to relay such leaks? How far should the press go in relaying reports which seriously breach the secrecy of a top agency of the United States government such as details of the super-secret National Security Council meeting in which the late U.N. Ambassador Adlai Stevenson was quoted as taking a minority position with regard to strategy toward Cuba and the Soviet Union?

Such is the maze of contradictory problems in government-press relations which now seems to prevail. Such practices grow out of government agency malpractices, admittedly, and surely they must be corrected. But their correction is not merely a government problem. For they grow out of a deteriorating journalistic tradition under which government agencies can count on the press, under the lash of television competition, to allow itself to be "used." For government, like sponsors, to be able to count on the press to relay reports of dubious authenticity or proven falsity, without checking or challenging, represents a deterioration of the function of news media which is dangerous in the extreme.

It is important to note that, though there is government censorship, it is not the kind one would expect, nor does it spring from the sources against which elaborate, Maginot Line-type safeguards have been erected. It does not come from the Federal Communications Commission, which conventional wisdom tells the American public, "has jurisdiction" over broadcasting. It comes from military, atomic, and other agencies which, under the law, are supposed to have *no* jurisdiction or authority over domestic broadcasting in the United States.

Nor does *this* type of government censorship seem to be as stoutly opposed by the broadcast industry as one would expect. The industry-military complex seems here to be fused and united into a single position or understanding on censorship which illustrates graphically the situation about which former President Eisenhower warned us. Here the interests of the military, and of the great corporations which are military contractors and at the same time operate the major networks and station groups, merge into a single complex in which public and private taboos and interests can no longer be discerned. It is this type of situation in so many places which makes it difficult to identify a single villain responsible for the serious blockage of the free flow of news in American broadcasting.

Through such a veil of secrecy and conditioning it is difficult even to raise the questions which need to be asked. Is it not perhaps true that there appear no longer to be any basic scientific secrets anywhere in the world? Is it not true that, as the UNESCO Preamble states, "Wars begin in the minds of men," which in the United States seem to be being militarily conditioned to a dangerous degree? Is it proper that from 20 to 40 per cent of the income of so many firms controlling broadcast communications media—RCA, ABC, CBS, General Electric, Westinghouse, RKO General, Sarkes Tarzian, 3M, and so on —comes from defense contracts, thus giving our communications media themselves a great stake and vested interest in continued tension and military contracts? Why are *these* facts not being more openly discussed, as democracy requires?

Is it well that the rest of the world should know that, reminiscent of DuPont in pre-World War I days, an American firm, Interarmco, sells military weapons and even planes to virtually either side in any nation or sub-nation that wishes them but that few Americans know of such "merchant of death" operations? Why is this practice not the subject of a few television documentaries? Might it not have been a good subject in 1965, perhaps? There seems to have been plenty of opportunity for such programs, and a great dearth of them that year. In his address at the National Conference on Broadcasting and Election Campaigns, October 13 and 14, 1965, Howard K. Smith declared:

> I was a judge for the Emmy awards this year. I sat through six solid hours of watching what were called documentaries. They were all very elaborate, and in beautiful color and must have cost a fortune to produce. But not one dealt with the untidy but fascinating world we live in. Most were a good two or three safe centuries away from today. . . .
>
> I could cite innumerable examples. CBS's documentary on TV ratings

was a careful mutual cancellation of facts and views signifying, in the end, nothing. . . .

NBC recently displayed the typical reaction of a declining form of expression; it sought to meet what is really a question of quality by heaping on quantity. Just as movies met their problem by making their screens three times bigger, they made their documentary three times longer.

The DuPont Award for broadcast commentary was not awarded last year; there was no one to give it to. The Peabody awards were given, but with the comment that the year was a poor one.

How wise is it for even General Mills and other sponsors, whom one would expect to have little direct vested interest in the continuation of militarism, to decline to sponsor anti-war programs and scenes, or to ask writers to minimize the horror of war? Is this obeisance to Pentagon policy in the public interest? Are the minds of Americans being prepared for war, or peace, as the UNESCO phrase suggests? How tolerable is it for the communications media so often to identify their interests with those of the military, with the blockage of possible peaceful solutions which this brings? Does this not deserve careful attention if the United States and the United Nations are to survive?

There *is,* no doubt, too much government censorship, particularly by the military. Any such censorship is too much in peacetime. All journalists should oppose managed news, and should fight for access to all materials which do not genuinely jeopardize our national security. However, bad as this situation is, it is not the source of most censorship in the United States. These other types now invite our attention.

The Sponsor as Censor. In a statement to the Cooperative League of the U.S.A., later published in the January 1965 issue of *Consumer Reports,* Senator Philip A. Hart of Michigan told of the cancellation of his scheduled appearances on TV to discuss truth-in-packaging legislation. As he stated, "Off the record, I was told advertisers had objected." More seriously, Senator Hart even raised the question whether educational TV would dare carry his presentations since the source of many of educational TV's foundation funds "are the major industries." Certainly there is business and sponsor pressure to leave certain things unsaid in American broadcasting. And apparently this pressure, though often carefully concealed, is more pervasive than is often realized.

Although it should be made clear that no villainy is intended by businessmen who block the broadcasting of materials thought to be adverse to their interests, it is regrettable that, by its abdication of the responsible editorial position needed, the broadcast industry itself has passed so much of the decision-making power regarding program content on to product-makers who are neither journalists, nor broadcasters, nor pledged or licensed to serve the public interest. It is unreasonable and unfair to both sponsors and the American public to have *any* part of such programming decisions exercised by sponsors. For, as a DuPont executive declared, ". . . Our interest is frankly commercial. We are a manufacturing concern, not a cultural foundation."[27] Nor do such firms feel any obligation to get into the news business, or controversy. It is perfectly reasonable to expect that, if the decision is left to the advertiser, it will be made primarily on the basis of the interest of his *firm,* not the broad public interest of the nation as a whole. Certainly a firm should not be *expected* to pay for the promulgation of views antagonistic to its sales and profit interests.

Even in news, where network executives have categorically and repeatedly denied such influence, sponsor pressure is a powerful factor. Martin Agronsky stated on a panel several years ago, "I was able in specific cases—I won't name stations or cities—to determine that on such-and-such a station a sponsor dropped me because of influence brought to bear by McCarthy supporters."[28] Gilbert Seldes has written:

> Responsible network and station executives deny that any news interpreter of known loyalty has even been discharged on account of his political opinions. They do not deny that under the system which permits sponsorship of news they can sell news time only when the interpreter is acceptable to the sponsor.[29]

That they do sell time on so regular basis would indicate that news policies are "reasonable" enough to meet the standards of sponsors.

In various hearings, sponsors have explained the basis of some of the considerations guiding their decisions. We are told, for example, that angry people, or sad people, or worried people, are not in a buying frame of mind. Therefore most advertisers prefer not to sponsor programs which will make people sad, angry, or depressed, or programs which might cause people to want to save, rather than *spend,* at least on the product being promoted. Realistic world news is bad for business.

Since some fifteen or twenty large companies provide approximately 50 per cent of the income of the broadcast industry, it is not surprising that the interests of these firms and their products have been loyally protected. It is not strange, either, that such giants frankly feel that, in exchange for the billions they spend on television, they have a right to expect that their products, their business tactics, and their anti-trust suits and other activities, should be treated with a little "extra fairness." Surely, they logically reason, the broadcast industry could and should consider them as *friends,* and treat them as such. Do *they* not finance broadcasting, they ask? How this blockage against criticisms of corporate giants, or corporate gigantism as a trend, affects the public interest, however accidental or unintended it may be, is the question raised here. This situation is less to be feared in the print media, where longer journalistic traditions prevail, and editorial policy is more independent of advertising, than it is in broadcasting where entrepreneurs and non-journalists determine what shall be done.

Looking over this thick web of private censorship, former FCC Chairman Newton Minow declared in 1961: "Since it is done by our own governmental licenses every broadcast day, it violates the spirit of the first Amendment and Section 326 of the Act just as surely as if we had done it ourselves."[30] This seems to be a fair expression of a very real problem, however innocent of censorship motives, as such, the businessmen responsible for it may be. Testimony by advertising agency representatives through the years has indicated that they see as legitimate the deletion of material which might be contrary to a sponsor's interest. No one agency or sponsor should be expected to see more than the tiny part of the blockage for which he is responsible. It is essential, however, that somewhere the total of these small taboos, each by itself insignificant, be brought together and analyzed. And it is time to challenge the widely repeated assumption that "What is good for the advertiser is good for the public." The interests of those specific companies which can afford television can in no way be expected to coincide with the total public interest. By adding together the taboos of sponsors, however petty each may be, we come up with a vast list of problems which broadcasting doesn't talk about. And many of those problems are national problems of such magnitude and importance that no one in a democracy, whether government, station management, or sponsor, should have the right to interfere with their full and free exploration and discussion.

Of course if and when these problems reach crisis proportions, they begin to be heard about even on TV and radio. This appears to be the situation regarding the connection between cigarette smoking and cancer, and the problem of car safety design. That these problems are now finally being discussed is fine; that they were avoided so completely for over ten years is less reassuring. How many of our problems can wait that long without becoming fatal?

A PARTIAL LIST OF SAMPLE SPONSOR TABOOS

In order to illustrate the type of petty pressures and taboos discussed above, a few typical examples from the hundreds reported in published sources are listed here:

1. Deletion from a program sponsored by Ford of a picture of the *Chrysler* building, and from a program sponsored by Chrysler of the name "Lincoln."

2. Deletion from a Camel program of the word "lucky," and from a desert program sponsored by another company, of camels; and asking a fighter, on a program sponsored by a firm which makes cigarette lighters, to ask for a light, instead of a match, as the script called for.

3. Changing the word "American" to "United States" on a program sponsored by a cigarette company other than the American Tobacco Company.

4. Insistence that villains smoke filter cigarettes on programs sponsored by non-filter brands, and vice versa.

5. Requesting a writer to reduce the smoking of cigarettes by Russians in a drama program. (Smoking is a sign of being good guys.)

6. Requesting an actor not to tap his cigarette before lighting it, because of the implication that it may not be fully packed.

7. The inability to get cancer announcements on or near programs sponsored by cigarette companies.

8. Deletion of the statement that "he'd rather fly" from a railroad-sponsored program.

9. Deletion of a scene in which a little girl refuses to eat cereal, from a program sponsored by a cereal manufacturer.

10. Deletion of the scene of a child becoming ill from eating too much candy to protect the sensitivity of candy manufacturers as sponsors.

11. The decision to change the version of feeding a baby from mother's milk to bottle, in view of dairy sponsorship.

12. Employment of an Irish actress on a program about the Dead Sea Scrolls, to avoid having too many Jewish actors or actresses.

13. Changing the villain from a given occupation or description to another type of individual because he might resemble the head of the sponsoring firm.

14. Deletion of an uncomplimentary remark about John D. Rockefeller from a program about Andrew Carnegie, in deference to the presence of a Rockefeller on the board of the sponsoring corporation (although this individual, had he known, might well *not* have objected).

15. Dr. Frank Stanton's declining to use the word "national" in congressional testimony, in reference to the broadcast audience, preferring to refer to the "nation-wide" audience, a phrase which does not include NBC's first name.

16. Pressures on behalf of the auto industry to keep to a minimum reference to auto wrecks as a cause of death of characters in dramas, Westerns, and other programs.

17. Request by an electric company that the title of Kipling's "The Light that Failed" be changed. Westinghouse bulbs don't fail!

18. Deletion of reference to suicide as a cause of death from programs sponsored by an insurance company.

19. Taboos by Procter and Gamble against showing "men in uniform . . . as villains" or "business as cold, ruthless." Special care in portrayals of the drug and grocery business on programs sponsored by drug, detergent, and food firms.

20. Deletion of the word "gas" from the phrase "gas chambers" in a drama about Nazi Germany, because of sponsorship by a gas company.

21. Deletion of recognizable Jews from such programs as Samson and Delilah, and showing the Negro in drama, for years, only infrequently and in stereotyped occupations, rarely as professionals.

22. Pressure from sponsors on Steve Allen to engage in no more such "controversial activities" as signing a petition for Caryl Chessman, joining the National Committee for a Sane Nuclear Policy, or referring in a program to a letter from a young viewer mentioning "the commercialization of Christmas."

23. Purging from Rod Serling's *Studio One* play, "The Arena," about the U.S. Senate, of reference to actual persons or problems. The result, in Serling's words: "An incredible display . . . of groups of Senators shouting, gesticulating and talking in hieroglyphics about make-believe issues—in a kind of prolonged unbelievable doubletalk."[31] (Query: What is the effect of such distortions on the creation of respect or disrespect for democratic machinery and processes?)

In addition to the petty sample taboos represented above, certain program *subjects* or areas are avoided as much as possible, out of consideration for sponsor (i.e., business and corporate) interests, generally or specifically:

1. *Poverty:* Until the last couple of years, few broadcast programs showed or recognized the existence of poverty in the United States. The November 22, 1958, issue of *The Nation* tells of the cancellation of a program by the late Ben Hecht, *Obit to a Nobody,* about eight Bowery derelicts. As *The Nation* commented, Hecht was suggesting that life is not all happy in the United States. "There is failure, despair, poverty and death. He broke a cardinal rule, he was condignly

punished, and we hope he has learned his lesson. Who does he think he is—Maxim Gorky?"[32]

In 1961, broadcasters, public officials, and hundreds of others protested the "unfair" film of BBC television's Denis Mitchell about Chicago. The poverty and ugliness it showed caused hundreds, *who had not even seen this magnificent documentary,* to join the effort to keep it off the air.[33] The need to preserve a happy atmosphere, conducive to purchasing generally, and the consumption of sponsor products in particular, is a strong pressure on broadcasters.

There is some evidence that since President Johnson's call for an attack on poverty, the broadcast industry curtain *has* been partially lifted in this field. How long this recent trend will continue, and how much will be shown or accomplished, still remains to be seen. That it required an official government campaign to break through and attract attention to the misery in which millions live is in itself revealing of the usefulness of government efforts to supplement or jog industry efforts.

2. *Private Utilities:* The broadcast media seem to have made themselves available to corporate-owned telephone, gas, electrical, and water companies who advertise heavily, for expounding *their* philosophies, while keeping to a minimum "socialistic" materials favorable to *public* ownership, cooperatives and other publicly owned TVA-type projects, even those essential to conservation, anti-pollution, public health, and other broad national interests. The selection of Merlin H. Aylesworth, formerly of the Colorado Public Utilities Commission, the Utah Power and Light Company, and the National Electric Light Association, as first President of NBC in 1926 set a pattern which seems to persist to this day. The question must be seriously raised whether these industries, and manufacturers in these fields, can buy immunity to criticism with their purchases of advertising, in addition to enjoying the over-all favoritism extended to all members of the corporate or business family community. Who is to challenge industry malpractices if industry-controlled media make such practices virtually exempt from critical examination? With no knowledge of such activities, how is the public to discuss or influence broad *public* interests?

3. *Liquor, Tobacco, and Coffee:* Serious students of the problem of alcoholism in the U.S. note the increase in fatal diseases traceable to

alcohol poisoning. Twelve hundred alcoholics are reportedly being produced each day. In 1958, Americans spent twenty-eight billion dollars for liquor and the consequences of liquor consumption. Yet the typical line in television dramas regarding alcoholic consumption seems to be "I really needed that drink." A similar situation has been true, and is still principally true, in regard to cigarette-smoking; the broadcast industry's attitude is cautious and compromising, as income from tobacco accounts would lead one to expect. In fact, the tobacco industry itself appears to have taken stronger steps in controlling cigarette advertising than the broadcast industry association itself, the National Association of Broadcasters, within a year of the Surgeon General's report. The NAB seems virtually unable to take drastic steps which might reduce the broadcast revenue of its members. Instead, in fact, the last re-election of Governor LeRoy Collins as NAB President was hotly debated, because of his urging the industry to take a firmer stand against TV cigarette ads. Medical figures on the effects of excessive coffee consumption, similar in many respects to those of alcohol and tobacco, indicate that this, also, is an important taboo area. How many programs on the air question the adverse health effects of too much coffee-drinking? Or too much consumption of virtually any heavily sponsored products?

4. *Air and Water Pollution:* Various kinds of industries seem to be responsible for most of the nation's most serious air and water pollution. Yet industry's responsibility seems not to be widely discussed by the broadcast media generally. Charles Winick tells of what more often happens: ". . . the plot of a television drama about how industrial plants were causing unhealthy smog in a West Coast community was changed. In a revised version, the plants were the leaders of the campaign to *eliminate* the smog."[34]

5. *Conservation:* In *Resources for Freedom,* a Summary of Volume I of a Report to the President, by the President's Materials Policy Commission, chaired by CBS Board Chairman William S. Paley, we read already in 1952:

> . . . As a nation, we are threatened, but not alert. . . . So efficiently have we built our high output factories and opened the lines of distribution to our remotest consumers that our sources are faltering under the constantly increasing strain of demand. As a nation, we have always been more interested in sawmills than seedlings.[35]

This report listed the many metals, fuels, and other materials whose domestic supply is now exhausted, and noted the alarming depletion and approaching depletion of others as a result of wasteful national practices. Yet there seems to be little evidence that Paley's committee's concern caused even CBS to urge any considerable slackening in present nationally suicidal policies, or to produce any significant continuing documentary or educational series of programs on water, metal, fuel, or forest conservation.

6. *Labor:* Pressures by various firms to prevent labor from even being allowed to *purchase* time on broadcast stations have been noted earlier.[36] Industry's side of labor hearings, as in the case of the Kohler strike hearings, was sponsored and televised. Labor's side, and testimony, was not sponsored; hence it was not televised. Strikes and labor demands seem nearly always to be given coverage which does not relate them to the profits of the industries concerned. As its natural enemy, of course, business should not be expected to be particularly generous or enthusiastic regarding labor. But how is what they do to be construed as public service of the over-all national interest, in which millions of citizens are laborers?

7. *Cooperatives:* In 1942, Senator Norris introduced a resolution calling for the investigation of NBC and CBS for refusal to sell time to cooperatives. The networks yielded to the extent of agreeing to sell time ". . . to advertise their goods but not their politics."[37] President Paley of CBS has also said that CBS will sell time to advertise products but not politics or ideas. Such industry practices, applied to cooperatives, labor, and other "socialistic" forces, generally, are in sharp contrast to the sale of broadcast time to corporations for promulgating *their* policies, politics, and ideas, however, as noted below.

Promoting Corporation Goals. In *Television Age,* December 2, 1957, the availability and usefulness of television for building the corporate image and promoting the corporate philosophy are described. "Today's most precious corporate asset, and greatest challenge, is people. The problem, then, is how best to reach them and communicate to them the corporation's ideas." This article describes how well television can reach the various publics. As the article points out:

. . . It is not just the top officials who must know a firm's objectives, but also staff members who prepare the reports and recommendations that affect its operation and profits. . . . The nation's capital—and state capitals—are all well covered by television. . . . These are the homes of thousands of government workers—the same people who, away from home, make decisions concerning all American business. The bigness of government today, national, state and local, fits with the size and penetration of TV in making personal contact on a mass scale.[38]

In any analysis of the extent to which networks and stations allow sponsors to censor or veto various facts or attitudes, evidence is, of course, not consistent. Networks will often give a firm "no" to a small company whose account it can afford to lose, while yielding if the advertiser is a large and powerful one. Preferential rate cards give large advertisers reductions to a fraction of the rates paid by small advertisers. While stations are licensed to serve the public interest, sponsors quite naturally buy advertising to serve *their* interests, even as against the public's (as in rationalizing practices hit by anti-trust or other suits). Sponsoring firms are interested in people as consumers, not as citizens in a democracy. Business firms are in business for profits, not for charity or public service. If their executives had been qualified for or interested in *public* service, they would have chosen different careers. Having chosen business, they should not be blamed. But, as observed earlier, they should not be put in the position where they either must or may determine the nation's informational, cultural, or political *program* fare, whose effects, other than sales or market effects, they are not qualified to assess or judge.

Broadcasting is a job for broadcasters, not for producers and salesmen of soap, cosmetics, cars, cigarettes, patent medicines, beverages, or military electronics equipment, however fine any of them may be in their chosen careers. News should not be "a service of Chevrolet," a local department store, a cigarette manufacturer, or any other sponsor. Their business is business. Controversy is essential to understanding, enlightenment, and decision-making in a democracy. But it is a poor practice for salesmen. Why then should they be blamed if they refuse to contribute funds to specific advertising approaches which will not advance, and may in fact reduce or harm, their sales or profits? Of course they will carefully censor scripts to be sure there is nothing objectionable from *their* point of view in programs they sponsor, contribute to, or even accept commercials or programs adjacent to. The Ford Motor Company carefully reviews "story lines, characterization and dialogue for every program we sponsor."[39] DuPont and General Motors seek to make sure that programs they sponsor avoid "anything of a controversial nature concerning any national or regional issue," as General Motors describes it, or "involvement in domestic or international subjects" as DuPont phrases it.

Although network officials in testimony have protested that networks *do* control, the situation which prevails when a large, powerful firm is the sponsor seems fairly clear. In his testimony before the FCC, September 29, 1961, James Whitney Cooke, vice president in charge of public relations for A T and T was asked: "You, yourself, have the ultimate judgment as to the cost, the music and the other components of the Bell Telephone Hour?" His answer was "yes." When he was asked: "What part in the supervision of the program, if any, is played by the network?," he replied, "Well, I believe they review the script . . . but beyond that . . . I personally do not see any great evidence of their presence. . . ."[40]

Armour and Company has stated: "You must not assume that we do not pay any attention to the contents of the shows into which we buy. On the contrary, we carefully consider the atmosphere of the shows that will carry our commercials." Bristol-Myers follows a similar policy, and adds, regarding scenes they may object to: "If the network refuses to change these scenes, we will occasionally withdraw entirely from this particular episode."

In his discussion of taboos, Lawrence Laurent quotes an advertising agency representative as saying:

> If I know that the sponsor of a program is a man, six-foot-two, with red hair, and freckles, I'm not going to permit the producer to cast a red-haired, freckle-faced giant in the role of a villain. Little thing, you may say, but it can be a real big deal in this crazy, mixed up TV business. . . .[41]

When former CBS Vice President James C. Aubrey was asked if sponsors should not be excluded from such a role, he told the FCC that it would not be a "wise course" to exclude sponsors from such participation.[42] The British Beveridge Commission, in the United States in 1949 to study our system of sponsorship, concluded: "By and large, the nature of the . . . programmes heard by the American people is settled, not by the networks and stations licensed to broadcast, but by businesses wishing to sell other things."[43] By adding up the taboos of each sponsor, however insignificant and justified (from a business point of view) each may look, American broadcasting ends up with a vast tabooed area of things not discussed. And generally, just as the more conservative trade associations of business have opposed food and drug laws, child labor laws, regulations on their operation, and so on, so has the sum total of sponsor pressure come to add up to a position in favor of big business and the status quo, and opposed to labor, higher taxes for education, small business, higher second-class postal rates, and scores of other such steps which may well be desirable in terms of the over-all public interest. At least it would appear that it would be in the public interest to have free and open public discussion of them. Even the very natural desire of the sponsor to have the commercial as perfect and attention-grasping as possible, since it is more important to him than the program, determines the kinds of programs America is allowed to have.

The situation we find in commercial broadcasting in this respect points up a fact about freedom which has been too little recognized. That is, that private corporations operating primarily for profit and the public corporation of government as controllers of communications both bring with them restrictions on freedom. One is reviewable by and responsible to the public via the ballot; the other is not. It is time that both types of restrictions were corrected. Since government is already under fire on this score, it is essential that the blockages resulting from private efforts, not called censorship, also receive the attention *they* deserve.

Censorship by Broadcasters Themselves. On April 24, 1957, Dr. Albert Schweitzer, upon receiving the Nobel Prize in Oslo, Norway, issued a Declaration of Conscience, begging, on behalf of the peoples of all the world, for a cessation of U.S. atomic testing until we could be surer of its effects on future generations. Neither the American networks nor the other principal news media of the United States gave this story the coverage given it in other countries. Whether or not it was "censored," it was kept from the people, although it was readily available and dramatic. Part of the reason it was withheld from the public, no doubt, was that Adlai Stevenson had, in the 1956 presidential campaign, called for a cessation of atomic testing until we could be surer of its effects. Most broadcasters, like the press, seemed not to want to favor this pacifistic proposal by carrying what appeared to be an endorsement of it by the internationally distinguished Dr.

Schweitzer. Politics, as interpreted by the networks, blocked it.

Virtually the only exposure Dr. Schweitzer's appeal received, belatedly, was via the *Saturday Review,* in its issue of May 18, 1957, for the print media, and the tape radio network of the National Association of Educational Broadcasters—then headed by this writer, in a joint effort with the *Saturday Review*—for broadcasting. This deliberate withholding by U.S. broadcasting of a passionate, urgent, humanitarian appeal by one of the world's most respected figures is one of the most shocking episodes in U.S. broadcast history. As an illustration of the selection process for items to be withheld from Americans by broadcasting itself, it is deeply disquieting.

Scores of journalists and writers have observed the tendency of U.S. press and broadcast media, as well as official sources, to withhold or falsify news—or merely to censor it. In his moving book, *Prescription for Survival,* the former Director General of the World Health Organization, Dr. Brock Chisholm, on behalf of starving millions has said:

> We know when the Food and Agriculture Organization of the United Nations tried to set up a world food council, it was the government of the United States that blocked it, as most people of the United States do *not* know. But we in other parts of the world *do* know, and we can't understand why.[44]

In case after case it appears that the broadcast industry itself has firmly blocked release to the public of certain facts. Although this blockage has sometimes been on behalf of the political party in power, or the military, with which large corporations are closely allied, most of it seems related to the financial and profit interests of corporations controlling broadcasting, either as station or network operators, sponsors, or a part of the business community generally, as opposed to the over-all national interest. This situation seems to prevail quite generally in spite of the fact that Dr. Frank Stanton has said: "I categorically assert that no news or public affairs program at CBS, however expensive to the sponsor, has ever been subject to his control, influence or approval."[45] What does further evidence show?

In 1931, H. V. Kaltenborn wrote:

> In 1924 station WEAF, in New York City, ruled me off the air because of my expression of liberal opinions. This station was then owned and

operated by the American Telephone and Telegraph Company. Each time I criticized a federal judge (who might have to pass on telephone rates), a labor leader (who supervised the company's labor contracts), or a Washington official (whose influence counted in the issue of a broadcasting license), one of the vice-presidents became frightened and protested. Finally the much-harassed vice-president in charge of broadcasting decided that he would be happier without my spoken editorials, even though the radio audience continued to enjoy them.[46]

Harry S. Ashmore, of the Center for the Study of Democratic Institutions, has said:

> . . . all the network commentators of my acquaintance at one time or another have been diverted from more useful pursuits to plead with a sponsor or his advertising agent that a dozen letters from the Citizens Council of Sunflower County, Mississippi, do not constitute a national boycott.[47]

Television and radio newsmen, particularly at local stations, are expected to share in large measure the outlook of their superiors. Otherwise they would not be hired. Therefore they do not need to be censored. Their make-up, the "word-to-the-wise" implicit in their very employment, knowledge of what "the chief" stands for, and wants his hearers to hear, and the subtleties of promotions and firings in the broadcast news area, are the only "censorship" that *needs* to exist. It does the job.

In 1958 Senator Wayne Morse declared that some networks "deliberately censored" news regarding his investigative efforts.

> The slanting and covert censorship of news is of great significance in a country such as ours, for it constitutes a fraud on the public, and one of which the public usually remains blissfully ignorant.[48]

The concept of how much news TV should present is of itself an interesting example of the "censorship" by management of the idea that television should devote at least as much time to news as it does to Westerns or comedies. In June 1958, New York City had forty-eight and one-half hours (ninety-seven programs) of audience participation programs alone, per week. The total time given to news was a small fraction of this number. What can be said to be the fate of news and public-affairs material rejected because it could not be crowded into the few hours set aside for news, information, education, or discussion? It was not and is not deliberately censored, of course. Yet it is kept off the air by "lack of time" as completely as if it had been censored or kept off for some other reason. And it is kept off by management decisions regarding the importance of news.

For years stations declined to give radioactive fall-out totals, because "the people didn't want them." A more valid reason seems to be that disturbing people is bad for business. How the public was to grow to want these facts, or to know that they were available to want, or that they were important to know, also represents an interesting type of question and blockage, short, perhaps, of deliberate censorship.

Or what is the result of sending the kind of untrained personnel most stations employ instead of trained reporters to cover an event? Cracks in the earth's crust are just holes in the ground to untrained observers. To trained geologists they may be omens of earthquakes. Journalists are trained to see and understand *significant* events. The most important developments are never reported if unskilled and untrained observers are sent out, or if those who are trained are forbidden to comment, interpret, analyze, or speak the truth frankly as they see it, because their reports might disturb business as usual. The information which does not get through is not, perhaps, actually censored. It is simply blocked or withheld by failure to employ and use good personnel who understand it. It *would* reach the public if proper personnel and standards were used and adequate time and resources were made available. What is this kind of blockage to be called?

Speaking to the Wisconsin State Historical Society in 1958, newsman Gunnar Back spoke of the

> . . . belt-line of the latest news . . . which is, as someone has put it, a glut of occurrences. . . . But, except for the contribution of the careful workmen in our craft, it's a flow of news censored by well-meaning ignorance, the inexperience of those who deliver it, and it suffers from time limitations and conformity to industry policy practices.[49]

Back recalls the "prodding from upstairs" which newsmen get, to emphasize *local* rather than national and world news. Allen Raymond, in *The People's Right to Know,* describes the "feeling of frustration and cynicism" that has come to prevail more and more as businessmen replace journalists as the superiors of newsmen. Reporters and correspondents learn how to "select" the kinds of news their bosses want to publish. "Anyone smart enough to be a Washington correspondent knows that his boss likes Ike," as one reporter told Raymond.[50] In view of "censorship by brevity and ignorance" which Gunnar Back describes, and the limitations Allen Raymond notes, how complete is the much-vaunted freedom of broadcast news in the United States? Is it not free only from *certain* people and pressures, and free only to do *certain* non-controversial things, which would seem to be a very narrow kind of freedom indeed?

The late A. J. Liebling suggested that, in order to understand the effect of investments and foreign holdings of U.S. corporations on foreign policy,

> A carefully reported survey of American holdings and operations in each country of, say, Latin-America to begin with, would seem to me an outstanding public service. The press might render . . . a great service . . . if it let the public know how things stand between say, the copper companies and Central America. Or the oil companies and the Middle East.[51]

In the broadcast area, questions might be raised regarding the pressures exerted on the United States government by fruit, oil, sugar, tobacco, and other companies with investments in Cuba since Castro's rise to power. Why are these enormous problems so little discussed in view of the overwhelming importance they have had in making United States foreign policy?

Almost all minorities, however small and atypical, are inclined to identify their special views and interests with the national interests. The story is told of the six tailors of the mercantile area on London's Tulle Street, whose petition for special privileges to the London City Council began: "We the People of England."

Repeatedly, broadcasters declare facts and policies favorable to themselves as "what the people want and need." Some doubt exists regarding the validity of such identification, either with the general public, their own newsmen, or representatives of the press of the print media.

On the basis of its product, at least, commercial broadcast management in the United States would appear to be less intellectual or artistic in its orientation than is the leadership of magazines and newspapers. *Ideas* are therefore relegated to a lower priority than showmanship or action. Since controversy in the area of ideas is taboo, for mercantile reasons, if there is to be conflict on television, it must take on obvious and *physical* forms instead. Violence, fist-fights, gun-fights, brawls, and similar forms result. Violence is the way to solve problems, personal and national. The clash of fists, bodies, horses, and anonymous cars, planes, and weapons, replaces the clash of ideas. Generally the industry appears to have been more concerned with its freedoms regarding profits, commercials, sex, and violence than with those in the arena of ideas. As E. William Henry, Former Chairman of the Federal Communications Commission, declared in an address April 4, 1964, "Your contrasting reaction to these two struggles . . . over-commercialization and Pacifica Foundation . . . cast a disturbing light on the basic motivations of an industry licensed to do business in the public interest."

What Henry referred to deserves brief comment. When the Pacifica Foundation station, KPFA, was in danger of losing its license because it engaged in the most open and frank discussion of all types of problems, without taboos, the broadcast industry generally neither protested, nor cried censorship, nor offered to help the lone, courageous station in its fight for the right to be controversial and free from censorship. As he observed: "Apparently not one commercial broadcaster felt obliged to make his views known to the Federal Communications Commission." When the FCC threatened to tamper with length and number of commercials, however, the industry's full lobby and public relations pressure was brought to bear. Bills were introduced into the Congress to forbid this.

> When you display more interest in defending your freedom to suffocate the public with commercials than in upholding your freedom to provide provocative variety—when you cry "Censorship," and call for faith in the founding fathers' wisdom only to protect your balance sheet . . . you tarnish the ideals enshrined in the Constitution. . . .[52]

Thus former Chairman E. William Henry of the FCC.

When it is carefully examined, the version of censorship to which broadcasters and networks hold is no more reassuring than that of sponsors. Chameleon-like, broadcast leaders and policies too often take on the coloration of the environment, which is corporate. The differences between sponsors as a genre, and broadcasters, disappear. The kinds of credentials these individuals have, the values they hold, and the materials they prevent the public from hearing and seeing, should be a source of deep concern to all citizens interested in access to truth, wherever it may be found.

In late 1963, the American Civil Liberties Union noted that CBS excluded a song satirizing the John Birch Society from the Ed Sullivan program, because it would have been "too controversial." In 1964, NBC vetoed a program on venereal disease that had been carefully prepared for the *Mr. Novak* series to help the nation recognize this tragic and dangerous threat to the youth of the land. The March 10, 1965, *Wall Street Journal* reported efforts by Xerox Corporation, a leader in the sponsorship of controversial programs, to secure distribution and broadcast in the United States of a documentary on the struggle of Jews for a homeland: *Let My People Go*. All three national networks refused to show it because "they show only documentaries they produce themselves."

These were broadcast management decisions, for, as David Sarnoff told the FCC: "The guarantee of freedom of speech . . . gives the broadcaster, as I understand it, the right to have programs of his own selection over his station, after that station is licensed."[53] However unrepresentative of the public, or of society as a whole, broadcast controllers and their qualifications are, they become the gatekeepers who determine what shall pass, or fail to pass, through the channels of the *public's* airways. Their sense of values, however deviant it may be from those of the intellectual, professional, or laboring populations, is the basis of policy in broadcasting.

As noted by Chairman Henry above, broadcasters seem considerably more interested in the right to carry as many commercials as they wish than in their right to discuss pacifism, integration, conservation, anti-trust violations, or in giving any significant allocation of time to labor, education, or religion. They do not seem to consider freedom as indivisible or as something that minorities deserve. Reports of professors dismissed or involved in the issue of academic freedom, for example, are likely to be considered a matter involving professors only. It is rarely suggested that the people of the nation have a great stake in whether or not professors (like newsmen), who are in a sense natural resources, are left free to find out and publish what only such specialists can produce. The scientific and cultural benefits which should come to a nation from such freedom on the part of its most disciplined and original minds are lost without such freedom. They need protection, less against government than against broadcasters who refuse them a voice, or who veto or censor what they wish to say. However sincere these broadcasters may be, they are considerably less than repositories or representatives of the accumulated public wisdom or public interest.

The Role of the Artist or Intellectual. Like professors and teachers artists, writers, or thinkers are likely to be looked upon as problem children of broadcasting. Such people usually are not high on the list of those professions respected most by businessmen, whose criteria of success are usually wealth and power, rather than learning, dedication, beauty, or courage. Since the program that is too powerful does not put the public in the proper mood for buying, what is broadcast by preference is material of just that level of mediocrity which will serve as a vehicle for sales—not an art form whose message or beauty, or challenge, the nation needs.

Censored, frustrated, bruised, belittled, rebuked, often laughed at, and oftener scolded, many of the most original and courageous scientists, educators, religious leaders, artists, and talented writers who have tried television as a career feel the disappointment and tragedy of being considered useless or trouble-makers. As a medium which might have created a resurgence of interest in art and beauty, and truth, however dangerous, which could have made the Renaissance seem pale by comparison, television is forced by its present masters to be primarily the dutiful lackey of sales messages conveyed in program vehicles cheap enough not to cause the contents (advertising) to suffer by comparison.

The creative artist and the intellectual, respected by some cultures, are brushed aside by the salesman who has taken over and who finds them troublesome. With the artists go their messages of warning and enrichment, unappreciated by the kinds of censors whom broadcasters assign to determine what the public shall have from the broadcast media, and unheard by the American public, which does not even know they are striving to be heard. Even satire and comedy, from which America might well learn much that might be useful to her sanity and survival, gradually come under the label of "controversial," and must be cast aside. As Groucho Marx once burst forth: "You can't kid about anything anymore. If you have an audience of thirty million and the sponsor gets eight letters saying his comedian offended them, he's terrified."[54]

John Bartlow Martin, in the October 21 article of his 1961 series for the *Saturday Evening Post,* quoted television director John Frankenheimer as saying that TV is no longer an art form, but a supermarket, existing solely to sell cigarettes, gas, lipstick, and so on. He recalls his days as a director. "What we all wanted to do was good things. They wouldn't let us. They told us, 'We don't want you guys'. . . .

So everybody left, everybody that's any good. . . . It was fun while it lasted. But it's over."[55]

At the local level, the problem of selection or censorship is in even more questionable hands. Per Holting, in his study reported in *Journalism Quarterly*,[56] documents case after case where pressure from the sales department or station management prevented television news departments from broadcasting certain items involving sponsors. By purchasing advertising, it appears, firms may often in effect purchase immunity from exposure of malpractices, or poor or unsafe products. (Further discussion of Holting's study appears in Chapter 5.) Whatever news reporting under this kind of system may be called, it is not free news reporting. If broadcast leaders wish to remove the barriers to the free examination of all problems, they themselves must free their newsmen from such pressures, so they may treat any subject whatever, whether or not it affects the sale of any given products advertised on television or radio. There must be nothing that cannot be spoken or thought about. Local businessmen—either as sponsors or sales or station managers—do not have the wisdom or qualifications to judge the importance of world and national events. Yet time after time, local station managers and sponsors cumulatively decide that half or more of the areas of the United States shall not see certain programs. Of the nearly two hundred stations which might carry NBC, CBS, and ABC programs like *White Paper, The Nation's Future, CBS Reports,* or others mentioned in earlier pages, less than half usually carry many of them. How much free access do viewers in the "censored" areas have to the ideas and facts they need for intelligent decision-making? How does this affect how these citizens will vote at the next election?

A typical illustration of one aspect of the problem is found in the efforts of station WBNY, Buffalo, years ago, to secure for broadcast *The American Forum of the Air,* which was not carried by the Mutual network station in that area.[57] Its request was turned down. Thus the network station can not only decline to carry certain programs, but also decide that the citizens of its area shall not hear this program from other sources either.

Comparable Blockages in Music and Other Non-News Materials. Although our principal concern here is with news, it is well to note that blockage is as complete, arbitrary, and monopolistic for music, educational, artistic, and other non-news programs as it is for informational programs. In the later chapter on blacklisting, the exclusion of certain artists and their works, on the basis of criteria other than quality of the product, will be discussed. At this point, however, a closer look specifically at the music situation in broadcasting might be useful.

On December 10, 1964 (in Civil Suit No. 64 Civ. 3787), the Department of Justice filed suit in the U.S. District Court in the Southern District of New York to force the broadcaster-owners of Broadcast Music, Incorporated, a music-licensing and publishing organization, to divest themselves of this ownership, because BMI and broadcaster-ownership "constitute a combination to restrain and monopolize" the music business. Since broadcasters own BMI and since, as the complaint states, ". . . songs must be performed on the air to achieve popularity"; and since "broadcasters determine which musical compositions shall be performed on their stations," this combination appears to violate Sections 1 and 2 of the Sherman Antitrust Act.

The Department of Justice in its complaint notes how BMI, like the NAB itself before it, was formed to oppose the demands of ASCAP, the American Society of Composers, Authors and Publishers, which seeks reasonable payment for the use of composer-member compositions. Since 1939, when the networks and the NAB formed BMI, to cite from the complaint,

> BMI has attained a position of dominance in the field of popular music used by broadcasters, including rhythm and blues, country and western, rock and roll and Latin music. . . . In 1962 BMI licensed 70% of the current hits listed in the combined polls of *Billboard, Variety,* and *Cashbox.* The BMI catalogue contains 84.1% of the top rhythm and blues songs listed in *Billboard's* R and B charts for five consecutive years. . . . More than 80% of the selections on the Hot 100 Records chart were BMI songs.

Why non-BMI music is excluded is obvious: broadcasters want to promote the use of the music, and thereby the profits and monopoly, of the firm they own. Why rock and roll, rhythm and blues, Western and Latin music are promoted, and classical and others forms of music—owned by ASCAP and other more classically oriented rival licensing groups not owned by broadcasters—are found to be less attractive to broadcasters, is also obvious. This apparent conflict of interest, and restraint of freedom, is mentioned as a case history here only as an illustration of the kinds of restraint which exist in various non-news areas. With this kind of manipulation and control available to them, networks and the broadcast industry are able to determine what music, art, drama, and other materials, as well as news, Americans will be allowed to see and hear. This denial, or difficulty, of access to a free market to the authors, composers, and publishers, as represented in the BMI case, also depresses the income of free artists.

It will be interesting to note what success the Department of Justice will have in its request that ". . . The defendant broadcasters be ordered to divest themselves of the stock of defendant BMI," thereby, once again, allowing factors other than monopoly ownership, economic controls, and profit and payola considerations to determine what kinds of music, and whose music, America may hear.*

This type of control, of course, extends to sports and other events as well, and even to the music that shall be played at football games. The University of Illinois band planned to play the Oldsmobile March for one of Illinois' televised games. Since Chrysler was the sponsor of Game-of-the-Week on NBC, however, this number had to be deleted from the band's program.

If the Justice Department's BMI suit is successful, similar steps may be desirable in other program areas, including news agency relations, in which commercial considerations appear to obstruct the free flow of artistic, sports, and educational as well as informational materials.

Conclusions. Through the years, local stations, which are by law the only units legally responsible, through licensing, for what they broadcast, have surrendered their functions to networks, syndicates, and film producers; they hear or see these materials for the first time at the moment they are broadcast. Networks, in turn, have surrendered various functions to advertising agencies, which in turn, have yielded much of this decision-making to sponsors, and so on in a confusing circularity of buck-passing, wherein the kind of confusion reigns that has been found in quiz, payola, rating, and other problem areas in broadcasting. Yet all these groups are of the same kind: all are part of the corporate complex. It has been alleged that this is the best way: that government meddling must be held at bay, since any controls would be "censorship." It is time to challenge that assumption. To believe after over forty years of commercial broadcasting that the programs the nation needs will result from the random accumulation of program types well-enough liked by beer, cigarette, soap, cos-

---

*According to a March 5, 1971, letter from BMI (Vice President Russell Sanjek) this case was settled in December 1966, "most government charges being withdrawn."

metic, automobile, steel, electronics, broadcasting, and other firms to gain and hold sponsorship, because they sell the product rather than because they are good or needed programs, appears to be dangerous naivete.

Efforts to remove present obstacles to freedom would not necessarily be censorship; they could well be *liberation from censorship*. What is needed is to free broadcasting from existing restraints and pressures which prevent the free flow of ideas, and the discussion of all our national problems, however unsatisfactory and uncomfortable such discussion may be to any specific interests such as business, labor, religion, or to any specific firms or individuals, and however radical certain proposed solutions may seem.

The truly great leaders of America have usually been not conservatives but innovators or radicals—daring, ahead of their time. The ideas we need most are likely to appear unorthodox and madcap, expressed by an eccentric, or a small minority not now allowed access to the broadcast media. Some way must be found to insure that they may be heard, so we the people may judge for ourselves, and have our imaginations re-activated. Requiring that such programs be broadcast is not censorship but liberation.

Requiring the labeling of programs that may be dangerous to children, or to unstable individuals, is not censorship. It works well in many free nations. Requiring stations to devote certain hours to the unrestricted and uncensored discussion of community, national, and world problems is not censorship. Comparing a station's promises, or network officials' public addresses and promises, with performance is not censorship. Requiring public and open reporting of profits taken in the use of the public's air is not censorship.

To assume that a few individuals on Madison Avenue or in a Hollywood office are adequate arbiters of American needs—of the public interest—is presumptuous. Of course, the individuals now in control prefer the present situation. They wish to keep the public quiet and uncritical, so as not to disturb their profit-taking, and their present prestige and power positions. These individuals and firms bear a heavy responsibility for the disinheritance this has brought already to many American citizens in the field of information and public affairs. They have failed to discharge it in the public interest, not because they are evil or intend to do wrong, but because they are the wrong men, with the wrong qualifications and perspectives, to see and judge the national interest. *Some* of the functions of broadcasting *can,* of course, be fulfilled within the framework of commercial and sales control which now prevails. But many of the most essential ones cannot. For these, alternative channels, educational, publicly owned, and supported on bases other than sponsorship, must be found. All of these, too, will contain *their* taboos, since freedom is always relative. But these taboo areas will be different, and new types of light will come through the efforts of other kinds of controllers.

But for all these services, certain national standards must be set by government in the public's interest. Regarding emphasis on violence, for example, Walter Lippmann, who has more consistently opposed censorship in principle than any other recent writer, and would have more to lose by real censorship, has said:

> For my own part, believing as I do in freedom of speech and thought, I see no objection to censorship of the mass entertainment of the young. Until some more refined way is worked out of controlling this evil thing, the risks to our liberties (of programs of violence and obscenity) are, I believe, decidedly less than the risks of unmanageable violence.[58]

Some nations, fully as democratic as the United States, feel that it is government's responsibility to safeguard the people against adverse effects or starvation in intellectual, political, informational, and artistic areas as well as in physical and health fields. In *The Public Philosophy,* many years ago, Walter Lippmann declared, "The freedom to speak can never be maintained merely by objecting to interference with the liberty of the press. . . . It can be maintained only by promoting debate."[59] It is this public debate—in political, educational, artistic, corporation, and all other fields—which has been smothered in the web of private taboos. The mass communications media, so used, become less and less communicative and more and more restrictive.

The Sixth Report of the Rockefeller Brothers Fund Study, *The Power of the Democratic Idea,* stated in 1960:

> The ideal of government by consent requires more than free elections and constitutional government. It calls for the existence of instruments of communication that men can use to get in touch with one another. . . . It means that these instruments of communication be generally available to the community rather than monopolistically controlled. . . .[60]

Democracy promotes discussion and self-criticism, not because of lack of faith or confidence or commitment, but because this is the only way in which imperfect citizens can find the truth needed to keep democratic inquiry and democratic functions operating. The citizens of the United States can face the truth on any subject. They should have access to it. Censorship is not something to be held at bay, as a threat, but to be shaken off. It is already within the gates, omnipresent and paralyzing, nearly everywhere one looks in commercial broadcasting.

At its best, censorship or "selection," is an exacting business which demands all the wisdom, special qualifications, safeguards, standards, integrity, and freedom from selfish motives that the censor (whoever he is) can muster. Even government, as a censor, appears to be imperfect in most respects by these criteria. But the broadcasting industry as censor or gatekeeper so flagrantly violates many of the criteria of freedom and integrity so frequently as to call for immediate and urgent study and change.

In an age when the electronic tools of communication already exist for the national and world-wide dialogue and understanding on which survival depends, it is intolerable to have these marvelous media controlled by salesmen to use predominantly for sales purposes.

Television and radio tell people what is true and what is important. If this job is falsely or imperfectly done, the nation will suffer. If broadcasting deliberately or unconsciously withholds truths people need, it is guilty of nothing less than treason. The responsibility of broadcast leaders in preserving world tensions and narrow nationalism can hardly be exaggerated. The burden they must bear for fostering old divisions and keeping old sores unhealed between East and West, North and South, and black and white, is a terrible one. While as individuals, Americans are sensible, generous, humble, and helpful, as a collective television audience, we are bitter, arrogant, intolerant, vain, vulgar, wasteful, cruel, and brutal. Firm and drastic steps to curtail the distortion now rampant and to release the damming blockage to free flow which exists must be taken quickly if the last vestiges of democratic freedoms in broadcasting are to be preserved. These media must be freed from their present chains before America meets extinction as a great and democratic nation, snug in the false conviction that its people are well informed.

NOTES

1. Federal Communications Commission, *The Communications Act of 1934, With Amendments and Index Thereto* (Washington, D.C.: Government Printing Office, 1961), p. 58.

2. Quoted in *Newsweek,* November 9, 1959, pp. 71-72.

3. Stan Opotowsky, *TV: The Big Picture* (New York: E. P. Dutton and Co., 1961), p. 222.

4. Clinton Rossiter, "The Democratic Process," in *Report of President's Commission on National Goals: Goals for Americans* (New York: Prentice-Hall (Spectrum Book), 1960), p. 72.

5. Sir Ian Jacob, in *E.B.U. Review,* Part B: General and Legal, No. 54 (European Broadcasting Union, Geneva, Switzerland), April 1959, p. 4.

6. Fourth National Radio Conference, *Proceedings and Recommendations for Regulation of Radio* (Washington, D.C.: Government Printing Office, 1925), p. 6

7. Cited by Robert Horton in *Broadcasting and Government Regulation in a Free Society,* an Occasional Paper, Center for the Study of Democratic Institutions (New York: Fund for the Republic, 1959), p. 15.

8. Newton N. Minow, Chairman, Federal Communications Commission, Address to National Association of Broadcasters Public Affairs and Editorializing Conference, Washington, D.C., March 1, 1962.

9. James L. Fly in *Broadcasting and Government Regulation in a Free Society, op. cit.,* p. 14

10. Editorial, *Broadcasting,* LVIII, No. 2 (January 11, 1960), 112.

11. National Association of Broadcasters, *Speaker's Guide for Television Broadcasters* (Washington, D.C.: National Association of Broadcasters, 1959). (Speakers' Packet)

12. Louis L. Jaffe, in John E. Coons (Editor), *Freedom and Responsibility in Broadcasting* (Evanston, Ill.: Northwestern University Press, 1961), p. 220.

13. William Carlisle, Address to Arizona Broadcasters Association, Apache Junction, Arizona, December 1, 1961. Also reported in *Static,* III, No. 1 (December 15, 1961), 16.

14. "Report on Network Hearings," *Broadcasting,* LXII, No. 6 (February 5, 1962), 53.

15. In John E. Coons (Editor), *Freedom and Responsibility in Broadcasting* (Evanston, Ill.: Northwestern University Press, 1961), p. 89.

16. Gene Wilkey, "Other Side of the Coin," Address at Southern Illinois University, Carbondale, Illinois, May 15, 1962, p. 22. (Mimeographed)

17. "Minow Puts Stanton and Co. on Grill," *Broadcasting,* LXII, No. 5, (January 29, 1962), 9.

18. Editorial, "Second Wind" (The Plotkin and Jones Reports), *Broadcasting,* XLVIII, No. 8, (February 21, 1955), 122.

19. Charles Winick, *Taste and the Censor in Television,* An Occasional Paper, Center for the Study of Democratic Institutions (New York: Fund for the Republic, 1959), p. 26.

20. *Associated Press* v. *United States,* 326 U.S. 1, p. 20. (*United States Reports: Cases Adjudged in the Supreme Court.* (Washington, D.C.: Government Printing Office, 1946), 326, 1-60

21. Allen Raymond, *The People's Right to Know: A Report on Government News Suppression* (New York: American Civil Liberties Union, December 1955), p. 37.

22. *Ibid.,* p. 47.

23. Thomas Braden, "Why My Newspaper Lied," *Saturday Review,* April 5, 1958, 13.

24. Fernand Gigon, *The Bomb,* translated from the French by Constantine Fitz Gibbon (New York: Pyramid Books, 1960), p. 98.

25. *Ibid.*

26. William J. Lederer, *A Nation of Sheep* (New York: W. W. Norton and Co., Inc., 1961), pp. 135-36.

27. Opotowsky, *op. cit.*, p. 86.

28. *The Television News Commentator,* with Eric Sevareid, Martin Agronsky, and Louis Lyons (Moderator), a Series of Television Programs Produced by WGBH-TV, Boston (New York: Fund for the Republic, no date), p. 9. (pamphlet, 13 pp.)

29. Gilbert Seldes, *The New Mass Media* (Washington, D.C.: American Association of University Women, 1957), p. 36.

30. Newton N. Minow, Address to Conference on Freedom and Responsibility, Northwestern University Law School, August 3, 1961. (Mimeographed)

31. Rod Serling, *Patterns* (New York: Simon and Schuster, 1957), p. 25. Reprinted in Harry J. Skornia and Jack William Kitson, *Problems and Controversies in Television and Radio* (Palo Alto, Calif.: Pacific Books, 1968).

32. *The Nation,* November 22, 1958, p. 371.

33. See Studs Terkel, "The Film that Burned Chicago," *WFMT Perspective,* 10, No. 10 (October 1961), 29.

34. Winick, *op. cit.*, p. 11.

35. President's Materials Commission, *Resources for Freedom,* Summary of Volume I of a Report to the President (Washington, D.C.: Government Printing Office, June 1952), pp. 1-2.

36. Harvey J. Levin, in his *Broadcast Regulation and Joint Ownership of Media* (New York: New York University Press, 1960), provides numerous case histories in which labor was denied time by Hearst newspapers, the Paterson (New Jersey) *Morning Call,* and other publications and firms.

37. Carl J. Friedrich and Evelyn Sternberg, "Congress and the Control of Radio Broadcasting," *American Political Science Review,* XXXVII, No. 6 (December 1943), 1017.

38. "Television and the Corporate Challenge," *Television Age,* V, No. 9 (December 2, 1957), 31-35, 46, 50-52. Quotations from pp. 32, 34.

39. Quotations regarding the policies of DuPont, General Motors, Ford, Armour and Co., Bristol-Myers, and Procter and Gamble are taken from statements of the firms themselves as part of a study conducted on this subject in late 1962 and early 1963. The full correspondence from responding firms, together with their published policies, when these were provided, are on file at the University of Illinois.

40. Hearings before Federal Communications Commission, Friday, September 29, 1961, Docket No. 12782, Transcript, pp. 7110-42. (Mimeographed)

41. Lawrence Laurent, "Commercial Television: What Are Its Educational Possibilities and Limits?" Chapter 5 in William Y. Elliott (Editor) *Television's Impact on American Culture* (East Lansing, Mich.: Michigan State University Press, 1956), p. 152. (Laurent also quotes *Sponsor,* February 20, 1956, and other sources in this connection.)

42. *Broadcasting,* LXII, No. 5 (January 29, 1962), 42.

43. "Note on U.S.A. Radio (September 1949)," in *Report of the Broadcasting Committee, 1949,* The Right Honorable Lord Beveridge, Chairman (London: Her Majesty's Stationery Office, 1962), pp. 289-90.

44. Brock Chisholm, *Prescription for Survival* (New York: Columbia University Press, 1957), p. 87.

45. Frank Stanton, "Parallel Paths," *Daedalus,* 89, No. 2 (Spring 1960), 352.

46. Hans V. Kaltenborn, "Radio: Dollars and Nonsense." *Scribner's* Magazine (May 1931), p. 496. Reprinted in Harry J. Skornia and Jack William Kitson,

Problems and Controversies in Television and Radio (Palo Alto, Calif.: Pacific Books, 1968).

47. Harry S. Ashmore, "Comment," in *Television: An Interview with Jack Gould, Television Critic of the New York Times.* Occasional Paper, Center for the Study of Democratic Institutions (New York: Fund for the Republic, 1961), p. 32.

48. Cited in Bernard Schwartz, *The Professor and the Commissions* (New York: Knopf, 1959), p. 251.

49. Gunnar Back, "The Role of the Commentator as Censor of the News," Address at Wisconsin State Historical Society, Madison, Wisconsin, January 25, 1958. (Mimeographed)

50. Raymond, *op. cit.,* p. 19.

51. A. J. Liebling, *The Press* (New York: Ballantine Books, 1961), p. 254.

52. E. William Henry, Chairman, Federal Communications Commission, Address to the National Association of Broadcasters, April 7, 1964, pp. 5-6. (Mimeographed)

53. Hearings, Federal Communications Commission, 1939, Docket No. 5060, Transcript, p. 8600.

54. Kenneth Allsop, "Those American Sicknicks," *Atlas,* II, No. 4 (October 1961), 288.

55. John Bartlow Martin, "Television U.S.A.," *Saturday Evening Post,* 234, No. 42 (October 21, 1961), 23.

56. Per Holting, "Where Does Friction Develop for TV News Directors?", *Journalism Quarterly,* 34, No. 3 (Summer 1957), 355-59.

57. This and similar cases of withholding programs from various areas are cited in Federal Communications Commission, *Report on Chain Broadcasting, U.S. Government* (Washington, D.C.: Government Printing Office, May 1941). The WBNY case is described on page 59.

58. Quoted in Seldes, *op. cit.,* p. 73.

59. Walter Lippmann, *The Public Philosophy* (New York: Mentor Books, 1955), p. 100.

60. Rockefeller Brothers Fund, *The Power of the Democratic Idea,* Special Studies Project Report VI, America at Mid-Century Series (Garden City, N.Y.: Doubleday and Co., 1960), p. 10.

Disquieting Practices:
Three Case Histories

Broadcast management's concept of news and its place in broadcasting in the United States, as well as its position on censorship by government and censorship by business, provides cause for concern. This concern mounts when one analyzes the position taken by the networks, and by the trade association and trade press, in three specific areas affected by the public interest: educational broadcasting, blacklisting (as a problem in civil liberties), and pay television.

This material reveals, as nothing else does, the nature of the business environment in which not only newsmen but other creative talent as well must operate, especially whenever controversial material or individuals are involved, or whenever the innovations or proposals involved might decrease the profits or increase the competition of the policy-makers.

Lawrence Lessing, in a biography of Edwin H. Armstrong,[1] has traced the story of RCA's litigation and opposition to FM (frequency modulation) and its inventor, until the latter, after some twenty years of court fights, committed suicide. The story of the tactics used and the pressures brought to bear by industry leaders enjoying monopoly positions, whenever these positions are threatened, are revealing and disturbing in some of their implications.[2] These three case studies are useful in making a closer analysis of the industry's real position on competition and the free flow of information and the arts.

Educational Broadcasting. From broadcasting's beginning, many educators were interested in having their own stations. The University of Wisconsin's station WHA is known as "the oldest station in the nation."

Already in the 1920's, proposals had been made for the reservation of frequencies for education, since educational stations were unable to survive in the face of frequent commercial station pressures. These proposals were opposed by the networks, the trade association, and much of the trade press. To this day, no standard AM radio frequencies are reserved for educational use, as they are in FM and television.

In 1931, when various pressures on existing pioneer educational stations had already begun to decimate them, the Radio Committee of the Association of Land Grant Colleges and Universities appealed for at least a certain number of wave-lengths for each state, which could be reserved as educational resources for educational broadcasting. The Federal Radio Commission declared that "a state does not have a fundamental right to the use of radio in its system of education."[3] The number of educational stations dropped from more than 200 to approximately 30 in a few years. Many of the educational stations left were forced to operate on frequencies shared with commercial stations, which were given preference. Others were condemned to daytime-only operation, or low power.

When President Franklin D. Roosevelt, convinced of the unworkability of the 1927 Radio Act, called for a new regulatory structure and a review of the entire broadcast problem, educators' hopes rose. The Wagner-Hatfield Amendment was introduced in 1934. It would have reserved part of the electronic spectrum for education's own stations. But soon an industry lobby arose to strike down this threat to the monopoly of commercial control. A revealing insight into the position taken by United States broadcasting leadership is provided in the *Congressional Record* of May and June, 1934. The May 8, 1934, issue of *Variety* magazine described the panic that the National Association of Broadcasters was in, "checking off names of Senators and trying to pull wires and get votes." The networks and the NAB warned that "the whole structure of American radio was endangered" by proposals for allocations of frequencies to education.

Although the Wagner-Hatfield Amendment was defeated, 42 to 23, educators still sought ways of gaining access to broadcasting. But for every educator who could be produced to explain why education needed its own facilities and frequencies, the networks and the trade association were able to produce "authorities" who "thought otherwise." This is one of the first illustrations on this scale of the use of broadcasting to *confuse* public opinion in order to achieve reenforcement of the status quo. This technique—producing counter-authorities in problem areas, from pay-television to the possible effects of TV on children—is by now a familiar procedure.

On October 17, 1934, in an address later published in brochure form by CBS,[4] William S. Paley, then its President, addressed the new Federal Communications Commission. The new commissioners wanted guidance. They listened with respect to this experienced broadcast leader who spoke for the industry.

Paley first warned against tampering with the commercial structure. "Radio, to be most effective," he said, "must be conducted on sound *business* principles. I do not believe any such realignment of existing facilities, as has been proposed, would result in a more effective service."

Why? Because CBS, business-managed, was doing and would continue to do the job better, at no cost to the taxpayer. In the first nine months of 1934, he pointed out, only 31 per cent of CBS time was sold. Of the 3,011½ hours of the other 69 per cent, which was the amount devoted to non-revenue producing programs, 810½ hours, or 26 per cent, "were definitely of educational or cultural content." He mentioned the fine CBS *School of the Air,* with its national committee of 33 distinguished educators, and its advisory faculty of 32 well-known teachers. CBS had set aside not only daytime hours but also "definite hours each week, between 6 and 11 o'clock" in the evening for fine public service programs.

The reason the educational interests of the nation could feel reassured about the future, without needing to have their own frequencies or stations, was that CBS and the other civic-minded networks would take good care of the nation's educational needs. Network control could be counted on:

Such program control is vital; and it acts as an important assurance that the extensive periods we are now devoting to educational, cultural, and informative programs generally, *will not be shortened in the future* [emphasis supplied] even if the time comes when we sell more than 30 or 31 per cent of our hours to commercial sponsors.

Thus the promise. Paley further told the newly organized Federal Communications Commission:

Commercial radio, in building up a wide general audience, can do far more for mass education and culture, during a few programs of brief duration which hold this entire audience interest, than could some station broadcasting such programs to a limited audience for many hours of the day. To change such a situation, to reduce the size of the available national audience by any procedure whatever, would be a blow to that very educational progress we all want to encourage.

Moreover, suppose education did get its own stations?

Would that not constitute a needless duplication of facilities, at a needless cost to the taxpayers? Especially when, in the judgment of so many of the educational and cultural leaders with whom we have cooperated, the present system . . . free to listeners . . . can do the job so effectively?

Respected industry leader and CBS President William S. Paley had thus spoken. His promises and statements, and those of the other broadcast leaders and the trade press in making it clear that it would be a mistake to allocate separate frequencies to education, effectively blocked education's effort to secure its own stations.

Before leaving Paley's testimony on this occasion, however, a few of its other characteristics and effects should be noted. In this address, he also articulated several principles which have prevailed ever since among broadcast leaders with reference to education.

First, the seeds of the *mass* concept of the media were firmly planted. Broadcasting's very name, Paley noted, suggests that it ". . . should never be systematically restricted to subject matter of interest only to certain groups within the larger commonwealth."

Then came what he referred to as the *axioms* which must guide the industry. The first: "to give the people what it wants to hear." The second: "to reserve some program space to offer what the program director believes people would like, if only they had an opportunity to hear it."

Then as a national leader, this young man gave the definition of education which was to prevail. CBS had ". . . not hesitated to classify a broadcast of the World's Fair opening as an educational program." It was indeed, he believed, "useful, informative and hence educative in our own American sense. All broadcasts which tend to develop in our nation a unity of national sense and feeling may be considered to have an important educational value, whatever their subject. The criterion of success in such educational programs," Paley said, was "a presentation so dramatic that the listener could distinguish it from pure entertainment only with difficulty."

Only in America would this definition of educational broadcasting, by a young man undoubtedly well qualified as a cigar company executive, but not necessarily qualified as an educational policy-maker, be quoted for a generation or more. Under this broad umbrella definition, entertaining or informational programs would be listed as "educational" until even educators who originally knew better, would cease to challenge such a definition. This permissive definition, no less than the later position of CBS in outright opposition to frequencies for education, helped delay and confuse the idea of educational broadcasting in the United States for many years.

During the next twenty-five years, each effort by education to secure special reservations in the broadcast media found industry's leaders ready. Commercial rather than educational stations were considered most in the public interest.

From 1948 to 1952, when it was apparent that changes in the rules would need to be made before television could become a major industry, a freeze on licensing was imposed by the Federal Communications Commission. This provided one last opportunity for education to appeal for frequencies. From November, 1950, through January, 1951, especially, a supreme effort was made. The Federal Communications Commission heard seventy-six witnesses. Seventy-one were in favor of reservations for education in television. But not Dr. Frank Stanton, who by now had replaced William Paley as CBS President and spokesman. Unlike Paley's open opposition seventeen years earlier, however, since education now gave some evidence of possibly winning its case, Dr. Stanton's testimony[5] principally raised questions. He wondered whether the economic problems of educational television would not be insurmountable, and expressed numerous doubts as to the wisdom of a decision to grant education frequencies in television. Certainly education found no support or comfort in either the networks, the trade press, or the trade association.

Judge Justin Miller of the National Association of Broadcasters, for example, was less restrained than was Dr. Stanton. Judge Miller definitely felt that "the reservation of channels is not the solution to the problem." For the present at least, "and for the future," he thought such reservations "would constitute a very serious waste of natural resources." Like CBS, Judge Miller, as NAB spokesman, believed ". . . it would be much less expensive for educational institutions to buy time on commercial stations and have the advantage of commercial know how."[6]

In his history of educational television,[7] which records much of this opposition and testimony, John Walker Powell describes the surprise of educators at the unexpected opposition to educational reservations by many commercial broadcasters, especially CBS and the NAB, from whom they had expected, at the least, neutrality. When the Joint Council on Educational Television (JCET) was created to press education's case, Powell notes, "CBS, identified by Telford Taylor (attorney for JCET) as the most articulate, able and dangerous of JCET's opponents, wanted the [educational] channels from Boston, Chicago, and San Francisco." UHF channels, CBS believed, were good enough for the educators. CBS was joined in bitter city-by-city resistance to educational allocations by Hearst interests, which were particularly embittered when a Milwaukee channel was assigned to education.

Litigation is a daily tactic of large corporations. But schools are generally not accustomed to this weapon, and frequently they merely surrender, as some two hundred educational radio stations did earlier. In this case, education, behind the JCET, and banded together in the National Association of Educational Broadcasters, was more stubborn. But the effort was costly. And the cost was the public's.

CBS, perhaps surprised at the shock of many people in areas where it so flagrantly put its own interests above those of public education and the public interest, later sought ways of brightening its tarnished image with numerous well-publicized grants and contributions to ETV and ETV stations. It allocated time, like 6:30 A.M. (but not prime time), to educational programs. Its contributions seem to have come only or principally after educational television was a *fait accompli,* or in areas where, by supporting the educational station, CBS could reduce the amount of *commercial* competition. Unfortunately these motives appear to have accounted for NBC's usual but more favorable position on educational frequencies as well. A number of other station groups, like Storer Broadcasting Co., opposed educational frequencies in certain areas and favored them in others, depending on how its own profits and power, market by market, would be affected.

In view of the record, the faith which educational broadcasters today can have in network leadership which yesterday did all in its power to doom their cause is, at best, somewhat tempered. When education needed friends, the networks and the NAB were not among them.

This is not to say that there were not many generous individual commercial broadcasters in the nation who *did* generously support education and educational radio and television. But the most powerful elements of the national leadership—the networks, the trade association, and most of the trade press—were either conspicuous non-supporters or outright opponents of educational frequency reservations for television.

The position of *Broadcasting* magazine, for example, was never in doubt. A typical *Broadcasting* editorial on educational reservations declared:

> If the public interest is truly to be served, as the Federal Communications Commission is charged to do by the law, the [educational] reservations must be withdrawn. . . . Television can educate at less expense and with greater effect if it does so through established commercial stations.[8]

If the Federal Radio Commission and the later Federal Communications Commission are accused, as they may well be, of having hampered, harassed, and delayed educational broadcasting from 1927 to 1961, when Newton Minow became Chairman, to be followed by E. William Henry (both of whom went firmly on record in favor of education), the power of the pressure on them by industry leadership should not be forgotten. The courageous efforts of Frieda Hennock, Clifford Durr, Paul Walker, James L. Fly, and Wayne Coy earlier, on behalf of education, were viciously opposed. The resistance of the commercial broadcast establishment to those who pressed for educational allocations was real and it was ruthless.

Even after the networks and parent corporations recognized that educational television was something with which they would have to live, their "support" seems to have been more conspicuous in words than in deeds. In an address to the National Association of Educational Broadcasters, October 28, 1959, RCA President John A. Burns proposed a crash effort on behalf of educational broadcasting. "There is urgent need for a full-scale program of Research and Development in education, comparable to the R & D programs now under way in defense and industry," he said.

> To achieve these aims, it is my proposal that we undertake a full-scale Research and Development effort in education, on both the local and the national levels. . . . To finance such a program of Research and Development, I propose that each state and locality set aside no less than two per cent of its education budget each year. The advent of new

electronic tools, especially closed-circuit television and its future deriva-
tives, makes possible an advance in methods of education comparable
to that made possible by the invention of the printing press in the fif-
teenth century. . . .

Burns concluded:

"There is a tide in the affairs of men," wrote Shakespeare, "which,
taken at the flood, leads on to fortune." Such a tide is running now in
education. It is up to us to take advantage of it—for the welfare of our
children and for the future of our country.

This address was given in 1959. During the next few years, the educational broadcast leaders to whom he spoke visited Burns and his
successor as RCA president, and met with David Sarnoff, RCA board
chairman, to secure RCA's financial assistance for this exciting project. Unfortunately the corporation, as late as 1965, was unable to
contribute any of the dollars needed to implement the inspiring words.

Robert Sarnoff, Chairman of the Board of NBC, reported in December, 1961,[9] what he considered were already tremendous contributions of NBC to education. During the past four years, he reported,
NBC-TV had broadcast 232 half-hour programs of an educational
nature. This, of course, amounts to 116 hours for the four years, or
29 hours per year. NBC, in other words, devoted to education, per
year, nearly as much time as it devoted to Westerns, detective programs, and light comedy per *week.*

Sarnoff's report does not state how many NBC stations carried
these programs. It is known that between one-half and two-thirds of
NBC-affiliated stations often do *not* carry NBC's non-commercial programs. This leaves large areas of the United States with no opportunity to view or use them.

Neither does the report say at what times, or which days of the
week these programs were broadcast. It is known that some of the
programs which NBC has boasted of carrying have been carried at
something less than ideal hours, such as between 1 A.M. and 7 A.M. If
one is to judge by the record, it would appear that education still does
not rank as high in NBC's estimation as one might hope.

In July, 1961, CBS President Frank Stanton delivered the commencement address at the Massachusetts Institute of Technology. It
was widely distributed. It was a statesman-like address calling for "an
Educational Marshall Plan." Dr. Stanton maintained that we are giv-

ing education too low a priority in comparison with economic, military, and other forms of aid, in our assistance to African and Asian nations. He said:

> In a world where the democratic idea is on trial in more places, under more desperate conditions, than ever before, we are practicing economic determinism, when we know from every evidence of our own experience that the only road to democratic fulfillment is educational determinism. . . . Only education—not manned flights to the moon, not new nuclear tests below the surface or in outer space, not webs of highways and patches of landing fields dotting half the planet—can ultimately prevent the sure collapse of a free nation unequal to its freedom. . . .[10]

There is mounting evidence to support Dr. Stanton's concern. Representatives of Asia and Africa at the European Broadcasting Union Conference in Rome, December 3-9, 1961, warned Americans that there are in the world 700 million children of school age, and over 600 million adult illiterates, who could be profiting greatly from educational uses of television. It is educational material to help educate these people that is most needed from American television. In fact, many nations beg for materials to help meet problems of literacy, agriculture, medicine, and public health.

The question that must be asked here is a very serious one: If the need for education is so great, why is it that films and television programs being sent to developing countries by CBS, NBC, ABC, and film companies seem to be the exact *opposite* of the *educational* assistance which Dr. Stanton says these countries need? If the need is as Dr. Stanton has defined it, should the networks be flooding these countries with television Westerns and comedies featuring entertainment? Should industry itself not be exercising some leadership in providing *educational* materials? What are CBS, CBS Films, Screen Gems, Columbia Records, and other CBS subsidiaries doing to help solve the problem which Dr. Stanton so urgently identifies? To match Dr. Stanton's words, what deeds by CBS exemplify the educational statesmanship he called for? Must industry export the type of films and television programs which create the anti-educational or non-educational effects which characterize most present television and film exports?

There are other commercial broadcasting practices also which have increased the difficulties both of education and educational broadcasting.

Traffic in station frequencies, for example, has already cost education dearly. In 1959, a group of educational institutions, led by New York University, sought to secure a television station frequency for New York. Education was outbid. The station equipment was worth perhaps a half-million dollars. The station sold for nearly four million. When education was finally able to buy a station in New York, it cost over six million dollars. Why should public education have to buy back from private exploiters what is public property?

A still more serious obstacle to education, however, is the low value given it by industry leaders. Broadcast leaders who say they respect education, but relegate it to inferior positions in their own firm's activities and scale of values, are not merely showing lack of respect for education; their deeds appear to contradict their declarations.

One thing the nation appears to need is to have the mass media show respect for education, and help create a demand for it. The authors of *A Design for Democracy,* a British Adult Education Committee study published in 1956, have said:

> . . . In the majority of people the desire for education is latent and requires to be aroused. To bring a group of students into existence is work which voluntary educational agencies are admirably fitted to perform. . . . The voluntary organization stands as a link between those whose duty it is to provide education and those who desire education. . . . Voluntary agencies must, therefore, be regarded as an integral part of the fabric of national education. . . . Neither universities nor local authorities can do much more than make provision for education. . . . [Other] agencies can stimulate, focus, and organize the demand for it.[11]

What broadcast stations and networks could do in this respect is considerable.

Bernard Berelson in *Studies in Public Communication* has observed, in speaking to broadcast spokesmen:

> It is the familiar vicious circle: You mass-media people create a climate unfavorable to an interest in serious education and then tell us that you can't change that until we produce a mass audience that demands serious educational fare from the media.[12]

In England, as well as in many other foreign countries, education has traditionally had a very *large* part of the attention, the staff, the budget, and the prime time of broadcasting. Education is not something put in unsalable time, or moved about, subject to commercial priorities. In Britain's BBC, educational programs have the highest priority; as author K. V. Bailey notes:

> In the BBC's Charter the powers of autonomy of the National Broadcasting Councils are defined in such a way that school broadcasting has a secure and inalienable place. No National Broadcasting Council may decide to replace school broadcasts with other kinds of programmes.[13]

In Japan, the number of stations devoted to education is approximately equal to those devoted to all other types of broadcasting. And the budget devoted to education and educational broadcasting is something over twice that of the United States in proportion to population.

Is the time not here when a few prime-time spots, with full production support, should be allocated by networks and commercial stations to American education—at least until educational broadcasting becomes as widespread, well-organized, and well-financed a national service as commercial broadcasting now is?

There is some doubt, on the basis of the record to date, that the present type of leadership in United States broadcasting will ever voluntarily provide the support which education must have. In a mass media system which considers intellectuals to be trouble-makers, how much effort will be devoted to creating more of them? If education is likely to produce intellectuals and educators, who are so frequently critical of television and radio, we can perhaps see why efforts on behalf of education by present broadcast leaders are likely to be something less than wholehearted.

Unfortunately, solid studies which compare the image of the educator and education in American broadcast media with those in other countries, reveal that education, educators, and the well-educated are all too often presented in a belittling or unfavorable light. More than likely, the teacher is a spinster or an absent-minded college professor. The serious student is the butt of many practical jokes. How likely is such a system to produce respect for education? And what are broadcasters doing generally to correct this denigration of the educational process and product?

Dr. Frank Stanton gave one answer in the January 23, 1962, FCC hearings. He said: "Our job is to provide the public with a ramification of programs and let them make their choices. Not to ram education down their throats. It's as simple as that."[14]

In an article entitled "Parallel Paths" in 1960, Dr. Stanton also said:

> . . . Democratic procedures, to some extent even democratic values, necessarily involve quantitative considerations, about which intellectuals are always uneasy. . . . The intellectual is highly impatient of much that is imperfect but also inevitable in democracies. . . . What do the intellectuals really want? Do they want us to do only serious programming, only programs of profound culture value? Or do they just want us to do more? And if so, what is more? . . . Or do not the intellectuals really want to stake out reserves, admission to which would be granted only on their terms, in their way, at their pleasure? . . .

"Intellectuals," Dr. Stanton said,

> . . . are a minority, one not really reconciled to some basic features of democratic life. They are an articulate and cantankerous minority, not readily given to examining evidence about the mass media and then arriving at conclusions, but more likely to come to conclusions, and then select the evidence to support them. . . .[15]

In many other countries the broadcasting systems are run by boards and individuals who are considered by the nation, as well as by themselves, to be intellectuals. It is perhaps not surprising that in those countries the intellectual and education are presented in a far more favorable light than they are in the United States, and that education receives a far larger share of the efforts of broadcasting than it does in the United States.

The time has come to challenge this situation. The definition of education that President Paley offered in 1934 and the present evaluation of education and its needs, as compared to those of commerce, are no longer adequate to our time. The nation needs a variety of educational broadcasting services. Why should we think in terms of only one educational network, co-existing with *three* commercial networks? Should educational television not be at least as large as CBS, NBC, and ABC all together? Why not at least as many, and as fine, facilities for education as for commerce? What does this nation value most? Certainly the time for a basic re-evaluation of our total broadcast structure with reference to educational needs and effects is overdue.

Commercial broadcasting's position on education and educational broadcasting represents a disturbing chapter characterized by the obstructing of educational values and ideas, whenever the establishment felt education's claims and needs would interfere with its own interests.

Blacklisting. At the time of the quiz scandals, Dalton Trumbo wrote in *The Nation:*

> In only one aspect of the scandal can we take real satisfaction: all who participated in the fraud were certified, loyal Americans. The elaborate system of blacklisting, by which the networks deny use of publicly-owned channels to those with whom they disagree, makes certain of that. Everybody connected with the shows had been cleared by the American Legion, The House Committee on Un-American Activities, the Senate Internal Security Committee, AWARE, ALERT, "Red Channels," sponsors' check-ups, the agencies' private eyes, the networks' corps of dedicated snoops and Heaven knows how many private nuts, crooks, and crackpots. The people who dived, and the people who won, and all who arranged the cheat and sponsored it, and distributed it . . . had never joined a "verboten" organization; they had never given money to unpopular causes . . . they were authenticated patriots . . . the Republic could take comfort that it hadn't been gulled by a gang of subversives.[16]

In referring to blacklisting, the secret listing of individuals not to be employed in television or radio, Trumbo was referring to one of the most sordid chapters in the history of United States broadcasting. Only now is the full story of this practice becoming widely known.

The first documented treatment of blacklisting in book form was Merle Miller's *The Judges and the Judged* in 1952.[17] In 1956, John Cogley brought out a two-volume study from which we shall quote later. Cogley's study, based on hundreds of documents, personal interviews, and letters, was followed July 10 and 11, 1956, by hearings by the House Un-American Activities Committee,[18] which produced a good deal of interesting testimony but received little press coverage and practically no TV or radio coverage. Except for brief but scattered stories of case-by-case examples of blacklisting, reported in the trade press, news magazines, and such liberal magazines as *Common-weal, The Nation,* and the *New Republic* in the late 1950's and early 1960's, no significant mention appeared until late 1964, when former CBS performer John Henry Faulk, himself the victim of the black-list and winner of a libel suit against blacklister Vincent Hartnett, brought documentation up to date and corrected any impression that blacklisting was dead with his book: *Fear on Trial.*[19]

The publication of a booklet entitled *Red Channels,* in June 1950, marked the start of blacklisting in television and radio. This booklet was published in New York by American Business Consultants, publishers of *Counterattack, The Newsletter of Facts on Communism. Counterattack* provided a list of 151 people who were allegedly pro-Communist. One of the great American tragedies lies in the way in which broadcast leadership reacted to this publication and other blacklisting steps which were soon to follow.

In *They Thought They Were Free,* Milton Mayer tells how totali-tarian tactics, which led to Nazism, came to Germany. One former Nazi explains it:

> . . . The world was lost one day in 1935, here in Germany. It was I who lost it, and I will tell you how. I was employed in a defense plant. . . . Under the law I was required to take the oath of fidelity. I said I would not; I opposed it in conscience. I was given twenty-four hours to "think it over." In those twenty-four hours I lost the world. . . . You see, refusal would have meant the loss of my job.[20]

A similar period of soul-searching undoubtedly confronted industry leaders in June, 1950. How agonizing the struggle with their con-sciences was, it is difficult to say. But in the decision made at that time, the future of civil rights in United States broadcasting—and of political freedoms and controversy on radio and television—was es-tablished.

The word was promptly passed down. Actress Jean Muir was fired from her General Foods, NBC program, *The Aldrich Family.* Her ca-reer, to all intents and purposes, was finished, although no solid evi-dence of pro-Communist activity on her part, the alleged reason for her blacklisting, was ever produced. The people whose phone calls caused her firing were members of the same pressure groups who were soon vociferously promoting Senator McCarthy and his crusade. Neither in the Muir case nor in later ones did the industry give evidence of checking to see whether the claims were true, whether the numerous "spokesmen" they heard from had received authorization from their memberships, or whether some of the groups quoted as subversive even existed.

Philip Loeb was fired from *The Goldbergs.* After many attempts to clear himself, including meetings with CBS President Frank Stanton, Gertrude Berg, and General Foods President Clarence Francis, Loeb knew he was doomed. After years of unemployment, and trying to clear himself, he took an overdose of sleeping pills in September 1955. His blacklisting was barely noted in the brief press mention of his suicide. Others to be fired were Ireene Wicker (the Singing Lady), Mady Christians, William Sweets, and some one hundred or so others, many of whom died broken in spirit and body.

Most of these cases were kept quiet. It was not until the fall of 1950 that word of them began to be generally known. The cloak of secrecy, and denial by the networks that blacklisting even existed, foreshadowed similar denials of such later practices as quiz rigging, payola, etc.

One bright spot in the stampede to sacrifice anyone who was accused was the attitude of Robert Kintner, then President of ABC, later NBC President, and until recently special Assistant to President Johnson. In the case of Gypsy Rose Lee, Kintner asked the accuser, Legionnaire Edward Clamage of Chicago, for proof that she was a Communist. None was forthcoming. She stayed. This position was not general, however. Kintner later received an award for his stand, conspicuously different from the usual network position. Undoubtedly, a firm, united stand by all the networks, excluding Communists and Fascists—but only on the basis of careful investigation, proper hearings, and valid evidence—would have stopped *Red Channels* and blacklisting in its tracks. No such position was taken.

Once the die was cast, the same thing happened to network and agency talent that happened to Voice of America employees following McCarthy smears. Victims' careers were ruined. Some committed suicide.

The demoralizing practice spread rapidly. John Cogley said of the industry after his months of investigation:

> It has, in effect, agreed to accept a basic limitation upon its right to hire. While this policy is accepted and the pressure continues, there is little chance that blacklisting can be brought to an end. . . . Most of the

executives at the networks, agencies and packagers were deeply disturbed by the institution even while they were creating it.[21]

Except when they were "deceived by dishonest outsiders," as in the quiz scandals, network executives have repeatedly alleged that they are in full control of their affairs, rather than yielding to sponsors, agencies, and other non-licensed groups. Dr. Marie Jahoda of the Research Center for Human Relations, New York University, questioned this:

> In itself it [blacklisting] is an admission on the part of the TV industry that prerogatives that should be retained by them can be usurped by outside sources. And once they have started to give in to these sources, they will have to give in more.[22]

Quoting a leading character actor, she continues:

> Everyone is afraid to offend. The fear is foisted by the networks who feel they have to please everyone. There is a fantastic amount of censorship which is labelled something else.[23]

The surrender of the networks and agencies was virtually complete by 1952. By then a writer, actor, producer, or director cited in *Counterattack* or *Red Channels,* which quoted each other as authorities, found it difficult or impossible to find work without being cleared. Since many specialists—actors, artists, composers, scientists, and others—are often not interested in or well informed about politics, they are often naïve. They also often support causes out of sympathy or impulse. *Red Channels,* it was apparent, was simply a listing of some of the most spontaneous and gregarious people in the industry, rather than politically sophisticated subversives or Communists.

Dore Schary, once head of production at MGM, declared that his activity as an outspoken Democrat was what led to his ouster from that job.[24]

Perhaps the most hair-raising aspect of blacklisting was the fact that if you were listed in the *Daily Worker,* or virtually any other list, however dubious or irresponsible, as attending a Communist rally, *Counterattack* or *Red Channels* would almost certainly report this.

The way in which the Communists' word was taken enabled them to destroy their enemies, with the aid of *Counterattack,* the networks, and the agencies. All *real* Communists had to do, to put the finger on a strong anti-Communist, was to list him as attending this or that rally, or to mention him as a "friend" in the *Daily Worker*. Cogley points out:

> Nearly all the official documents cited by the professional anti-communists are tabulations of names made by the communists themselves. No hearings have been held to determine whether or not the use of these names was authorized. In some cases they were not authorized.[25]

Although networks, agencies, and others connected with blacklisting continued to deny its existence, and many of them still do, an elaborate secret checking and clearance procedure was set up. This "clearance" procedure is reminiscent of McCarthy days, when State Department employees who were fired could rarely find out what the accusation against them was, or who made it.

Cogley's description of the problem of clearance, as encountered by one actor seeking clearance, deserves quotation:

> . . . Although he must "clear himself," it is also necessary for him to convince various key people that his "clearance" is legitimate. By and large, the persons this actor encountered are the ones who deal with clearances: George Sokolsky, Jack Wren of BBD & O, the top security officers at CBS, various American Legion figures. If this group is convinced of a man's sincerity or, in the case of executives, "defensibility," he can work. . . . The informal "clearance" board is largely right-wing in its political orientation. If a performer has a strong prejudice against associating with Hearst columnists or American Legion officials, or rejects their definition of "effective anti-communism," he will find it difficult if not impossible to "clear himself."[26]

Of the networks, CBS set up the most elaborate procedure and precautions. Where NBC and most agencies turned this sticky problem over to their legal departments, CBS assigned Vice President Joseph Ream to it. CBS instituted a loyalty oath for all employees to sign under pain of losing their jobs. Some left rather than sign. It required the employee to certify that he had not belonged to any of the organizations listed as subversive by the Attorney General. If he had, he had to provide an "explanation" that would satisfy CBS that his membership was not meaningful. The signed oaths were kept sealed in CBS files. In considering the morale of network employees, the existence and uses of such oaths should be kept in mind. It appears to be similar to the numerous devices used by certain other organizations to keep their people "in line," and to establish a corporate conformism acceptable to broadcast controllers.

One of the "heroes" of the story of blacklisting was Laurence A. Johnson, a Syracuse, New York, supermarket operator. Johnson had for several years been taking it upon himself to exert various pressures on food manufacturers who were television sponsors to force them to refrain from engaging certain individuals accused by Johnson and his vigilante-like groups in Syracuse of being identified with the Communist movement. "With Johnson in the ring, the industry spokesmen do not have to feel foolish when someone asks just how real the "economic" threat is . . . Johnson *is* the public."[27]

Johnson's weapon was the threat of a boycott. He was willing to remove from his supermarket shelves, he said, the products of companies whose television programs hired people whom he, *Counterattack*, the American Legion, or others like him considered Communist or subversive.

As far as the actual effectiveness of boycotts was concerned, their threat seems to have been worse than their reality. One executive quoted by Marie Jahoda reported that he was not very much impressed by letters accusing performers of political discrimination of one kind or another:

> . . . He had learned to ignore such correspondence when he realized that the largest number of such letters he ever received in an individual case was 200. On the other hand, when one favorite show altered its time schedule, 8,000 letters of protest came in. Nevertheless the show lost nothing of its popularity on the new schedule. Several executives said they knew that some of their biggest sponsors were annoyed by the interferences of one Mr. Johnson . . . and ignored his threats of boycott without damage to themselves.[28]

However hysterically and unprofessionally network executives behaved in this case, therefore, there seems to be no evidence that boycotts did any significant harm when those in a position of responsibility stood up to them. All it took was "guts."

In his home town, Johnson was considered to be a "patriot" who was frequently carried away by his zeal. Few of his fellow citizens could understand why he was taken so seriously at the national level. Representatives of the Syracuse University radio and television center and the six local stations met early in his crusade to discuss what to do. They unanimously decided that they would not listen to protests from Johnson which were not "adequately documented." The Syracuse station people had difficulty understanding why the big executives in New York were so frightened by his usually baseless charges.

There were many errors in listings. The wrong Smith, the wrong Pollock, and so on. Many people still cannot find work because of such errors. One actor was listed as having been a member of the Abraham Lincoln Brigade in Spain. Once he found what the accusation was, he was able to prove that he was not even out of the United States during the period listed. When *Counterattack* editors listed Harry Belafonte, and he was able to prove the falsity of their accusation, they offered no apology or retraction. Blacklisting meant finding that no one would hire you, but not knowing why—or even what list you were on.

Since Hazel Scott was the wife of a Congressman at that time, she had a chance to testify under oath on her nine *Red Channel* listings. As she ran down the list, she declared:

> One of these listings was for an appearance, by direction of my employer, which was perfectly proper at the time. Another was ostensibly a series of benefits for orphaned children. As soon as I found out otherwise I discontinued my activity. Still another involved the use of my name three years after I played a benefit for a group which thereafter merged with one that developed a bad name. A fourth advertised that I was a guest of honor at a dinner I never went to or even heard of. Three others I refused to join. The remaining two I never heard of.[29]

In some cases, listings and accusations were meaningless. The "organizations" to which the person allegedly belonged did not exist. Or the accused was out of the country at the time a meeting he allegedly attended was held. Or he had been listed against his will. Roderick Holmgren who, with William Gailmor, Lisa Sergio, and a score of other familiar names in the news field, was fired, and found his career as a commentator (over station WCFL, Chicago) ended, thanks to *Red Channels* listings, admitted that the listing in *Red Channels* was accurate. He had been publicity chairman for the National Labor Conference for Peace. He had taught some classes at the ill-fated Abraham Lincoln School. But it was never clear why or how these two facts proved that he was unfit to be a news commentator.

Such was the type of evidence which networks accepted as adequate to blacklist talent. If they were themselves so completely a part of this kind of a witchhunt in private industry, with how much conviction could they be expected to oppose such tactics in government? How could they really have felt about McCarthy and his tactics, at that time, whatever their protestations, when their own were so similar?

Much of the pressure to which networks yielded was from sponsors. This is consistent, of course, with their position regarding sponsor sensitivities, as observed in earlier chapters. The views of many sponsors were very clear. The President of the American Tobacco Company explained: "We would disapprove of employing an artist whose conduct in any respect, 'political' or otherwise, has made him or is likely to make him distasteful to the public."[30]

The spokesman for Westinghouse Electric, which itself owns and operates stations, declared:

We buy "Studio One" as a package from CBS through our agency, McCann-Erickson. These two businesses, as well as all of us at Westinghouse, have a great stake in our capitalistic society. It is therefore in our own best interests never to engage in any activities that would jeopardize the free enterprise system.[31]

The President of Columbia Artists Management declared:

The public performer . . . must observe an axiom of show business, which is not to engage in contentious nonconformism. . . . Active participation in politics . . . is incompatible with his profession. . . . Judgment of the performer's behavior is on a public relations level. Wherein merit may lie on any question is irrelevant.[32]

The ease with which performers could be made "controversial," however, is too often forgotten. If Mr. Johnson of Syracuse phoned a few corporation executives about you, you *became* controversial, whether you had ever engaged in or even heard of politics. Blacklisting had little to do with what you *were* or *did*—only with what someone accused you of doing or being, without your knowing what the accusation was, and without their ever having to confront you.

Fortunately, there were refreshing protests against the witch-hunts. Dorothy Waring, of Waring Enterprises, as well as Henry C. Brown, Jack Barry, and other talent agency individuals, urged networks and sponsors to refuse to allow a few smear letters to intimidate them. They called for valid criteria for determining who was a Communist, since, in the blacklist practice used, more innocents and anti-Communists were likely to be ruined than Communists or Communist sympathizers. Kay Conran, artists' representative and agent, said: "Even more than I dislike Communists, I dislike 'witch-hunters.' " Robert Schultz denounced the un-Americanism of the blacklist. He maintained that the accused should have the right to be confronted with the evidence, so that legal procedure could be followed. But such views were in the minority. The networks held the whip hand, and had the last word.

While broadcasting and the movies were yielding to blacklisting, what was the legitimate theatre doing? It was itself demanding a Congressional investigation of alleged Communist activity in the theatre, instead of yielding to witch-hunters. In 1941 Bert Lytell, President of Equity, had urged the Dies Committee to investigate his profession. In August 1955 the House Committee on Un-American Activities held hearings. Twenty-two of the twenty-three witnesses called took one of the invokable amendments, which McCarthy and broadcast leaders all too generally considered adequate to prove the witness to be "unfriendly." Then they went back to work. Some actors who had invoked the Fifth Amendment were given new contracts at higher pay and for a longer period of time than before. Professional ability still counted on Broadway.

The mass media, especially television and the movies, are big business, controlled by corporation ethics, morality, and values. The decisions about blacklisting were therefore made by people more interested in profits than in art or civil rights. They had it all over Broadway for size and power. Where Madison Avenue and Hollywood capitulated to the pressures, however unproved, almost as soon as they were applied, the theatre, by contrast, laid down a program to fight the pressure, through the joint action of unions and management which enjoy a far better relationship in the theatre than in broadcasting. Beneath the denials they issue, it is hard to see how broadcast executives can fail to feel a sense of shame over their record. The theatre can be proud that it did not succumb to pressures to blacklist.

When Laurence Johnson tried his tactics in the theatre, accusing an actress, he was ignored. When Jack Gilford, under contract to the Metropolitan Opera, was listed in *Red Channels,* and the Legion demanded that the Met fire him, the Met stood firm. Gilford stayed.

Broadway and the Met could both hold their heads up with pride. How different television and radio would be today if the networks had done likewise!

It is possible that some form of super-patriotism motivated industry leaders who kow-towed to the Johnsons, McCarthyites, *Red Channels, Counterattack, Daily Worker* listings, and other unproved and often false accusations. In their decisions to administer summary justice without due process, however, they violated the very civil rights which Communism itself deprives people of.

Even the federal government, which was faced with the problem of individuals cleared for access to classified documents, urged caution and care. U.S. Attorney General William F. Tompkins wrote:

> The nature and extent of membership in a designated organization is but one factor to be considered in determining the qualifications of individuals for employment with the Federal Government. . . . The Board has determined the Communist Party of the United States of America to be a communist-action organization. However, under the Act no action against individuals can be undertaken until the Party has exhausted its appellate remedies.[33]

Many good writers, actors, producers, and newsmen left broadcasting, never to return. Second-rate talent, individuals with few convictions, and unlikely to antagonize their corporate bosses, came to clutter the channels of the nation's most available communications system. Many of those who stayed could never be the same, after the compromises they had to make with their own consciences. Edward P. Morgan, formerly with CBS, remarked: "The lists, as well as the whole climate of opinion of the past few years, put into the minds of even the best men something which was not there before—a care about the words they used, an instinct to cover themselves on controversial issues."[34]

Like courage, morale is a very complex thing. What was, and still is, the effect of the demonstration of lack of intestinal fortitude by "chiefs" on their staffs? On those "thrown to the wolves" and their families and friends? On affiliated stations and agencies? On broadcast leaders in other countries? Today blacklisted writers write under assumed names, or they split fees with other writers who are still in the clear. But blacklisting affects *what* as well as *who* shall appear or be discussed. What can you write about in an environment of compromise, suspicion, and fear? What writers want to be called subversives because they attack urgent but controversial social problems? When the FCC sought to get performers and writers to testify regarding blacklisting, many declined, saying "they couldn't afford that kind of publicity." The analogy to gangster terrorism, or to life in totalitarian lands, is frightening.

The broadcast industry would have us believe that blacklisting is no longer practiced. This assurance can be given little credence when it comes from a leadership which denied its very existence when it was at its height, just as it denied quiz rigging and other malpractices, even while they were going on. In 1960, Rod Serling found that two actors he wanted for *Twilight Zone* were still on the blacklist. In 1963, Pete Seeger found he was still on the blacklist, when ABC-TV, supporting previous actions by the other networks, vetoed his proposed appearance on *Hootenanny*. "The boys upstairs," the program staff found, would allow neither Seeger nor The Weavers on the program. Scores of documented cases running into the 1960's indicate that, though it may be less frequently practiced than it used to be, since fewer "suspicious" or controversial individuals are even *proposed* as talent or writers, blacklisting is still very much with us.

In *Private Governments and the Constitution*, Arthur S. Miller, student of the corporate ethic, writes:

> . . . where the exercise of private power becomes sufficiently obnoxious, Congress can and does step in to redress the balance of power and, at times, to try to protect individual liberty. . . . It is just as important that legislative bodies should be able to protect persons from oppression at the hands of private groups which exercise power indistinguishable from that exercised by government as it is that the courts should be able to protect them from oppression by officials whose power is more generally recognized as governmental.[35]

If a factory worker or a government employee is fired because his loyalty is questioned, is he not normally accorded a hearing, and due process of law? To what extent do television and radio employees enjoy similar rights and protections? How applicable to broadcasting are fair labor practices and civil rights protections?

After his careful study of blacklisting, and those who practiced it, John Cogley wrote:

If the American businesses which together comprise the radio-TV industry are to assume the burdens of government, they must also assume responsibility for dispensing justice. They cannot have it both ways. They cannot argue on the one hand that economic considerations come before all else, and, on the other, speak glowingly of the contribution "business statesmanship" is making to a business-oriented democratic society.[36]

In his acceptance address for the Frank Luther Mott Research Award of Kappa Tau Alpha, at Boston University, April 26, 1961, Dean Leonard Levy of Brandeis University well summarized the dangers of such practices as blacklisting. He said:

. . . With hardly a whimper we witness the erosion of small encroachments, insensible to the permanent damage being done to the First Amendment as a result of emergency measures having become permanent. . . . The media of mass communication and the courts to a lesser degree, are responsible for a failure of nerve, a treason to the First Amendment, in not using their mighty pipelines of information and opinion, their superlative educational facilities, to condemn violations of freedom of expression, whatever the degree, or the source, or the victim. . . . If these rights are to survive and flourish, they require . . . devotion to the life of the free mind and an ability to see clearly and steadily that freedom itself is at stake whenever the freedom of any, even the most unimportant or obnoxious, is abridged.[37]

And a Rockefeller Brothers Fund Study concluded:

. . . Without the presence of civil liberties, no social order can claim to be a democracy. . . . A democracy must of course set limits to the individual's right to carry his beliefs and values into action. But if it adheres to its commitment to civil liberty, in spirit as well as in form, it does not require the citizen to conceal or deny his beliefs and values. . . . Within very broad limits the citizen is free to speak, to publish . . . to worship . . . and to associate with those he chooses. And so he is able not simply to enjoy his privacy without interference but to give his inner beliefs and feelings at least some external form.[38]

It appears from the study of the effects of television and radio that broadcasting has at least as powerful effects as drugs and foods. That some control over their purity and quality is now indicated appears obvious, in spite of industry resistance based on profit motives. But in the broadcast industry's behavior as an employer, equal dangers appear to prevail. To allege that this is a private concern of the networks is hardly acceptable, in view of the profound effects of broadcast industry practices as a bellwether for the nation and as the pattern-setter for several thousand broadcast stations in most of the communities of the United States.

Taking one foreign system as an analogy, we find the books of the BBC open. BBC employees are on a status comparable to that of civil service. Their right to hearings and appeals—to insure that valid evidence, not opinion or unproved accusations, govern action—is established. Even so, the Beveridge Commission in 1950 felt the need for broadcasting to provide an example to the nation in this respect, even more clearly, and recommended further steps to insure that all appeals would involve genuine hearings and rehearings whenever necessary.

To say that, since broadcasting in the United States is controlled by industry, what happens to station, network, and agency staffs and talent is not the *public's* business hardly seems like operation in the public interest. Whether a speaker comes to the public over publicly owned or privately owned facilities, his civil rights should be unimpaired. So should the public's right to hear what he really thinks. For all great minds are in this sense public property—a national resource. To block the free flow of a man's mind and convictions is no less an offense than to block the movement of his body. The latter is called slavery. What can the former be called?

Just as standards for the qualifications of personnel in broadcasting need to be established—as rigid and objective for people who prepare programs as for those who prepare prescriptions, so must fair labor and personnel practices be established for the broadcast industry. Then and only then will blacklisting and other violations of civil and personal rights in broadcasting be brought to an end.

Pay Television. The story of pay television provides one of the most graphic and fearful examples to date of the withholding and distortion of facts, the protection of monopoly position at the expense of the public interest, the misuse of control of broadcast facilities for the fabrication of public opinion, and manipulation by large groups of both congressional and individual voting.

In the November 1964 election in California, voters were asked in a referendum to vote whether or not pay television should be allowed in California. By a vote of more than 1,500,000 votes, Proposition 15, as it was called, was defeated, and pay television, as planned and developed by a corporation headed by Sylvester Weaver, former NBC President, was outlawed.

This represented one of the greatest successes to date of the anti-pay television forces, which had already built up one of the most vicious records in any industry for misrepresentation and blockage of information.

Fortunately, such selfishness and tactics are becoming too flagrant to be overlooked any longer. In its November 20, 1964, issue, *Life* devoted an editorial, "Stupid Question, Stupid Answer," to the California experience. *Life* described the "viciously misleading campaign" which the network stations and theater owners conducted with

> . . . STV cast as a masked bandit robbing school children and old people of their "right" to enjoy TV "for nothing". . . . While San Francisco network affiliates refused to sell Weaver air time, they aired on their own behalf such jingles as *Pay-TV/Before You're done/you'll charge for air/And rent the sun.*

Life raised the question of the validity of the referendum, which appears to be "a two-edged tool of government," in which not the people, but special interest groups in control of mass media ". . . Write [laws] to their own specifications."

The coalition of network stations, theater and restaurant owners, and a few other groups which opposed pay television, hired advertising executive Don Belding to head their campaign to kill it. Approximately $1,000,000 was made available to him. Although both the California and the United States Supreme Courts later ruled that the referendum which killed pay TV was unconstitutional, the organization that was intended to provide an alternative service to advertising-based TV had meanwhile been liquidated. In the New York Sunday *Times* November 15, 1964, television columnist Jack Gould had written correctly: ". . . with the collapse of the West Coast undertaking, the cause of pay television has been set back indefinitely and perhaps irretrievably." Thus ended one more "battle to be born" by a new service which would be competitive with advertising-supported television. A quick look at the general position of the networks and the NAB on pay TV will be useful, as a part of the assessment of the extent to which these groups operate in the *public* interest, whenever this interest conflicts with their private interests.

In May of 1957, after it had accumulated some seventy thick volumes (a stack 18 feet tall) of testimony and evidence over a period of several years, the Federal Communications Commission proposed to allow controlled tests of pay television to explore ways in which it could be authorized to operate alongside the present commercial system. This proposal precipitated a campaign of vituperation, distortion, and political pressure tactics—which included specific legislation introduced into the Congress—which has perhaps never been equalled in the mass media. Some of the principal features of this campaign are examined here.

The principles involved in the pay television issue can be examined without reference to the specific types proposed. Whether the system uses a coin-box, monthly-rental system, or some other device or procedure for collecting the payment, and whether it uses broadcast channels or telephone wires for sending the programs, what is involved is a service which, like magazines that take no advertising, would enable the consumer to pay directly for not otherwise available programs if he wished. In other words, he would pay in money instead of in subjection to commercials, interruptions, and other characteristics of the present advertising-supported system. The consumer would vote for programs *directly* rather than by the indirect route which advertising-supported television now provides. By the latter system, if the *product* is faulty, the program, however good, is likely to be considered a failure, since the final criterion of success, even transcending ratings in the long run, is whether the program sells the *product*. In the present system, in other words, the program is secondary, a by-product of television's advertising role. In pay television it is primary—the *only* product involved in the transaction.

The principal exponents of various types of subscription-supported television have been the Zenith Radio Corporation with its Phonevision, now jointly controlled with RKO General in a New Haven experiment; International Telemeter, a subsidiary of Paramount Pictures; Skiatron Subscriber Vision, promoted by the late Matty Fox; and Subscription Television, Inc., STV for short, the California project mentioned earlier. TeleGlobe, Blonder-Tongue, Angel Toll-TV, TelePrompTer, and some other firms are also interested, and have done some development work and exploration of pay television potentials. It will be noted that most of the companies listed would be essentially newcomers to broadcast programming—firms not now in power positions in the present network and advertising-based systems.

Various systems have already been tested, so there is no longer any question as to whether they are electronically or mechanically feasible. Zenith's successful Chicago tests in 1951 were followed in 1953 by tests by Telemeter in Palm Springs, California; in 1957 in Bartlesville, Oklahoma, by a theatre group using phone lines instead of through-the-air distribution; in 1960 in Etobicoke, a suburb of Toronto, Canada by Telemeter; more recently in Hartford, Connecticut, where Zenith and RKO General have been conducting an experiment on Channel 18; and in California, where STV was ready to be launched when the referendum stopped it.

Although proponents speak of first-run movie films and plays, various types of professional sports events, operas, and so on as likely program offerings, the system is obviously adaptable to any type of programming which people, rather than sponsors, will support. Since the money paid by the subscriber would not have to be shared with advertising agencies and other middle men, each of whom takes his percentage share under commercial television, minority audiences not adequate to justify programming under the present commercial system should be more than large enough to finance pay television offerings.

Several sports managers, such as Walter O'Malley of the Los Angeles Dodgers, have looked forward to pay television as one way of putting sports on a sounder basis than they are at present. Some spokesmen see this as a way of rescuing certain sports from the desperate straits to which they have been reduced in some areas by present television practices. The financing of adequate baseball farm clubs, minor leagues, athletic clubs, and other means of keeping sports on a grass-roots base are particularly stressed. Similar hopes have been expressed by various theatre and musical groups, which believe pay television would provide sufficient support for a national experimental theatre, for example.

Although there has been no final decision on acceptance of advertising, a great deal of the support for pay television comes from individuals and firms who insist that it must carry no advertising whatever. Surely if pay television is to be an alternative to advertising-based television it should not itself be allowed to accept commercials. Only in this way would the unique advantages of a completely different type of fiscal base, as well as a wholly different approach to programming, be realized.

In studying the tactics and arguments used to oppose pay television, it is essential to distinguish between the real and alleged motives of the networks, the trade association, much of the trade press, and the large station groups which most aggressively participated in the anti-pay television campaign.

One of the principal unmentioned motives for opposition was and is undoubtedly the realization on the part of those now receiving the majority of profits that, once people begin to ask, and know, about the finances of television, the American public's present abysmal ignorance about the economics of television would be at an end.

In all nations television has costs. The exact costs can be computed for each system and compared. Some systems are more wasteful than others, and some are more efficient and freer from taboos. A public which knows what kinds of costs are involved, however, and what the choices are, can make more informed decisions than they can in a system in which the figures are not public property, and are concealed as they are at present. Other motives for opposition to pay television are of course those of powerful monopolies in all ages everywhere. If railroads had won their fight to restrict the use of trucks for hauling freight; or if *advertising*-based magazines had sought successfully to have laws passed making it unlawful to publish magazines not based on advertising, the analogy would be more obvious.

The principal problem involved in the campaign of opposition was how to make corporate and profit interests appear to be the public interest. That this seemingly impossible task was so well accomplished is a tribute to the public relations skill, the tremendous power of commercial television as presently operated, and the great support the networks and larger stations received from friends in the Congress. In a careful study of the factors involved in the pay television problem in December 1960, *Sports Illustrated* referred to "the Stantonesque talent for identifying his own advantage with the National Purpose,"[39] which characterizes the usual approaches and declarations of such network spokesmen as Dr. Frank Stanton of CBS.

As the battle grew more heated, and as it appeared that some sort of a test would have to be agreed to, the Federal Communications Commission was forced to attach all sorts of obstacles and conditions to tests of pay television which opponents hoped would so delay it, and make it so costly, that it could not succeed. One of the effects of this tactic has been to discourage smaller newcomers who would not have the funds for all the tests, litigation, and other expenses with which pay television has now been saddled. The only firms able to afford pay television tests today are large corporations, individually competitive, but similar in kind to the networks themselves. To that extent, in keeping out different kinds of possible innovators, the campaign against subscription television has already been successful. It has kept out the small, new businessman. If, in spite of the opposition, pay television is finally approved, it is likely to appear upon the national scene bearing all sorts of trappings, chains, and controls hung upon it by those who sought to sink it. These accouterments may come to plague their originators, if the latter, convinced that they cannot defeat it, decide to join the movement, or move in and control it themselves. For there is considerable evidence that, if pay television does succeed, unless prevented by law or regulation, the same Sarnoffs, Paleys, and Goldensons who now ring up advertising-based television profits will be collecting pay television's fees.

One of the most amazing accomplishments of the campaign opposing pay television was its success in conveying the impression that *the industry generally* was opposed to it. This was the impression conveyed by the networks, as well as by the trade association and most of the trade press. For instance, the spokesmen of the National Association of Broadcasters, after telling the Senate Committee on Interstate and Foreign Commerce, April 25, 1956, that under pay television there would, in his opinion, be no more free World Series, dramas, or musicals, and that "the only loser will be the public," concluded: "I have spoken at length as a representative of the television industry."

The right of the NAB to speak for the entire industry was and still is less clear than would appear from such declarations. Many stations did not and do not belong to the NAB, which is a voluntary trade association. Many stations which *did* belong to the NAB did not agree with the NAB's stand on pay television. The Intermountain Broadcasting and Television Corporation, for example, 80 per cent owned by Time, Incorporated, and 20 per cent owned by G. Bennett Larson, filed a statement saying it wished to make it clear that the views of the NAB were *not* the view of that firm, for it *favored* pay television.

Central Broadcasting Company of Eau Claire, Wisconsin, in its filing, pointed out the *advantages* of pay television for small market stations. The brief filed with the Federal Communications Commission declared:

> It is apparent that there is insufficient economic support from advertising for the kind of national television service envisioned by the Commission. . . . Subscription television offers a "reasonable source of adequate economic support for a truly national system." There is nothing

legally improper or "un-American" about a system requiring the entertainment consumer to pay. . . .[40]

The late Edgar Kobak, who was at one time President of the Mutual network and at another an NBC Vice-President, was convinced that the nation *should* try pay television. He saw in the review precipitated by its consideration an excellent opportunity to study many other desirable changes as well. He urged that pay *radio* as well as pay television be considered; that hearings on this possibility be covered by television-radio; that there be an investigation into how charges would be made and who would be paid; that a study should be made of whether the government should not charge for licenses; and that the government look into the rights of set owners who now pay "very large sums annually" for maintenance, electricity, etc.

In giving the impression that "the broadcasting industry" in the United States opposed pay television, therefore, the networks and large stations gave an impression that was rigged and inaccurate. This predisposition to conceal certain facts has been found in other connections.

The big and rich stations *did,* of course, oppose any challenge to their monopoly and profits. And having the biggest voice, they were the ones who were most heard and quoted. However, it should be understood that the anti-pay television campaign described here, and made to look like a united or unanimous effort of "the broadcast industry" was, instead, one in which the larger interests prevailed over the smaller and frequently more numerous pro-pay–television exponents, many of whom did not dare speak up for fear of losing network affiliations or suffering other retaliation.

The Charleston, West Virginia, *Gazette-Mail* on March 25, 1958, pointed out in the last few lines of an angry editorial how the networks treated a local station which dared to oppose their anti-pay television campaign:

> . . . While we wouldn't be caught dead saying it ourselves, we've heard it whispered that this trio of giants have within themselves the makings of a television cartel capable . . . of bringing Congress to heel and of getting a corner on the spoken word in the United States. . . . There's certainly some evidence of heavyhanded dealing right here in Charleston, where one of them flippantly cancelled its contract with WCHS-TV and said, "Go peddle your viewing audience somewhere else."

The fear that the networks would fail to renew contracts with stations that became too independent, was one reason why more stations, some of which were very much interested in pay television, dared not disagree publicly with the networks. For network affiliation often means life or death to a small station.

But these were the least of the network and station activities opposing pay television. One of the principal techniques used was to devise questionnaires and surveys to prove how indignantly the public opposed pay television. Lawrence Hughes explained the tactic in the *Saturday Review*. NAB President Harold Fellows, he wrote, declared that:

> . . . "every survey and poll that I have seen shows that an overwhelming majority of the people opposes the use of free channels for toll purposes." But as every ad man knows, survey results may rest on how questions are worded; what questions are asked, and the fact that, other things equal, people are inclined to vote for the known and against the unknown. Also, at this stage, the Subscription forces have far fewer researchers and press agents at their command.[41]

When the *Saturday Review* itself asked its subscribers what they thought of pay television, in connection with an article by Irving Kolodin, nearly three-fifths of all respondents said they believed it *should* be authorized as a test so the public could at least choose. The flood of mail was quite different from that stimulated by industry questionnaires and broadcasts.

The questionnaires used by pay television opponents to prove that the public was opposed to pay television were excellent examples of the same kind of rigging that was being used in quiz shows, rating uses, profit statements, equipment bids, and other functions of many of the firms involved. How would you reply to a pay television questionnaire if you were told that it was estimated that under pay television, programs would cost you over $400 a year as compared to *nothing* under the present system? Or if you were told that, if pay television were allowed, free television would no longer be able to offer popular programs? Or if your children came crying to you, asking you to do something to keep free television from being "destroyed," as "the man on television" said it would be if pay television were permitted?

The United Nations Declaration of the Rights of the Child, to which the United States is a signator, pledges that children are not to be exploited for commercial or selfish interests. In their anti-pay television spot announcements and programs, scores of stations did not hesitate to warn children that their favorite programs would be killed by pay television. If they didn't want to lose their favorite programs, they were urged to make sure their parents didn't stand for this. "Tell them to wire or write their Senator, or Representative." Thus public opinion was manufactured via the exploitation of children on the basis of fabricated threats. Of course the public was opposed to what the network spokesmen *said* pay television was, and would do. But this was far from a fair picture. It was on the basis of such rigged "surveys" and impassioned pleas that millions of indignant citizens sent letters and wires of protest to their Senators and Representatives, urging that pay television not be allowed to kill free television. This "spontaneous" uprising of an indignant public, following one-sided editorializing, spot announcements aimed at exploiting the ignorance and gullibility of children as well as adults, and full-page newspaper and magazine ads, illustrates the power of big television to implement campaigns which are based on misleading the public, as was done in so masterful a fashion in California in 1964.

A considerable number of newspaper editorials at the time discussed and condemned the vicious campaign of misrepresentation regarding pay television which was launched in early 1958. However, there were *no* such editorials in many parts of the country, for in many areas the largest television stations and the principal newspapers are already owned by the same firms. In a great many areas, other television stations have allowed newspapers to buy interests in a television station. In Champaign-Urbana, Illinois, for instance, where a particularly vicious campaign of misrepresentation was carried on, both competitive newspapers own stock in the principal television station, the only one then on the air. This kind of foresight on the part of many station managements, in purchasing immunity from press criticism and opposition by allowing part of joint ownership of the television station by the local press is not to be belittled. It doesn't require a very large slice of a television station to keep some newspapers friendly. This is a factor to be considered in assessing the extent to which what are thought of as normal intermedia criticism and correction, which will balance each other out and expose the truth, can take place.

A few newspapers, however, did ask good questions. Several, for example, noted the paradox whereby, while RCA, NBC's parent, was fighting off an anti-trust suit, which it considered an invasion of or limitation on private enterprise, NBC was appealing to the same government to invade and limit the free enterprise rights of smaller business firms: pay-television exponents. It appeared an odd situation indeed when giant corporations were calling for regulation to kill pay television, a new type of business, before it got started, while calling for more freedom from regulation for themselves and asking that the government's power to regulate be limited still further.

Campaigns were set up to inform PTA's, women's clubs, and other educational groups of pay television's danger to freedom and all the American way stands for. Speakers stumped the country with petitions ready to sign. These petitions were then obligingly sent in by commercial stations as a "service" to gullible people who often signed without ever hearing an opposite viewpoint, stampeded into signing them as they would sign a petition against poisoning their water. Leonard Goldenson in fact said: "To permit such a test is equivalent to starting an epidemic to test a new vaccine."[42]

One trade magazine, as a service to its constituents, printed a complete script with production directions for a half-hour live dramatization of the "evils" of pay television. The title was "Now It Can Be Tolled." The prospective producer was informed that the script gave him "an entertaining and informative programming tool for stations seeking a ready-made anti-fee-television presentation." The stations which presented this or similar programs, with no fair representation for pay-television proponents, illustrate the kind of fairness which broadcast leaders quote in support of their right to editorialize or report court trials. This script indicated that the fee to be charged would be enormous. The leading character in the drama was elected "pay viewer of the year" because he spent $5,721.23 in a year to watch pay television. A child is pictured as having run up a bill of $712 in two evenings while mother was in the hospital and he was being cared for by a babysitter.

The effectiveness of this scare campaign, in which an ignorant public was misled and convinced that pay television was a villainous hoax, was noted in an editorial in the *Lyons* (Kansas) *Daily News*. The editorial on January 24, 1958, told of the frantic call of a woman which typified the response of many callers who had seen the network presentations. She urged the paper to publish an editorial warning people that their free television was about to be taken away from them. There were lots of helpless old people who would suffer from this deprivation. The people should not allow this to happen. She urged the paper to urge readers to make sure their Congressman killed pay television once and for all. The editorial noted how similar this would be to having newspapers warn people to oppose television because it would kill off newspapers and magazines.

The sort of language used to stampede the public into helping their large commercial brethren preserve their monopoly was illustrated in the speeches and testimony of network and NAB spokesmen. They spoke of pay television "highjacking the American public"; the "blackout" of the best of free television which pay television would bring; and the "booby trap" it constituted—"a scheme to render the television owner blind, and then rent him a seeing eye dog at so much per mile—to restore to him, only very partially, what he had previously enjoyed as a natural right." One of the more remarkable lines found, time after time, in some variant form: *"We* have no economic axe to grind."

Calling the arguments of pay-television exponents "the sheerest kind of sophistry," and "intellectual quicksand," opponents painted a black picture indeed of the fate of the American viewer if pay television were approved. Lawrence M. Hughes remarked in the *Saturday Review* article mentioned earlier:

> In a forty-eight-page report on "Free Television and the American People," CBS seeks to alarm possible Subscription viewers by showing that a twenty-one hour week of paid programs—including two baseball games, two films, two plays, one opera, two "stellar variety shows" and six hours of miscellany, each for 50 to 75 cents—would cost a family $9.10 a week or $473.20 a year. Had CBS projected this estimate to all 42 million television homes in the country, it would have provided Subscription promoters with an annual "potential" of $19.9 billion, or more than 14 times as much as all 300 network and all 4,000 "spot" advertisers now spend in "free" television.[43]

The tactic which CBS used, if applied to "free television" would involve choosing selective examples and then extrapolating them. For example, since the television tax on toothpaste (the part of the price which goes to television advertising) for the average family is $1.00 out of the total $5.00 spent per year on toothpaste, or 20 per cent, the average family's television tax under the present system is "obviously" 20 per cent of its expenditures. For a family spending $10,000 it would be $2,000, for a $20,000-a-year family $4,000, etc.

Since, as Goebbels taught, repetition is important, the $473.20 figure, fabricated for the occasion, became the statistics of the defense. Richard Salant, later head of the news department of CBS, and other CBS officials used it. CBS-owned and CBS-affiliated stations used it. Newspapers enlisted in the campaign used it. It was quoted and requoted thousands of times, as if it were authentic or accurate. Master riggers were at work.

NBC's Robert Sarnoff did not like to quote CBS figures. He and his staff made up their own. So did RCA's David Sarnoff. They were equally frightening and misleading. Fear words and clichés such as "Television is a delicately-balanced economic mechanism," were strewn about like chaff. Pay-television exponents were denounced for wanting to "ride piggy back" on public frequencies.

Of course, "over-riding all other considerations" was the deep concern of the "unselfish" network spokesmen for the public. Concern over profits was barely mentioned except in such assurances as Dr. Stanton's that of course they, the networks, had no axe to grind. One of the most remarkable achievements was to make the whole attack on pay television look like an effort to have *more* competition rather than *less*.

The elder statesman of the industry, David Sarnoff, perhaps best encapsulated the passionate appeal of the commercial networks for protection against even allowing the public to find out how pay television would work. He told the Federal Communications Commission on June 6, 1955:

> It would be tragic for this Commission to authorize pay television to cripple this great democratic medium for the free dissemination of ideas, education and entertainment "to all the people of America." My earnest plea to the Federal Communications Commission is: "Keep American radio and television broadcasting free to the public."

Again and again, the public was told that more service, and more competitive services, would somehow result in *less* service. It will be recalled that this was the argument Paley had used against education, of course, as early as 1934. Pay television, its opponents declared with prophetic dollar-vision, would black-out free television.

Pay television would fail, it was predicted by some, because people would realize they were being robbed, and would refuse to pay. Or if it did not surely fail, it would succeed. If it succeeded, CBS testified in

June of 1955, such *success* would be disastrous to the public interest. It was inevitable that a blackout of even a few markets to advertisers would start "a cycle of destruction of networks and favorite programs."

The slightly double-talk nature of the arguments becomes more apparent the more closely they are perused. The faithful manner in which affiliates coast to coast picked up the same figures, epigrams, epithets, and threats developed by NBC and CBS speech-writers for presidents and board chairmen to recite as impassioned defenses of the public's rights, was amazing. Even the most obviously false and hackneyed arguments received amazing circulation and mileage. Some network affiliates even outdid their parent networks in their one-sidedness. As a result of bitter protests, CBS originated a program, *Right Now!*, though it was broadcast in a Sunday afternoon spot where not too many viewers would see it. Many stations declined to carry even this much of the pro-pay television side.

As a result of this one-sided campaign, the FCC issued scores of reprimands. Its September 17, 1958, letter to Midwest Television, Inc. in Central Illinois is fairly typical. After noting that in the 3-day period between January 17 and January 19, station WCIA broadcast "72 identification, station break and spot announcements expressing opposition to subscription," and 13 editorial programs urging people to write their Congressmen, and after noting that the station's women's program was devoted to an "explanation" of a resolution passed by a group opposing pay television, the FCC observed: "However, it does not appear that you presented any other material on this subject, such as, for example, the CBS program *Right Now!* broadcast on the network Sunday afternoon February 2, 1958, which was carried by a number of CBS affiliates and on which both sides of the issue were presented by responsible representatives." After considering WCIA's various protestations regarding the efforts it had made to be fair, the FCC concluded:

> Considering all the above, the Commission is of the view that WCIA's presentation of the subscription television issue was one-sided, without adequate efforts having been made to secure the presentation of the other side by responsible spokesmen. Accordingly, it is the Commission's conclusion that your presentation . . . was contrary to the policy enunciated by the Commission in its Report on Editorializing by Broadcasting Licensees and did not meet the standards of fairness called for under the circumstances.

However, it added, with strange logic, ". . . the Commission is not disposed to impose sanctions on the basis of your omissions. . . ."[44] WCIA, of course, continues its operation, and its opposition to pay television. The scolding, like the California Supreme Court decisions, did not come until after the job had been done.

Dr. Stanton warned that the networks would be destroyed.

As programs and audience are drawn away from free television, circumstances may well force affiliates, as a matter of self-protection, to turn to pay television. As this occurs, the stations would, of course, be unavailable as outlets for free network broadcasting. And without a nationwide aggregate of outlets, there is no network. . . .

The destruction would be total:

In these circumstances, network television as we know it today, cannot survive if pay television is successful. The American economy is deprived of an important instrument of marketing. A source of entertainment and of information is hijacked from the American public.[45]

Network editorials, which network officials had promised (when they were seeking the right to editorialize) would be devoted to the *public* interest rather than to their own *private* interests, were devoted to pay television. Presidents and board chairmen appeared in person. Under Commission rules the stations must seek out and allow equal time to representatives of opposite views. The record indicates wholesale violation of the promises the networks made in order to get the right to editorialize.

In asserting that free television quality would suffer, that outstanding programs and stars would inevitably move from free to pay television, that sports programs would disappear, that public service, religious, educational, children's, and other minority programs would have to be curtailed or abandoned, that the movie industry would probably gain control of pay television and make billions of dollars out of the helpless public, that pay television would black-out free television, and that if pay television came, the networks themselves would have to abandon the role of public defenders and join the villainous pay television plunderers in order to survive—to mention only a few of the scores of threats made to the public in order to manipulate it—the broadcast industry set a sordid example of scare tactics and rigging of facts and figures which cannot be erased. They are a part of the record for all time. They raise serious questions regarding the ethics, morality, and truthfulness of much that the industry has done to preserve the status quo.

While asking for freedom from regulation by others, the industry seems to have misused its own power as an agency of social control. The techniques used in opposition to pay television were apparently designed not to get both sides of an important public issue out into the open for rational discussion, but for the manipulation of the public and the concealment of the public's interest.

This is one of the most dramatic examples in recent years of the use of the electronic mass media to mask realities, distort facts, and manipulate and create public opinion. That this was done with impunity reveals the impotence of present regulatory procedures and agencies to control misuse of these media and malpractices by their operators. Many stations received reprimands for their violation of the fair practices provision of the right to editorialize. Like apologies after elections, which do not change the ballot results, they were too late to halt the formation of public opinion regarding pay television. All those stations which were reprimanded seem to have survived to do the same again whenever it serves their interests. Some have already repeated their tactics of misrepresentation in regard to UHF and de-intermixture, with impunity.

Here, as has so often been the case, the industry's interests were made to appear to be the public's interests. Those who opposed the position of the networks were referred to as "deviate cases." The most abusive terms were used to arouse the public. One spokesman was quoted widely as calling pay television "legal and licensed piracy of the free air waves" and warning of "the monopolistic stranglehold this retrogressive device would have on the public."

One of the most interesting aspects of the anti-pay television campaign still remains to be examined. Since the broadcast industry controls access to the public through the airwaves, and since the Congress contains a large number of Senators and Representatives who are themselves owners or beneficiaries of free television stations, the industry's tactic was to insist that the public and the Congress decide, thus shifting the decision away from the FCC, the agency to which Congress had earlier delegated the responsibility for regulating broadcasting and developing new kinds of services. The speeches of impassioned Congressmen and Senators of that time attest to their loyalty to the controllers of electronic media who had favored them with free time or who had been able to win their confidence and friendship in other ways.

The Committee Against Pay As You See TV decided to maintain that the Federal Communications Commission had no right to authorize even a *test* of pay television. Although this appeared at first to be a wild effort, unlikely of success in view of the fact that the Federal Communications Commission was clearly vested with full responsibility for broadcast matters of this sort, it worked. The Committee then proposed that the whole problem be referred to Congress. There, they knew, they had friends and could maintain control. And they did.

If applied to magazines, this committee's reasoning would be equivalent to saying that if someone wishes to start a magazine that proposes to take no advertising, being supported only by direct payment on an issue-by-issue subscription or newsstand basis, an act of Congress would be required. This decision Congress itself accepted. In tribute to the industry's lobby power, it should be noted that this position was not only proposed, it was made to stick. New York's Congressman Emanuel Celler introduced a bill which would have imposed a $10,000 fine and a possible prison sentence for even *trying* pay television. Thanks to the efforts of the old hands who were the leaders of the industry, pay television was labeled not only un-American but criminal. One important lesson taught the nation by the pay-television case, therefore, is this: Under present conditions it appears that big television and radio have enough power and control so they can, with confidence, have disputes referred to Congress, or the people, both of whom they've now learned how to control and manipulate with considerable success.

When, a few years later, the right of the Federal Communications Commission to authorize a test of pay television was referred to the United States Court of Appeals in Washington, D.C., the Court declared: "Surely, the Commission's power to see that this area of the public domain is used in the public interest is not less for 'paid' television than for the existing system of so-called 'free' television."

The Washington *Daily News* of March 17, 1962, noted, in its discussion of this decision:

> There is no more moral reason to outlaw pay television than there would be to outlaw a circus, or bowling, or baseball, because they compete for the public's entertainment dollar with movies, or "free" televi-

sion. We don't by law quash a new soap just because it competes with existing soaps.

The industry lobbying activity against pay television included dinners and parties for various government officials, Congressmen, and others in positions of influence. At one such party CBS network and affiliate executives were hosts to some thirteen hundred government notables and wives, including members of Congress and the Federal Communications Commission. Seating arrangements insured that broadcasters from the home state would be able to get their messages across to their Congressmen or Senators. This was a non-broadcast service which CBS was happy to provide at no extra charge.[46]

Affiliates scheduled cocktail parties, breakfasts, and many other functions as a part of the behind-the-scenes influence brought to bear in this single case. They were very successful. Congressman Celler's bill proposing that anyone charging the public for television should be fined up to $10,000 or be sentenced up to five years was one of the most extreme proposals, but hardly the only one. They still stand in the *Congressional Record* as monuments to the lobby power of the broadcast industry leadership of the time.

The Waukesha, Wisconsin, *Daily Freeman* on March 1, 1958, wrote:

The home television set proved itself a powerful lobby weapon during the current fight over free versus pay television. It was so powerful, in fact, that by comparison with conventional lobbying techniques for inspiring letters to Congress, it has no equal. The House Commerce Committee received 50,000 pieces of mail on the pay television question—the biggest volume staffers remember receiving on any issue. Practically all the letters were against pay television. On February 6 the Committee adopted a resolution asking the Federal Communications Commission to delay its tests of pay television. The Senate Commerce Committee did likewise February 19. . . . It appears pay television as a big development in the industry is dead for the time being. Meanwhile, so also is the theory that competition is the life of trade in our free-enterprise system.

The *Capital Times* of Madison, Wisconsin, summed up the lobbying, the politics, and the public's interest in an editorial January 26, 1959. It wrote:

As matters now stand the more discriminating viewer must accept the poor and often insulting programs that are devised to attract the mass audience at which the beer, cigarette and toothpaste ads are aimed. He has no choice. He either watches the shoot-em-ups and skull crushers or he turns off his set. . . . The established television interests and the politicians in Washington are denying him that right. And in doing so they are crudely and audaciously misrepresenting the facts. . . . Members of Congress are very reluctant to antagonize the big networks because they can provide hundreds of thousands of dollars of free advertising. They can invite their favorites on the special shows that emanate from Washington. . . . Congress is obligated to established television interests. What chance has the public got in such a situation?

The anti-pay television campaign of the broadcast industry, or rather of a numerically small but financially powerful part of the industry which included the networks, the trade association, and much of the trade press, illustrates control of public opinion of the most vicious nature. This approach said, in effect, that people shall *not* have the right to pay for pay television, even if they want to. It declared that the public shall not even have the choice of something which might compete with the present commercial broadcasters' monopoly, however much the public, if it understood, might welcome this alternative service.

In preventing the development of a different *type* of commercial broadcast support, a very basic and fundamental decision is involved. An editorial in the October, 1959, *Progressive* pinpoints the broader issue:

The freest media of public communication today are books and the theater. These forms claim the work of our most valued creative artists. What keeps these forms free indeed is their economics. A book publisher, in considering a manuscript, has to ask himself: Will enough people buy this book at a fair price to make it profitable? Similarly with a producer of a Broadway play. Each is bound by his self-interest to disturb his audiences, if they want to be disturbed, make them laugh if they want to laugh, break down taboos if they want that. If he doesn't, his competitors will. The only product the publisher is concerned about selling is his book, the producer his show, both directly to the audience. Neither is required to tailor his product for selling another man's merchandise. The creative artist is free only when he is able to offer his art directly to the public for acceptance or rejection. Pay television promises a direct creator-consumer relationship for the first time in the history of American broadcasting. It is a most exciting promise.

In the sabotage of pay television, the possibility of many new types of broadcasting, by education, industry, science, and public services was scuttled. By what right a small leadership group, with a tight monopoly, presumes to make such decisions for a nation is a question which must be asked here if democracy still has any real meaning.

What application of the pay-television *principle* could bring the nation in the form of alternative services is almost beyond imagination. It is not necessary to think only of currently visualized *commercial* (though non-advertising) uses of pay television which involve *coins*. There are medical and educational uses, for example, which might involve sending doctors keys or slugs (to be used instead of coins) so they may receive "scrambled" demonstrations of surgery or other items which it is not wise to broadcast on open circuit. New surgical or radiation developments may mean life or death to patients tomorrow. Unless such non-mass uses are promoted widely, as variants of pay-television *principles* would enable them to be, these uses will never fully develop. Coin-box or key approaches may provide a way of financing credit courses in extension and adult education. By trying to kill pay television, such uses, which would become possible as offshoots of pay television only if it is allowed to develop, are also killed. Certainly, technically, all such uses of "subscription television" non-mass approaches can be helpful in education which, by nature, is the opposite of "mass" media uses of these media.

The Tulsa *Tribune* on January 23, 1958, pointed out that big industry is not merely presuming to decide whether there shall be pay television or not.

> . . . What the television tycoons are really saying is that if you want to see good shows without commercials, you cannot see them in your home—no, not even if you are willing to pay for the privilege. You must load the kids in the car and drive to the nearest theater. Your home entertainment is to be reserved exclusively for what the Presidents of NBC, CBS, and ABC choose to give you. . . . We have here a very fundamental issue. Do the electronic screens in America's living rooms belong to NBC, CBS and ABC or do they belong to the people who have bought them? Is it in the interests of "free enterprise" to give the three networks dictatorial power over what one shall see in his

home, or shall the homeowner be allowed to buy a program if he thinks it's worth the price?

The services which the pay-television approach to broadcasting would make possible could benefit education, save lives, stimulate writers and artists, and open the way for new business. There is no question of the rights of the commercial industry to fight for how it shall run its own business. But in exercising, or seeking to exercise, a life-and-death influence on what kinds of business there *shall be* in the United States, or who shall have access to instruments *they* now control in dog-in-the-manger fashion is another matter. They are not even the inventors of these instruments. They are only their exploiters.

Robert Sarnoff and Frank Stanton have declared scores of times that broadcasting must give the public what it wants. If the public wants pay television, however, this rule seems not to apply. The networks quickly convince the public to "unwant" anything which they, as custodians of these instruments, don't want it to have. Since broadcasting can determine what the public shall want, leadership seems to reason, the thing to do is to educate the public to want what the networks think it should have, viz., what they find most profitable. Then they deprecate or destroy all that might interfere with their monopoly.

This manipulation reveals the hypocrisy of the posture of the networks in blaming the public for its low tastes. If the industry can train people virtually overnight to hate pay television, which they had never even heard about before, and to take definite action to oppose it, they can train people to do, or like, virtually anything which concerns them. The way in which such power is to be exercised is one of the principal questions facing the nation. It is the principal reason for this chapter.

In the case of the *Associated Press* v. *the United States,* cited earlier, it will be recalled, the Court decided: "Freedom to publish is guaranteed by the Constitution but freedom to combine to keep others from publishing is not." The Chicago *American,* March 10, 1962, commenting on the decision of the United States Court of Appeals upholding the right of the Federal Communications Commission to authorize pay television tests, declared "The court ruled that the Federal Communications Commission has an 'affirmative duty' to help develop and improve the nation's communications facilities by experimenting with new systems; otherwise, it said, television would permanently be stuck where it is now." The *Wall Street Journal,* March 14,

1962, also commenting on this decision, declared that the Court "concluded that 'unless the future of television is to be confined to its present state, the Federal Communications Commission must be reasonably allowed opportunity to experiment.' "

The question whether preventing the Federal Communications Commission from carrying out its legal function is in the public interest needs to be raised. Since this was done by Congress itself, it also raises basic questions about the relationship of the interests of Congress to those of the public, the Federal Communications Commission, and the industry. Is Congress, under present conditions, really more capable of looking after the public interest than the Federal Communications Commission is? Is a pay-television referendum now "the voice of the people," or the shouting of a lynch mob, aroused by television as a power structure itself? How free are non-utility type services like broadcasting to be left to determine political policy? When the railroads sought to curb the development of motor transport (in what was only a forerunner of the tactics of the networks, behaving like utilities) were they not soon forced to desist?

The pay-television case reveals the orientation of United States commercial broadcast leadership today as perhaps no other case history can. Sons of the corporate ethic, the networks and those stations which cooperated did not hesitate to use the most ruthless tactics of corporation warfare, as well as one-sided propaganda, to protect their interests.

The concern here is not with whether or not pay television shall eventually come into operation. It undoubtedly will come in some form as a part of the alternative services the nation will develop. It will not, of course, be the kind of pay television it would have been if the networks had not forced pay television itself to become big and ruthless in order to survive. The new, the small, and the idealistic have already been frozen out. To that extent, the networks have already won. Only their kind may now operate pay television.

The larger concern is rather for the lesson in monopoly, selfishness, rigging of facts, ruthlessness of tactics, and perversion of "public opinion" which industry leaders provided for all the world to see, while pretending that it was the public's interests, rather than their own, that they represented, because they "had no economic axe to grind."

This position, and this tactic, should be sufficient to justify including in eventual regulations controlling access to pay television, provisions for excluding networks and stations who did so much to kill it.

If present broadcast industry giants were allowed to control pay television, their monopoly would only be intensified. Their threats that pay television would kill free television must be remembered, for they could cause this to happen. If they move into positions of control in both services, they can throw their emphasis on whichever service they prefer. Their power to transform their threats into self-fulfilling prophecy should suggest the safeguards which pay television regulation must provide when it is finally approved.

Finally, from all three of these case histories we can learn much about the concept of the public interest which appears to guide present national broadcast leadership, and how likely it is to allow truth, unimpeded, to flow through the channels it controls as effectively as if it owned them. Surely some change in this situation is needed.

NOTES

1. Lawrence Lessing, *Man of High Fidelity: Edwin Howard Armstrong* (Philadelphia and New York: Lippincott, 1956).

2. See Columbia Broadcasting System, "The Cost of Shifting the U.S. Television System to UHF—Only," September 22, 1955. (18 pp. plus tables, mimeographed)

Further testimony and data recording network and NAB opposition generally to UHF can be found in: U.S. House of Representatives, *All Channel Television Receivers and Deintermixture,* Hearings before the Committee on Interstate and Foreign Commerce, 87th Congress, Second Session (Washington, D.C.: Government Printing Office, 1962).

3. Federal Radio Commission, Docket No. 984, June 26, 1931. (In the case of the University of Wisconsin) (mimeographed)

4. William S. Paley, "Radio as a Cultural Force," New York, Columbia Broadcasting System, October 17, 1934. (Brochure)

5. Federal Communications Commission, *Sixth Report and Order,* April 1952, contains "exceptions" and alternative proposals filed by CBS, the NAB, Dumont, and numerous other stations and groups.

6. *Ibid.*

7. John Walker Powell, *The Story of Educational Television: Channels of Learning* (Washington, D.C.: Public Affairs Press, 1962).

8. Editorial, *Broadcasting,* 46, No. 12 (June 21, 1954), 114.

9. Robert W. Sarnoff, Address to TV and Radio Affiliates, Beverly Hills, Calif., December 7, 1961, p. 5 (mimeographed).

10. Frank Stanton, Commencement Address, Massachusetts Institute of Technology, June 9, 1961, pp. 5, 8 (mimeographed).

11. Adult Education Committee of the British Ministry of Reconstruction, *A Design for Democracy* (New York; Association Press, 1956), pp. 118, 120-122.

12. Bernard Berelson, "The Great Debate on Cultural Democracy," in *Studies in Public Communication,* University of Chicago, No. 3 (Summer 1961), p. 9.

13. K. V. Bailey, *The Listening Schools* (London: British Broadcasting Corporation, 1957), p. 107.

14. "Program Hearings Fail to Orbit," *Broadcasting,* 62, No. 5 (January 29, 1962), 46.

15. Frank Stanton, "Parallel Paths," *Daedalus,* 89, No. 2 (Spring 1960), 347, 351, 352.

16. Dalton Trumbo, "Hail, Blithe Spirit," *The Nation,* October 24, 1959, p. 243.

17. Merle Miller, *The Judges and the Judged* (Garden City, N.Y.; Doubleday, 1952).

18. U.S. House of Representatives, Committee on Un-American Activities, *Investigation of So-Called Blacklisting,* 84th Congress, Second Session, July 10 and 11, 1956 (Washington, D.C.: Government Printing Office, 1956).

19. John Henry Faulk, *Fear on Trial* (New York: Simon and Schuster, 1964).

20. Milton Mayer, *They Thought They Were Free* (Chicago: University of Chicago Press, 1955), pp. 177, 178.

21. John Cogley, *Report on Blacklisting* (New York: Fund for the Republic, 1956), Vol. II, *Radio-Television,* p. 30.

22. Marie Jahoda, *Anti-Communism and Employment Policies in Radio and Television* (New York: Research Center for Human Relations, New York University, December 1955), pp. 253, 254. (Printed as pages 221-81 in Cogley, *op. cit.*)

23. *Ibid.,* p. 235.

24. Elizabeth Poe, "Blacklisting and Censorship in Motion Pictures," in *Mass Media* (New York: Fund for Adult Education, July 1959), p. 17.

25. Cogley, *op. cit.,* p. 19.

26. *Ibid.,* p. 62.

27. *Ibid.,* pp. 102, 103.

28. Jahoda, *op. cit.,* pp. 254, 255.

29. Cogley, *op. cit.,* pp. 20, 21.

30. *Ibid.,* pp. 100, 101.

31. *Ibid.,* pp. 192, 193.

32. *Ibid.,* p. 205.

33. *Ibid.,* pp. 219, 220.

34. *Ibid.,* p. 85.

35. Arthur S. Miller, *Private Governments and the Constitution,* Occasional Paper, Center for the Study of Democratic Institutions (New York: Fund for the Republic, 1959), p. 10.

36. Cogley, *op. cit.,* p. 209.

37. Leonard W. Levy, "Legacy of Suppression: The Past and Present," Kappa Tau Alpha *Yearbook,* 16 (1961-1962), 18.

38. Rockefeller Brothers Fund, *The Power of the Democratic Idea,* Special Studies Project Report VI, America at Mid-Century Series (Garden City, N.Y.: Doubleday, 1960), p. 30.

39. M. R. Werner, Henry Romney, Margot Marek, and Eugenia Frangos "The $6,000,000,000 Question," *Sports Illustrated,* December 26, 1960. (Reprint, p. 8).

40. The testimony of this firm and the other principal protagonists and antagonists of pay television are summarized in a Special Digest issued June 11, 1955, by *TV Digest,* then based in the Wyatt Building, Washington, D.C. Excerpts quoted here are from this issue, unless otherwise credited.

41. Lawrence M. Hughes, "Free Choice or Free TV?", *Saturday Review,* February 22, 1958, p. 66.

42. Desmond Smith, "Pay or Free? The Coming TV War," *The Nation,* May 18, 1964, pp. 504-6.

43. Hughes, *op. cit.,* pp. 39, 41.

44. Federal Communications Commission, (Public) file, Letter of September 17, 1958 (Reply No. 8429, Docket #62706), to Midwest Television, Inc., Champaign, Illinois, pp. 1, 3, 4.

45. *TV Digest,* Supplement, June 19, 1958.

46. Werner, et al., *op. cit.,* (Reprint, p. 7).

5

Broadcasting from the Courtroom: Problems and Approaches

For many years the broadcast industry has been requesting the right to broadcast trials direct from courtrooms. On August 26, 1954, for example, CBS President Frank Stanton broadcast nationally an editorial, over both CBS television and radio, asking that "the curtain of silence," which blocks such broadcasting, be lifted. For some ten years the pressure for access mounted with some evidence of success.

Then the Warren Commission, in its report on President Kennedy's assassination, indicted TV, radio, and the press for many dangerous practices which provided "dramatic affirmation of the need for steps to bring about a proper balance between the right of the public to be kept informed and the right of an individual to a fair, impartial trial."[1]

Thereafter, in domino-like sequence, several reversals followed for those pressing for more access to the courts and more freedom in the treatment of pre-trial publicity. The conviction of Billie Sol Estes was reversed in 1965 on the grounds that press behavior had made a fair trial impossible for him. The Supreme Court decision stated that "Televising and broadcasting parts of his trial over [his] objection deprived him of his right to due process under the Fourteenth Amendment." In 1966 the Supreme Court reviewed the conviction of Samuel Sheppard and concluded that he had not received a fair trial because of the behavior of the press.* Several volumes of studies devoted to this problem began to appear. One, fairly typical, having surveyed radio and television in connection with court and police activity, declared: ". . . Some of the incidents described are so unnecessary and so clearly obnoxious to the administration of justice that little can be said in defense of such practices."[2]

---

* In the November 1966 retrial, Dr. Sheppard was acquitted.

Recognizing that they may have been delinquent in certain respects, broadcasters themselves began to observe stricter controls. One of the most constructive efforts in this direction was the guidelines procedure set up in a published memorandum issued by CBS News, while Fred Friendly was Director of News at CBS. It was first reported in the May 28, 1965, *New York Times.* After setting down procedures to prevent premature publicizing of pre-trial confessions and previous records of the accused, this memorandum states: "CBS News, regardless of how newspapers or other stations in their regions may sensationalize, should set a tone of responsibility in both coverage and language. That is really the meaning of this memorandum."[3] A proposal by CBS for a study to be carried out by the Brookings Institution aroused considerable interest, and it appeared that the study would be made. A new research project by the Twentieth Century Fund was announced. Under the title of *Free Press—Free Trial,* the project set out to "examine the responsibility of the press in a free society to report on court trials and the judicial process without prejudice to a defendant's right to a free and unbiased trial."[4]

Great care was taken as the retrial of Dr. Sheppard began. While such problems were in the news, Richard Speck was arrested, charged with the murder of eight student nurses in Chicago. The guidelines established for his trial provided that the news media would report only matters already on the court record and would not seek out or interview either witnesses or jurors as they had done in the past.

TV and radio especially, but all the press in general, found their cause set back considerably from where it had been three brief years before, when the American Bar Association redrafted and reaffirmed its Canon 35. It was this Canon of the American Bar Association which had been the special target of efforts by the broadcast industry for years, and indeed it stands today, in the forty-eight states where it has been adopted, as the principal barrier to broadcasting from the courtroom. It must be made clear that this Canon is not a law, but merely a provision in the Canons of Judicial Ethics of the American Bar Association, which is essentially a code of the legal profession. The applicable paragraph of Canon 35 of the Association's 36 Canons reads:

Proceedings in court should be conducted with fitting dignity and decorum. The taking of photographs in the courtroom, during sessions of the court or recesses between sessions, and the broadcasting or televising of court proceedings, detract from the essential dignity of the proceedings, distract participants and witnesses in giving testimony, and create misconceptions with respect thereto in the mind of the public and should not be permitted.

This wording, an improvement over earlier versions, which included the words "are calculated to detract . . ." etc., was adopted by the Bar Association's House of Delegates February 5, 1963. It was essentially a restatement and reaffirmation of a position originally taken thirty years before, following publicity excesses attendant upon the Bruno Hauptmann trial in the Lindbergh kidnapping case.

Against this Canon the broadcast industry has steadily protested. In his address to the assembled CBS Radio Affiliates, September 13, 1962, CBS Board Chairman William S. Paley declared:

> Hearing chambers and courtrooms closed to direct coverage by major news media are wholly inconsistent with the democratic objective of an informed people. . . . All of us—in broadcasting and out of it—ought to fight this stubborn and pointless discrimination in every way we can until it goes the way of every other survival of the dark ages.[5]

John Charles Daly, while still vice president of ABC in charge of news and special events, told the American Bar Association, July 15, 1957:

> The people have a right to know. . . . We have an obligation to ourselves, to the public, and to our way of life to accept nothing short of full freedom of information and access. We cannot and will not stop short.[6]

Numerous resolutions of broadcast organizations and associations of newsmen through the years have supported the position of Stanton, Paley, and Daly.

It should be noted, however, that television and radio representatives are not *excluded* from trials by Canon 35. Only certain types of equipment and certain types of activity are excluded. Broadcasters, like the press, may send their reporters, and these reporters are free to broadcast what they observe, just as newspaper reporters are free to write about the trial.

Because on this point the television industry seems often to have misrepresented the nature of its exclusion, the fairly long clarification given by the Supreme Court in its (Billie Sol Estes versus Texas) decision should be noted:

> The television camera is a powerful weapon. Intentionally or inadvertently it can destroy an accused and his case in the eyes of the public. While our telecasters are honorable men, they too are human. [The problems involved] are real enough to have convinced the Judicial Conference of the United States, this Court, and the Congress that television should be barred in federal trials by the Federal Rules of Criminal Procedure; in addition they have persuaded all but two of our States to prohibit television in the courtroom.[7]

The statement goes on:

> The right of "public trial" is not one belonging to the public, but one belonging to the accused. . . . So long as the television industry, like other communications media, is free to send representatives to trials and to report on these trials to its viewers, there is no abridgement of freedom of the press. . . . [This right] does not bring with it the right to interject themselves into the fabric of the trial. . . . The distinctions to be drawn between the accoutrements of the press and the television media turn not on differences of size and shape, but of function and effect. . . . Courtroom television introduces into the conduct of a criminal trial the element of professional "showmanship," an extraneous influence whose subtle capacities for serious mischief in a case of this sort will not be under-estimated by any lawyer experienced in the elusive imponderables of the trial arena.[8]

> . . . Thus, the evil of televised trials, as demonstrated in this [Estes] case, lies not in the noise and appearance of the cameras, but in the trial participants' awareness that they are being televised.[9]

It must be recognized that this is one of the most difficult problems besetting the legal profession, or broadcasting, which aspires to be a profession. This is not merely or primarily a problem of broadcasting; it is also a problem of the efficient administration of justice. It is not a problem of right versus wrong. It is a question of a clash between two rights. The First Amendment, providing for freedom of speech, press, and religion, comes into conflict here with the Sixth Amendment, which provides for a fair and speedy trial for every individual accused of a crime. These conflicting rights must be reconciled somehow. But in any solution the right of the public, of society as a whole, and of broadcasting as its instrument, must be weighed carefully and responsibly against the private rights of the individual citizen, as set forth in the Bill of Rights, which is primarily concerned with protecting the rights of the individual citizen against the rights of organizations, institutions, or governments.

Numerous documents have been prepared by the broadcast industry as guides to behavior which, it is alleged, would insure that broadcasts of court proceedings would not adversely affect the administration of justice. Most of these plans however, as will be noted later, seem based on a failure to understand fully the role and function of the court and the trial in American life.

Yosal Rogat has written:

> Probably it must be assumed not only that judges desire to find the truth, but also that they have some kind of special knowledge, or technique, *e.g.,* magical or scientific, by which they can approach "non-subjective truth." Only with the aid of such assumptions can we explain the extent to which men voluntarily submit their disputes to the arbitration of courts; why they feel bound by the decision of a court, entirely apart from being forced to accept it; and why, even including the losers, they attach the importance they do to "having their day in court."[10]

The late A. J. Liebling, the distinguished journalist, has noted that ". . . One of the tests of a society is the fairness of its criminal justice; this need must not take second place to the public's taste for the morbid and sensational." If fair trials are made impossible by mass media pressures, he adds, "the judicial process must be protected by removing the trial to a forum beyond its probable influence."[11]

In most cases, broadcasters pressing for access to courtrooms state that their presence will not prejudice the *outcome.* This is to miss much of the point of due *process,* most or much of whose value lies in the process itself, not just in the decision. As Yosal Rogat says further:

> It is essential to remember . . . that we are concerned with the way in which a trial is conducted, and not simply with the decision arrived at. It is the purpose of a trial to apply reason and objectivity to a dispute; and there is much more to its legality than a just outcome. There may be no doubt that a Negro has murdered a Caucasian, but the level of legality attained may depend on whether he is tried and convicted in New York or Mississippi.[12]

In many respects, television coverage might well constitute as significant and real a part of the environment as geography—being in New York as opposed to Mississippi—already is.

In all civilized lands, courtrooms, like operating rooms for surgery, are very special kinds of places. They are intended for intimate and intensive activity of a very special nature. It is to be noted, in passing, that the Freedom of Information Committee of the National Association of Broadcasters would change this. In its publication, *Broadcasting Public Proceedings,* it states: "Throughout the country many courtrooms and hearing rooms are antiquated, and it is hoped that broadcasters will be able to work with local officials to provide modern broadcast facilities as new buildings and rooms are designed and constructed."[13]

Historically and legally, however, it is for good reasons that courtrooms are neither theatres, auditoriums, stadiums, nor amphitheatres. Even in the environment now provided, the judge may, and must, without violating any public rights, sometimes "clear the courtroom." Only in People's Republics and People's Trials are court procedures made into public shows.

The Committee on Radio and Television of the Bar of New York notes the cases in the U.S.S.R. where public trials have been held, both in earlier years and for Francis Gary Powers in the more recent U-2 case. Castro's trials, too, were reminiscent of amphitheatre trials of centuries ago. It has taken centuries to get justice and trials free from such an "entertainment" environment, in which justice no longer seems to be the principal objective.

The transformations which take place, once televising enters, are subtle. The Ruby trial recordings came to be played in spots regularly occupied by the Johnny Carson show and the late movies, to audiences trained to expect entertainment at that time, after the news. Is this the framework appropriate to the educational function television says it wishes to fulfill with its broadcasts from the courtroom?

The rights of the public in regard to courts are well stated in a court decision in the case of *United Press* v. *Valente,* when press representatives sought to compel a judge to allow them to be present and publish news of an entire trial. The court said:

> The public interest in a public trial stems not from a right of every citizen to be a spectator but consists in keeping the fabric of Society from being injured by the destruction of the civil rights of the individual.[14]

In his treatise on *Constitutional Limitations,* the great legal scholar and professor at the University of Michigan, Thomas M. Cooley, has explained:

> The requirement of a public trial is for the benefit of the accused; that the public may see he is fairly dealt with . . . and the requirement is fairly observed, if without partiality or favoritism, *a reasonable proportion of* the public is suffered to attend, notwithstanding that those persons whose presence could be of no service to the accused, and who would be drawn hither by a prurient curiosity, are excluded altogether.[15]

The guarantee that a court be open to the public

> . . . is not to satisfy the curiosity of the mob. . . . It is not for educational or entertainment purposes . . . [Courts] are open to prevent secret trials or Star Chamber proceedings. . . . They are open because of our natural aversion, as a freedom-loving nation, to any proceeding held in secret . . . especially judicial proceedings.[16]

As Canon 36 of the Bar Association's Canons of Judicial Ethics points out, a trial is "an inquiry to ascertain the truth." Any right which conflicts with this primary one must take second place.

Trials were never designed, nor probably could they survive, as spectator events. It is perfectly natural for tickets to be sold to sports events. Even the activities of cheerleaders do not significantly prevent the normal course of sports events. They may even help. The theatre, too, would be nothing without the audience. The course of both sports and theatre is deeply affected by the audience, which becomes a part of the event. Part of the success of both events depends on the dynamic feedback from the audience. Court trials and courtrooms, however, were designed to prevent precisely this relationship between the public and the participants in a trial. They are workshops in which intensive, undramatic, undisturbed, concentrated probing occurs.

As a part of his argument for access to courtrooms, John Daly cited the excellent record and credentials of the broadcast industry. He said: "I point again to a mature, responsible industry. The directors of news operation in our media will never sacrifice justice or a man's rights in the interest of a sensational story." Let us look at the record, as he urges us to.

After considerable discussion and planning, television and radio was granted full access to the proceedings of the United Nations. How much and how well has this right been exercised? How much has it helped the causes of peace and the U.N.? One example of an approach which should cause some concern has already been mentioned: the Khrushchev shoe-pounding incident at the U.N. How well was it reported by TV and radio? Are these the types of criteria of significance that television would use in the courtroom? Will the visual, the dramatic, or the vulgar blind us to the basic, the significant? Is this the kind of selection of significant facts that broadcasting would make for trials?

In sports, broadcasting has succeeded in winning almost universal access. With what effects? As television has taken over, professional football teams have begun to call a special time-out each period to permit time for commercials, and the game has lengthened. More and more plays are missed as commercials run over. Or game broadcasts are not carried to completion because of other commercial commitments. Baseball, which used to ban beer and cigarette ads even from the baseball field fences, now is principally an advertising medium for such products. The average big league game now lasts approximately thirty minutes longer than it did before it was broadcast, and rhubarbs, raspberries, colorful characters, and other extraneous audience-attracting features seem to be featured far more than they were in the pre-broadcast days, when the sport was more humdrum, but more purely and uniquely a sports event than "a show."

In the days when broadcasting was requesting access to sports events, broadcasters promised much, pointing out that they would only report what was happening anyway. They would not manage, change, or control, they said.

Many years and many millions of dollars later, on April 20, 1964, ABC President Thomas W. Moore made a speech to the Hollywood Advertising Club. He said that the time has come for sports to adapt themselves more closely to the needs of television scheduling. He then explained in some detail how the schedules and contests in baseball, professional football, college football, golf, hockey, auto-racing, and even regional Olympic meets, could be better adapted to television coverage. Sportswriter Red Smith, a couple of days later, was moved to point out in his syndicated column that "ever since the hucksters of television got their grubby little paws into sports, it has been inevitable that sooner or later they would want to rewrite the script for their own convenience and profits. . . ." Is it not similarly likely that, once inside the courtroom, broadcasters may well have numerous suggestions for improvements in the administration of justice, beyond the one already noted above, regarding improving the design and construction of courtrooms?

In the public interest, television was given permission to report American political conventions to the nation. On the basis of the record, former President Eisenhower and others have said television should henceforth be banned from the convention floor. He has been supported by several of the nation's best newsmen themselves. Has television been a success where it has entered such arenas? Has it helped or hindered the democratic process? That, not entertainment "popularity," should be the crucial question.

We have noted a number of instances of "staging" in reporting events which may become humdrum, like the time when Southern Democrats, in what looked like a gesture of secession, took off their badges and threw them on the table—for the television audience—and then, when the cameras were turned away, put them back on. Is this broadcasting reality? Will similar practices and criteria prevail if television covers trials? Unintentional as many of these effects may be, and unobtrusively as they may have crept into broadcasting, they are real. Will court proceedings be more successful in resisting the demands of the populace, and the powerful magnifying and sometimes distorting effects of television? Have we not learned rather, that, however hard television may try, it is so far *incapable* of leaving events unchanged?

John Daly, in his appeal for access to courtrooms, from which we quoted earlier, has said: "a camera can no more produce a circus than a seismograph can cause an earthquake. Both simply record what is there."[18] In view of the instances cited earlier of the respects in which television serves as a news-maker, even when it seeks only to be a news reporter, this statement seems subject to serious challenge. Time and again, as has been noted, the appearance of a television camera and crew on a scene causes people, often self-consciously and unintentionally, to "act" as they would not otherwise do. Good television producers naturally prefer to send pictures of things happening, rather than not happening. The failure of broadcast leadership to recognize or acknowledge what they have been doing casts serious doubts on their ability to keep promises to leave courtroom proceedings unaffected if they are admitted to them. Promises of good behavior were made as a condition for television to cover the Jack Ruby trial, for example. How did this work out? The March 15, 1964, *New York Times* quoted presiding Judge Joe B. Brown who "accused the national television networks of breaking their agreement regarding the first live video coverage of a jury bringing in a verdict in a murder trial. . . . The networks offered no formal reply to the Judge's charge. . . ."[19]

Radio, Television and the Administration of Justice, from which this quotation was taken, lists scores of documented cases in which TV or radio or both interfered with the course of justice or fair trial. Several of these are very revealing of the extent to which broadcasters kept promises to behave responsibly.

In the Frank Sinatra, Jr. kidnapping case, a certain Hollywood "starlet" told TV and the public that she had received a phone call from Frank Sinatra, Jr., "while he was allegedly held captive." When she later took the stand "her story proved to be a fabrication which she refused to substantiate by sworn testimony."[20]

On March 22, 1961, Station WBAL-TV in Baltimore broadcast a program "in which nine of the twelve jurors purported to re-enact their deliberations . . . [and] comment on the evidence and [to] express their opinions as to the guilt or innocence of the accused and whether or not he should receive the death penalty. . . . On March 23 sentencing was postponed."[21] The court stated:

> . . . The effect of such a spectacle on the administration of justice is, we think, bound to be unfortunate. . . . Witnesses called on to give disagreeable or embarrassing testimony may be reluctant to do so voluntarily if they know that their testimony and their credibility may subsequently be discussed by the jurors on a television program.[22]

The longest list of TV and press problems, of course, was found in the Oswald case, in which responsibility for the assassination of Oswald came dangerously close to being placed squarely at the door of TV and the press. Police requests to reporters to stand back were ignored, in disregard of both the law and agreements.

> They would push forward. . . . The press and the television people just took over. . . . Police Chief Curry had instructed the reporters that they were not to ask any questions and try to interview (Oswald) in any way, but when he was brought into the room they immediately began to shoot questions at him and shove microphones into his face. It was difficult to hear Oswald's answers above the uproar.[23]

And the blinding TV lights in the eyes of police guarding Oswald,[24] as the Warren Commission suggested, made seeing Ruby or others impossible. Communications were disrupted. "One reporter admits hiding a telephone behind a desk so that he would have exclusive access to it if something developed."[25]

A noted radio and TV commentator on October 21, 1964 noted the lack of rules, codes, or controls among newsmen.

> . . . When an important or climactic event occurs and there is no seasoned or responsible press officer in command, then there should be some way in which the press itself might exercise some restraint. . . .
>
> How do we bring some order and responsibility out of chaos?[26]

The sort of chaos he referred to has been illustrated by a case in which newsmen fell across a witness on a stretcher, whose leg had recently been amputated, and others reported in the New York study. In Cleveland, for example, in the case referred to earlier, the press demanded Dr. Samuel Sheppard's arrest while evidence was still being sought. As Justice Frankfurter said:

> . . . Circulation-conscious editors catered to the insatiable interest of the American public in the bizarre. . . . Special rooms in the Criminal Courts Building were equipped for broadcasters and telecasters. In this atmosphere of a "Roman Holiday" for the news media Sam Sheppard stood trial for his life.[27]

In another case, broadcasters and part of the press of Chicago called Barry Cook, before his trial, "a murderer who loves that kind of gore."[28] He was later *acquitted*. In California a young man named Rexinger was accused of a sex crime. Newspapers, television, and radio called him a sadist, psychopath, and ex-convict. Before he came to trial the *actual* perpetrator of the crime came forward and confessed. In New York a "vicious killer," as the broadcast and press media referred to him, was found innocent on the basis of evidence at first withheld by the police.

In California, Caryl Chessman went to his death on the basis of less than conclusive evidence.[29] Why is it not better known that the California Supreme Court ruled Chessman's right to procedural due process had been violated, that the evidence was circumstantial and never proved, or that various reporters complained that *their superiors* would not allow the presentation of Chessman's side in the case? California Governor Edmund G. Brown's virtual concession that he could no longer resist the power of public opinion (created by television, radio, and newspapers), regardless of his doubt about Chessman's guilt, is shocking and dismaying. This is a frightening example of mob action, generated by the media, whose efforts did not constitute news reporting but the focusing on policy-makers of pressures which apparently could not be resisted. Whatever television and radio management *intended,* or *thought* they were doing, it appears that they created much of the pressure which left Governor Brown no alternative but to let Chessman die. Reports of the court trial, as provided by the correspondents from various foreign countries, cast serious doubt on his guilt. It is too little known by Americans that millions of people in a score of those countries signed petitions of appeal for at least a stay of execution, and that the news media of many nations, as well as their citizens, were shocked at what looked to them like a miscarriage of justice in these United States.

In cases like the Chessman case, the public, even under present conditions, can be whipped into a howling mob. Authority can be stolen from duly constituted law, and yielded to lynch law. The court, and our system of justice, loses control. But justice, unlike elections, cannot be determined by majority vote, any more than a majority of people can simply *vote* that an individual has or does not have a certain disease.

If it is protested that these are rare cases, it must be asked how many innocent people must suffer, or have their careers ruined, in order that television and radio may have special privileges? What is a fair price? Or should *any* such tragedies or slip-ups be considered too many? As of today the "inadvertent slips" seem all too common. It would not seem enough for *most* TV newsmen or photographers to observe the rules *most* of the time. Since violations seem to be so frequent, strict professional codes of procedure by broadcast journalists themselves, with enforcement penalties with real teeth in them, might be in order before TV asks for a "second round" of test cases or a second chance. Certainly the effects of all too many "demonstrations," or trial runs to date are disturbing.

One of these effects is economic. Costs to the court system of retrials are already mounting steeply. Even greater are the costs in efforts now necessary to get as jurors intelligent people whose minds are not already made up. These are real problems. In some cases, pre-trial publicity and the pressure of the mass media on jurors have delayed trials for years. Mistrials and the difficulty of finding unprejudiced jurors increase both the time and costs of justice. Some retrials come only after individuals have been wrongly imprisoned for many years, as was true for Dr. Sam Sheppard. These delays (during which accused but innocent people may suffer, witnesses may die, etc.) and economic costs have been described by many legal writers already as a "clear and present danger to the administration of justice."

Television coverage also may have economic implications by punishing the poor, but leaving the well-to-do free from the disgrace of public exposure, as in the case of the fourteen young people arrested in a deb party in New York, August 31, 1963. All but two had funds, or friends with funds, to secure counsel and bail. Only the two who were unable to secure counsel were extensively photographed, as if they were somehow more guilty than the others. As the New York study states, the police yielded to press and TV pressures "in direct violation of Rule I, Part II of the Appellate Division."[30] Without these pressures, there would have been no such photographing or unequal justice.

This raises the question also raised by the Warren Commission report. Would it have been possible for Jack Ruby to shoot Oswald if it had not been for the blinding TV lights in the eyes of the police protecting him?

Wherever TV goes, at the present stage of photography, TV lights blind both police and suspects. The efforts of many individuals to shield their eyes from these lights are interpreted by the public as "hiding his face," an admission or evidence of guilt—an example of the often forgotten factors which often make public opinion.

Instead of arresting offending photographers for violation of security regulations at the Oswald questioning, and thereby antagonizing the press, police admitted that they allowed them to interfere "with the movement of people who had to be there."[31] The press threat to "reveal" or "expose" possible police brutality to Oswald helped intimidate Dallas Police Chief Curry, who said that he "felt it was necessary to cooperate with the news media representatives, in order to avoid being accused of using Gestapo tactics in connection with the handling of Oswald."[32] In this and many cases, press and TV representatives blatantly violate police orders and the law. Should obedience to the law perhaps be one prerequisite to securing credentials?

Other practices and tendencies inconsistent with legal procedures are also notable in present types of news coverage. One is the inclination to equate arrest or accusation with guilt. Except in cases where the accused is a friend of the media, rarely does television or radio seem to remind the public of the accused individual's *innocence* until he is proven guilty. Is the implication of such coverage not usually that if one is accused, one is guilty? Is this habit of the news media not already in contradiction of the constitutional concept that one is innocent until proven guilty? Such questions, annoying as they may seem to the broadcasting industry, need to be asked before additional freedom of access to courtrooms is granted to television and radio. Since it is alleged by broadcasters that their efforts, if they are given more freedom, will serve to aid in law enforcement, let us look at some other TV and radio habits which arouse reservations. Is it true, as Father Drinan, Dean of the Boston College Law School has claimed, that ". . . the media now distort the legal profession and actually caricature the whole thing, because the only thing that appears . . . about the law is sex, rape, divorces, and the more lurid criminals?"[33] If that is even partly true, and many criminologists, penologists, educators, and sociologists believe it is, should a period of good behavior, in which television proves that it can picture law and justice responsibly and accurately, perhaps not be required before television cameras enter the courtrooms of the nation?

If direct reporting from courtroom trials becomes possible, what will be the effect on witnesses? Judge Willard L. Phillips of Kansas City addressed his legal colleagues on this matter on February 27, 1962. He said: "I am sure you have experienced the difficulty frequently encountered in procuring the attendance of some witnesses under existing conditions. Imagine what would happen if these witnesses knew they were going to appear on nationwide television."[34]

Other attorneys and judges have noted how television has an exhilarating effect on some witnesses (the extroverts) and an inhibiting effect on others (the introverts). How will television help the judge solve the problem of the introvert who can't even speak because of being on television? Or the extrovert who calls: "How am I doin', Ma?" How long before lawyers will have to hold screen tests for witnesses? Or what is to be done about witnesses who don't *want* to be on television (though they'd be glad to testify in a quiet court, away from cameras, the press, and television) and therefore deny that they saw the accident, or crime? How sure can television be that it may not help cause perjury, or stimulate a witness to contempt of court once television takes over? What kind of insurance will television take out against acts of retaliation in crime cases against witnesses who would not be widely exposed except for televising? Will televising help or harm in the problem of securing and using witnesses generally? How will the need to face friends and neighbors after the trial affect witnesses and jurors whose every agonized or confidential thought or gesture or expression may have been broadcast?

How is the accused ever to secure a fair trial, even with all the extra costs and precautions made necessary by television coverage? How, for example, can he receive a fair trial, even with a change of venue, since the Sixth Amendment to the Constitution states: "In all criminal prosecutions, the accused shall enjoy the right to a *speedy* and public trial, by an *impartial* jury *of the State and district wherein the crime shall have been committed . . .?*" (emphasis supplied).[35]

And what will happen to the judge? The National Association of Broadcasters pamphlet, *Broadcasting Public Proceedings,* referred to earlier, contains suggestions for "the strategic placement of fixed microphones at the judge's bench, at the witness chair, and possibly at the counsel table."[36] Never can the judge escape. Stomach rumblings, itches that need scratching—all are now to be televised. The analogy to Big Brother is frightening.

How would *you* like to do your job under the steady glare of a television lens? Or try to concentrate on the fate of people, left in your hands, under such circumstances? Or how would you as a defendant like to have your fate decided by a judge now charged with keeping an eye on a dozen new problems and distractions which television has introduced, besides concentrating on evidence and testimony? Edward Bennett Williams describes the problem:

> Trial lawyers and trial judges know that the search for truth is tortuous enough without putting it on stage. Television turns all participants into actors. If they are unwilling actors, their essential dignity as human beings is offended, and this will affect their conduct. If they are willing actors, there is a grave danger that the litigant, whose life, property or liberty is in jeopardy, may be adversely affected by participants who are more concerned with the effectiveness of histrionics than with the compliance they owe to their oaths. And this goes for all participants—lawyer, judges, witnesses, litigants and jurors.[37]

Superior Court Judge Henry S. Stevens, of Phoenix, has explained:

I am one who takes copious long-hand notes and so my eyes are not constantly on the courtroom. . . . Frequently I am able to refer to my notes . . . without calling upon the court reporter to search the record. . . . If I am required to police the cameras I cannot devote myself to the job which is at hand to the best of my ability.[38]

It has been urged by many broadcast groups that Canon 35 be withdrawn and that the decision be left to individual judges. Attorneys and judges who oppose this position have pointed out that leaving such decisions in the hands of an individual judge places an undue burden on him and leaves him at the mercy of the press and television, in the manipulation of public opinion. This should be a rule of the profession, not a procedural matter subject to change. If a judge antagonizes the industry, television is likely to try to get him defeated in elections or appointments on this basis only, even though he may otherwise be the best man for the job. This is a decision to which individual judges should not be subjected.

Judge Stevens, after bitter experience, wrote the American Bar Association's Special Committee on Proposed Revision of Judicial Canon 35 on February 6, 1962: "Woe be unto that judge who has sufficient courage to exclude photography in a celebrated case. . . . I know from bitter experience that disfavor with the press can be a pretty rough ordeal."[39] It is perhaps significant that the places where judges have yielded, and have allowed access to television, have generally been where the judges are *elected,* rather than appointed—as in Colorado, where, for the John Gilbert Graham trial, televising by delayed recordings was allowed. Thomas K. Younge, former President of the Colorado Bar Association stated:

There is no question in my mind that the individual judges of the Supreme Court were each aware that they must sooner or later stand for reelection and would need the support of the newspapers in their campaigns. I believe they were thereby influenced in their decision, which as you know was to abolish Canon 35 and permit the taking of pictures and the broadcasting of proceedings at trials.[40]

In several states, the attitudes of judges on this problem have been polled by students for master's theses, term papers, and special studies. Judges, generally, appear deeply concerned with the problem presented by the broadcaster's demands. Not because they are anti-broadcasting, or unsympathetic to the desirability of having greater national understanding of legal procedures, or even because they have something to hide, but because of the kinds of problems here suggested. Trial judges frequently point out how much control they have already lost over juries and, particularly, over prospective jurors who are exposed to the mass media daily. Increasingly, the press already appears to determine to a considerable degree the outcome of many doubtful cases. How many additional outside and vigilante pressures the American system of justice can endure is a serious question being asked increasingly by judges and lawyers concerned with the problem. The demands of broadcast owners and managers for access to courtrooms for television cameras and microphones for live broadcasts as well as for TV personnel, who are already allowed, are not surprising. Consistently, through the years, broadcast management has resisted any limitation on its freedoms. Once rights are secured, they are often neglected. In his statement before the Federal Communications Commission, March 1, 1948, on behalf of the right of broadcasters to editorialize, Dr. Stanton announced elaborate plans of CBS to originate regular editorials. However, he pointed out, "Even if we felt we could not fulfill the responsibility and did not exercise the right of editorializing, we would nevertheless want the right, as a matter of principle."[41] Once the right was secured, as Dr. Stanton has later admitted, it was, indeed, neglected. (See p. 357.)

In the same way, once Dallas stations secured the right to air recordings of the Ruby trial, taping soon became sporadic and incomplete. Stations which had fought fiercely for access began to stay away. This record is significant for what it promises for the future if similar rights were granted nationally.

Whether the power of veto, or selection, is better lodged in the broadcast industry than in the legal profession is dubious. In view of the problems newsmen have had with broadcast management, and the frankness with which many leading newsmen like Edward R. Murrow, David Brinkley, Walter Cronkite, Howard K. Smith, Edward P. Morgan, Chet Huntley, and others have expressed concern about the effects of TV on the events it covers, it is surprising that news broadcasters associations so generally have pressed for access to courtrooms.

This position is particularly surprising since newsmen perhaps come closer to being professionals than any group in broadcasting, with the possible exception of engineers. In their demands for entrance to courtrooms, newsmen are applying some of the same types of pressure to another profession, viz., law, that they themselves have been subjected to, from management and sales, for several years. It might have been expected that members of a group aspiring to professional status would see the problems of another profession as fraught with professional implications and problems for *all* professions and professionalism itself, and to have defended *professional* standards, as such, everywhere. As we have already observed, the fate of professionals in broadcasting, whether they be writers, artists, musicians, or newsmen, is not a record of either great recognition, high status, or great independence. To see news "professionals" helping to pit broadcasting, which is essentially a business, against the ethics and canons of another *profession,* seems something of a paradox.

The way in which newsmen, through the years, have yielded to management and sales pressures perhaps partially explains their position. This situation has been fairly widely studied and documented during the last ten years.

In his study of pressures on newsmen which reduce their freedoms, Per Holting[42] noted the pressures on behalf of sponsors, but exerted largely by sales and station management, to cause certain items to be used, others not to be used, and still others to be changed, on news broadcasts. Sponsor cancellations and threats of cancellation, Holting found, are an important factor in causing newsmen to compromise with ideals and standards taught them as journalists. Unfortunately, newsmen have resisted such pressures less vigorously or effectively than almost any other group in journalism, although they seem to talk about them a great deal.

As documented by Holting, the position of newsmen in broadcasting is far more subject to sales and other non-news pressures than it is in the magazine or newspaper business, whose managers are more likely to be journalism-trained. Radio and television news staffs and organizations, therefore, are likely to include more non-journalistically trained individuals than are similar newspaper groups. These are likely to include large proportions of disc jockeys, salesmen, and commercial announcers as opposed to qualified journalists. This may be a practical explanation of the position these groups take on such problems as access to the courtroom.

The 1963 study of influences on news broadcasting in the state of Illinois[43] is revealing on this point. Several interesting facts emerged which are relevant here.

First, although thirty years ago even Judge Justin Miller of the National Association of Broadcasters stated that news broadcasts should be free from commercials, and twenty years ago newsmen nationally had nothing but contempt for the Gabriel Heatter practice whereby newsmen themselves read the commercials, it was found that in nearly three-fourths of the stations of Illinois today, newscasters, willingly or not, deliver commercials. Many are apparently consoled for their desertion of their professional role by talent fees which supplement their regular salary as newsmen. In 62 out of 100 Illinois station news departments, however, so-called newsmen are also doing *other* commercials—apparently any commercials, for any programs or sponsors, which they are asked to do. In the face of management and sales pressures, news professionalism seems to be being increasingly compromised in this respect.

A few other facts from this study are equally relevant here. For example, fifteen of the news directors reporting said they didn't *like,* but still had to *use,* jingles and sound effects to introduce and close newscasts. The over-riding of the standards of journalism by those of "showmen" seems firmly established. No widespread instances of strikes or other organized or individual acts of refusal on the part of newsmen thus affected have been noted.

The January 4, 1960, *Bulletin* of the Illinois News Broadcasters Association carried the farewell message of its President, Harold Salzman, of Chicago Radio Station WLS. He pointed out how fortunate Illinois was in having so few newcasts dominated by disc jockeys and sound effects. He declared,

> We must resist efforts of managers to "ding-up" what they think will pass for a newscast with sound effects, weird weather reports, phony predictions of things to come, out-dated gossip, screaming praise for themselves, and a starvation diet of good news. A housecleaning is needed to sweep out the jazzed-up newscasters, fender-benders, sensationalists, alarmists, carnival barkers and others whose approach to broadcast news is frenzied and irresponsible. . . . A strong, professional news staff can marshal a force against which the juke-boxers have no defense. . . .

It appears that 1960 was a year of decision for newsmen in the same way 1957 had been a year of decision regarding what to do about blacklisting. In both cases those individuals involved yielded, as did the Germans described by Milton Mayer. Within a few months,

Salzman's own station was not only using such sound effects, but was also making and exporting recordings of them nation-wide to other so-called radio news departments. Journalism in that station and in other stations of the state and nation had just lost another round to salesmen, showmen, managers, and their values and pressures. This forecast the type of defeat of news values and standards which the 1963-64 Illinois study revealed. And the newsmen on the staffs seem to have gone along with this decision, both in 1960 and in the later years studied.

Here are a few other facts from this study. They should be useful in forecasting how firm and successful newsmen are likely to be in resisting domination of courtroom coverage, if it comes, by those who are not qualified newsmen:

1. Several news directors reported that they had to be careful about news stories that might displease station sponsors, or friends of the manager. This is relevant to courtroom coverage, of course. Suppose such individuals become involved in court cases, once broadcasters have access to courtrooms. Will they be excluded?

2. In three-fourths of the stations reporting, newsmen admitted that management or sales departments influenced the selection, deletion, or handling of various news items from time to time. What is to be considered news depends largely on management and sales decisions. This raises the question of whether, and to what extent, journalistic criteria as opposed to sales and other criteria, would govern what is done as court coverage. Good journalists' values may be trustworthy. But are the judgments of non-professional, non-journalists to be trusted in such matters? Several of the newsmen responding, in fact, stated that they could not even now report, as news, legal suits in which station sponsors or friends were involved. Undoubtedly any trials involving such suits of sponsor-friends would similarly be left unreported by such stations.

3. Several of the Illinois newsmen responding to this study reported that they could *not* report as news the opening of a new store or shopping center unless it bought advertising from the station. Conversely, even if they did not, as journalists, consider the events newsworthy, many of them had to report, in newscasts, often with on-the-spot film, the opening of stores, however

insignificant, which were sponsors of the station. This criterion of news significance is disturbing.

4. In various panel and interview programs, the selection of people to be interviewed as newsworthy was reported as more than coincidentally related to firms and individuals who were considered "friends of the station" on the basis of sponsorship or other "connections." Will newsmen be able to prevent this happening in connection with court cases, when they are unable to prevent it from happening in the other programming which the station already does? On the basis of such experience, if the court begins to probe into testimony regarding anti-trust suits and practices of sponsors or corporate or personal friends of the station or its management, how long would it be before the sales department or the manager would insist that the news department "lay off"? How fair would this kind of coverage be?

5. In this study of Illinois news departments, one repeated complaint was that news departments, already operating on smaller budgets and with fewer personnel than sales departments, in many cases are heavily overworked, understaffed, and unable to offer high enough salaries to secure enough first-class people to do the news job they want to do. Some of them are so limited in their budgets, which are usually set by non-news trained sales or management superiors, that they complain of being able to make only two or three long-distance phone calls a day to run down news leads. This is a very revealing illustration of how management wants its funds used. Is it reasonable to believe that if these news departments are given the additional responsibility of covering courtrooms, they will be *less* overworked and understaffed? How many hours a day will qualified news personnel be available and prepared to spend in the courtroom to insure that the pro and con, the cross-examination as well as the testimony, the poor laborer as well as the cheesecake, are fairly covered?

On the basis of the record in broadcast journalism in the last few years, it would appear that the *general* (not the unanimous, of course) impression might be that when the boss or sales department barks, too many newsmen jump. The performance of newsmen appears increasingly to be a precarious struggle between defending their professional integrity and holding their jobs. All too often the latter

seems more important. They can be replaced—they are often remind-
ed—probably by adolescent disc jockeys, who will achieve higher ratings.

One mark of a true profession is that there are some things one
won't do for money. For many so-called newsmen this list seems to be
getting shorter each year.

The broadcast news profession in its present state, in other words,
is characterized more by yielding to management and sales pressures
than by refusals to yield. If the record of the past is to be believed, it
is safe to conclude that, in covering trials and court proceedings, as in
covering super-market dedications or lawsuits of friends and sponsors,
newsmen will do as they are told, or they will be fired. And what they
will be told to do can fairly well be anticipated by noting what broadcasting has done so far. The fact that broadcast executives, like
ABC's Leonard Goldenson, have stated unequivocally and repeatedly
that television is primarily "show business" should indicate whose
values will continue to prevail.

Part of the problem of covering courtroom proceedings, of course,
is the lack, in the organization of either stations or networks, of a department qualified to cover such a field. Generally, for documentaries,
whatever subject they cover, responsibility has been given to the news
department as a catch-all because of the absence of a better qualified
department or staff to assume responsibility for them.

Is it not quite possible that responsibility for courtroom coverage
does not belong in a news department, any more than the programs of
science, music, drama, history, education or law are properly a function of news departments? All probably deserve departments of their
own, if they are to be adequately treated.

More disturbing, however, is the fact that the disciplines, traditions,
and criteria which prevail for news appear to be precisely the opposite
of those which must prevail in the courts or in legal matters. Due process is rarely exciting or unusual. This contradiction and dilemma can
perhaps most clearly be stated as follows:

> Newsmen normally define their values in terms of *news,* i.e.,
> deviations or exceptions from the normal, whereas the court
> seeks *truth,* which is the *sum total* of the typical and average,
> slowly accumulated by due process and discounting for the atypi-
> cal which would "make news." How qualified newsmen are to
> report the uneventful, which "due process" so generally means

—the search for truth, however dull—is a serious question. The very training of newsmen as journalists, however good they may be as newsmen, is likely to make them unfit to see the *over-all truth* instead of the *deviation,* unless checked and balanced by legal training and qualifications and legal disciplines.

A second question revolves around the very great danger which results from *any* kind of televising of trials. The problem is seen in a disquieting effect of television already observed by many psychologists. This problem, or effect, has been dramatized recently in the case of bystanders who have stood by and allowed murders, crimes, and violence to take place before their very eyes, without interfering. To what extent is this related to the habit, and conditioning, whereby people daily witness television violence on their screens, where, they recognize, they are powerless to do anything about it? Being so largely a fiction medium, television seems to transform much of what it broadcasts, including news, into a passing parade, erasing the boundary between reality and fiction in the viewer's mind. Would it not, therefore, be a dangerous disservice to broadcast courtroom trials, at least before this problem is partially solved? At present there is a widespread impression of unreality in news about wars, events, and peoples as gleaned from the atypical glimpses of them which television provides. Will television do a clearer job of reporting what is going on in courtrooms than it does of reporting U.N. meetings or educational developments, or news from those places where we *are* allowed to have correspondents and cameras?

The oft-repeated allegation that television reports things faithfully and as they are, perhaps needs to be challenged again and re-examined more closely in terms of the specific problem involved in access to courtrooms. In his CBS editorial, broadcast nationally on August 24, 1954, for example, Dr. Frank Stanton stated: "After all, radio and television hear and see exactly what happens. . . . They are the public's mirror, reflecting things exactly as they are."[45] This concept now seems to be proven false.

By its very nature and the potential of its lenses, television can and does distort. On television, things are often not what they seem. With different lenses the small and unimportant can be made as large, and important, as the large or great. A man's nose, or a small child, can be made as large—and fill the screen as completely—as the whole man. The part can be made to "equal" the whole. The tiny can be made to fill the whole screen as completely as the enormous, just as, via radio, the cheapest commercial jingle, or solo, can be made as loud as the greatest symphony. In this respect, television wipes out differences in size, changing what is seen from "real life" scales and models to distortions of natural relationships. In this sense, television is not a reality medium; it is a fictional, "unreal-making" medium. It contrasts with and differs from life, in such subtle ways, however, that in seeing unequals made equal by television, the average individual is likely to lose all sense of ratio, proportion, and difference. This equalizing and leveling effect of television is too often forgotten by its masters, who claim for it accurate presentation or reflection of reality.

The dangers of this characteristic, however, applied to court procedures which are devoted to establishing relationships, causes, and reality, should be obvious enough to require that safeguards be established to anticipate them. Since a courtroom is a place in which conflicting pressures meet, and must be balanced and weighed, the dangers offered by a medium which can change relationships and ratios at will, making the large look small and the small large, must be taken into account. Otherwise television viewers may see only distortions of what the court sees.

* * * * * * * * * * *

SOME PROPOSED CONDITIONS

Although several problems have been raised which indicate dangers which would be attendant upon the presence in the courtroom of equipment for direct broadcast, under present conditions, practices, and safeguards, it is possible to visualize conditions under which such broadcasts *might* be safely carried out and be in the public interest.

In fact, the purpose of the analysis of problems contained in this chapter is to recognize that the problem *must* be solved, and to suggest some necessary steps for its solution. We must work at this problem, devising codes, procedures, and safeguards until it is possible to televise courtroom proceedings. The author most fervently endorses the position stated by the New Jersey Supreme Court:

> An answer to problems such as are presented here must be achieved. Fair criminal prosecution and exercise of the guaranty of a free press are not incompatible with the constitutional right of a defendant to a fair trial by an impartial jury. Only the will to recognize and subscribe responsibly to that fact has been lacking.[46]

The conditions and practices documented in this volume *are* disquieting. They are endangering justice in America. We must set about correcting them, and establishing conditions under which both free press (by TV, radio, and the print media) and fair trial (for the innocent until proven guilty in a court of law) can exist peaceably together. One of the conclusions of the Warren Commission report stated: "The promulgation of a code of professional conduct governing representatives of all press media would be welcome evidence that the press had profited by the lesson of Dallas."[47]

In the remaining pages, some suggestions toward this end are offered. Undoubtedly this list is both incomplete and imperfect. Individual readers, as well as the legal profession and broadcasters, are invited to suggest desirable revisions, deletions, and additions which can finally become a statement of conditions which will make broadcasts from courtrooms safe and desirable.

As a preamble to the guidelines and conditions which need to be established, the broadcast industry should clearly set forth the purposes it would seek to serve by such broadcasts. This statement should be positive, not negative, or defensive, as most previous statements have been; and it should be related to the administration of justice in the United States. Prescriptive as well as proscriptive guidance is necessary if broadcasting from courtrooms is to serve the public interest in positive ways.

This statement should make it clear why broadcasters need access to courtrooms with their unique instruments for live broadcasts. Why are delayed broadcasts not adequate? What abuses in United States justice will this help correct? How will such broadcasting result in the *better* administration of justice, thereby serving the public interest? How will the search for truth be made *easier* by such broadcasting? What is needed is broadcasting's statement of how, by such broadcasts, it will serve the public interest, not merely the prurient curiosity of sensation-seekers. Once this approach is established, conditions essential for such broadcasting can be set forth. The following sample conditions might serve as points for discussion in such a consideration.

1. Before requesting access, broadcasters should guarantee that the special correspondents to be accredited for this purpose will be fully qualified, and their qualifications should be stated. A correspondent or reporter qualified for the foreign service should know languages; for medicine one should have medical training; for science, science train-

ing, and so on. A court interpreter for television should be both qualified as a journalist and trained in the law. If only one of these disciplines is available, the legal qualification should take priority. Jointly, the legal profession and the broadcast industry should be able to devise standards to insure accurate and faithful reporting by qualified legal reporters.

Access should not be expected for the kind of reporter described by Dean Erwin N. Griswold of the Harvard Law School in the July 1962 *ABA Journal:*

> . . . The man in charge of the set [camera] whispered to one of the lawyers to get his d— co-counsel to stand aside, as he was getting between his camera and the witness. The lawyer lost his temper, but remembering he was on television, did not dare say what was on his mind and was left speechless. By the time he had regained his speech, an important question had gone by, and an unwarranted impression had been made on the jury.[48]

The individuals in charge of such broadcasts, in short, should be legally trained correspondents, qualified to maintain balance and retain the significant in reporting. They should be comparable to those available on the staffs of most foreign broadcast systems, or United States newspapers and magazines—specialists in such fields as medicine, labor, industry, science, education, and so on. Until the *proper people* can be put in the courtroom in charge of the equipment, the doors should remain closed.

2. The station or network agrees that facilities will be kept in operation in the court at all times throughout any given trial. Selective recording of atypical parts, or hit-and-run type coverage, will not be acceptable. Such assurance must be from management levels, since it has been demonstrated that news department promises, however sincerely made, are frequently over-ruled; the news personnel who make them are also frequently dismissed in case of difficulty. Until broadcasters are prepared to provide the care, personnel, time, and effort required to do this job properly and responsibly, they should not presume to enter the courtroom.

3. The station or network agrees, if it is to cover *certain* trials, that *regular* coverage of courts will be carried out. In this way friends and enemies of broadcasting will be treated alike, and both will be given a fair chance for access to the medium. Court coverage can also thereby

be placed in proper perspective, rather than offered as a "spectacular."

4. To avoid competition for *firstness* in coverage, trials will not be covered *live* unless carried continuously or in their entirety. A partial account of a trial can be no more faithful than a partial account of a football or basketball game. Certainly it is as important to the nation as those events, and should be covered with equal care and by equal specialists. As noted earlier, television and press have a long record of false reports and similar failures traceable to a race for firstness. Therefore, a race for scoops must be prevented by a plan to be worked out and submitted in advance by television itself. This may well include the pooling of facilities, the observance of release dates and times which will not affect witnesses, jurors, or sentencing, and similar provisions.

5. No sponsorship of court proceedings should be allowed.

6. Penalties for various violations must be agreed to in advance. At present, the news media, even when they are proved to be the cause of mistrials or other costly developments, are free from penalty. Some correction which would make the media responsible in some legal way for irresponsibility—perhaps on the British model—might well be considered. Such steps are necessary principally because, though broadcasting has codes, their flagrant violation is seen daily, and since they contain no real penalties, they are essentially meaningless.

In the medical, legal, and other professions, means exist, within the profession itself, for disciplining members for infractions, or even disqualifying them from practice. Until such professional approaches are developed by broadcasting itself, the courts or other outsiders may have to establish these penalties or conditions. The Supreme Court of Florida, for example, recognizing the problems caused by the mass media and the pressure they exert on court decisions, has recommended adoption of British and Continental European practices whereby pre-trial comment on the merits of a case can be held in contempt of court.[49] As a result of his study, Dr. Donald Gillmor recommends that provisions be made for punishing contempt by the press or mass media as a "clear and present danger to the administration of justice."[50] Certainly there should be some way of holding irresponsible press organs responsible for the publication of information prejudicial to due process before it is admitted into evidence, the publication of names and addresses of jurors, and similar practices.

7. Some provision, such as Senator Morse's proposed Senate Bill

1802, to amend the Federal Criminal Code, should precede television access. Senator Morse's bill would "forbid any employee of the court, defendant or attorney to publish information not already properly filed with the court which might affect the outcome of any pending criminal litigation."[51]

8. Satisfactory procedures must be established to guarantee that the editing of tapes will not result in the kind of one-sided presentation illustrated by the Kohler hearings cited earlier. Unless satisfactory review procedures can be applied, excerpts should not be permitted for fear of the distortion which may result. To entrust the selection of excerpts either to management, with its conflicting interests, or to the often young and immature individuals who so often make up news staffs today, would be a great and real danger to the cause of justice.

9. Before the coverage of any given case, or court session, is undertaken, the station would file with the court a plan of coverage, setting forth the steps it agrees to take, in order to assure full, complete, and unbiased coverage.

In consultation, broadcasters and Bar Association representatives undoubtedly can work out far better provisions than these, which are intended only for purposes of discussion and as points of departure for the careful study needed.

In a discussion at the University of Missouri in April 1964, John H. Colburn, editor and publisher of the Wichita *Eagle and Beacon* referred to certain provisions in the joint bar-press codes adopted in Oregon and Massachusetts, which he recommends. Slightly paraphrased, these include, briefly:[52]

1. Avoid editorializing that might prejudice a trial's outcome, until the trial is over. The accused must be presumed innocent until he is either convicted or acquitted.
2. Don't call a *crime* a *murder* until there is a proper indictment.
3. A case should not be considered "solved" on the basis of police statements. Only courts decide guilt.
4. A statement from the accused should be called a *statement,* not a confession; it should be made clear whether or not he was advised by counsel in making it.
5. Don't let individuals (police, attorneys, prosecutor) use the press for personal publicity, or as a sounding board.
6. Be careful not to identify as "suspects" individuals merely questioned by the police.

Such suggestions as these are to be welcomed in the joint efforts needed to establish adequate safeguards for the difficult and exacting activity which courtroom coverage by television, when approved, will constitute.

So far, neither the code of the National Association of Broadcasters nor network leadership seems to show a real understanding of the problems involved. Although the brochure *Broadcasting Public Proceedings* specifies "qualified newsmen," nowhere are qualifications prescribed or spelled out. Much is said about the concealment, or partial concealment, of cameras and microphones, the use of rubber-soled shoes, and the speed of films which might be used, but little is said regarding the purpose or over-all fidelity of reporting such broadcasts, for which centuries-old court traditions and procedures would now be changed. The assumption that, once television is in the courtroom, and once it proves itself silent and not visually distracting or conspicuous, the problems will be solved, is to miss the *main* problems involved. What safeguards will be provided, and how, against interfering with due process—either with reference to the judge, the jury, the witnesses, attorneys, or the defendant or the plaintiff—still remain to be spelled out before this effort can be considered a satisfactory approach to the problem. It is hoped that a study such as that suggested by Dr. Frank Stanton, possibly by the Brookings Institution, may be helpful in these regards.

If this analysis strongly opposes allowing broadcast personnel to enter the sacred precincts of courts of justice with facilities for live broadcasting *until significant and drastic changes are made in applicable broadcast practices, personnel, and standards,* it is because the stakes are high.

Courts are the last resort of desperate citizens. A judge is not selected to represent the public, but the law. If conditions conducive to concentrated deliberation, and freedom from pressure, are lost by the courts, the faith with which people voluntarily submit their disputes to the arbitration of the courts will also be lost. Where, then, are the helpless, the desperate, or the injured to turn? How then will disputes be settled? By those methods now being illustrated nightly on TV in Westerns, or by Mike Hammer, James Bond, and similar popular heroes? In the terms normally shown on television, whereby murder justifies murder, and a tooth for a tooth is exacted? Or must do-it-yourself forms of justice and violence be resorted to? It is true that in a few cases courtroom access seems to have worked. But scores of incidents, especially recent tragic ones in Dallas and Cleveland, prompt caution. Even in examples cited as success stories, such as the Colorado trial of John Gilbert Graham, there are words of reservation.

Judge Peter Holme, Jr. of Denver, in the ABA study and report of 1962, said that it was his firm impression that "Colorado's experience has borne out most, if not all, of the misgivings expressed by those who opposed photography and televising of courtroom proceedings."[53]

Dr. Donald M. Gillmor has warned:

> . . . until more reliable knowledge concerning the influence of inflammatory press publicity upon judges and jurors has been incorporated into legal thinking, *the only responsible assumption may be* that the mass media *are* capable of impairing the fair administration of justice. Ignoring the possibility of such effects might grievously jeopardize the constitutional right to a fair trial. . . . One thing seems certain. If self-discipline is not exercised soon in this area of news reporting, legislation of some kind is inevitable.[54]

There is more involved, therefore, than merely the problem of access to courtrooms. And it is fervently to be hoped that broadcasting itself, with the legal profession, will establish the necessary conditions, without inviting governmental action.

In early January of 1965, the Philadelphia Bar Association adopted a policy statement which drastically limited the information which attorney-members could give the press and TV before a trial is concluded. Guidelines suggested by the journalistic honorary, Sigma Delta Chi, followed. These were discussed on a CBS program. At that time Harry Reasoner said:

> This highly complex problem of free press and fair trial is not going to be settled in Philadelphia. The American Bar Association has begun a study that will take three years. And the conflict may not be settled in that time either. But the problem will not go away. All sides, it seems to us, are aiming at fair press and fair trial.

In the face of this problem, neither continued pressure from the broadcast industry for entrance, as is, nor continued refusal by the legal profession seems desirable. Both courts and broadcasting are a part of our culture and age. It would be defeatist indeed to decide that the nation, and these two groups, is incapable of working out conditions that will not only allow courtroom coverage but also improve present broadcast and general mass media treatment of criminal, civil, and court problems generally. Certainly "trial by newspaper," retrials because of mass media publicity, character assassination of innocent individuals, and other malpractices noted in earlier pages are not necessary or inevitable in a great nation that values justice.

Just as responsible parents must decide that there are certain things that their children are not yet ready to undertake, on the basis of the maturity displayed in other kinds of situations, so the American public and the legal profession must decide that broadcasting *does not yet seem ready,* on the basis of the practices, values, personnel, and traditions it now displays, to undertake this task and responsibility. Just as saying No to a child at a given stage does not mean lack of affection or confidence for the future, however, so saying No now should not mean lack of faith in broadcasting's potential for handling this task, perhaps with distinction, *eventually.* Surely the great instruments of television and radio, carefully used by properly trained professionals, can and should *help* the causes of justice and law enforcement in America.

To repeat, as the Supreme Court stated in its *Estes versus Texas* decision:

> The television camera is a powerful weapon. Intentionally or inadvertently it can destroy an accused and his case in the eyes of the public. While our telecasters are honorable men, they too are human. [The problems involved] are real enough to have convinced the Judicial Conference of the United States, this Court, and the Congress that television should be barred in federal trials by the Federal Rules of Criminal Procedure; in addition they have persuaded all but two of our States to prohibit television in the courtroom.[56]

For the time being, therefore, the television industry is faced with the need to get its own house in order before it can with optimism seek entry into courtrooms. As Chief Justice Warren wrote in the *Estes versus Texas* decision:

> I recognize that the television industry has shown in the past that it can be an enlightening and informing institution, but like other institutions, it must respect the rights of others and cannot demand that we alter fundamental constitutional conceptions for its benefit. We must take note of the inherent unfairness of television in the courtroom and rule that its presence is inconsistent with the "fundamental conception" of what a trial should be.[57]

Broadcasters still have far to go. While working cooperatively with the legal profession to develop conditions which will be acceptable and workable for courtroom coverage eventually, broadcast management and news personnel alike should work toward the achievement of true professionalism. Only thus will a repetition of many of the unfortunate practices described in earlier pages be made impossible in the future.

In the final chapter some approaches to such professionalism are suggested.

NOTES

1. *Report of the President's Commission on the Assassination of President John F. Kennedy* (Washington, D.C.: Government Printing Office, 1964), p. 242.

2. *Radio, Television and the Administration of Justice: A Documented Survey of Materials,* by the Special Committee on Radio and Television of the Association of the Bar of the City of New York (New York and London: Columbia University Press, 1965). "Introduction," p. VIII.

3. *Ibid.,* p. 279.

4. *Newsletter* of The Twentieth Century Fund, Winter 1966, p. 1. This study has now been published in book form. See Alfred Friendly and Ronald L. Goldfarb, *Crime and Publicity: The Impact of News on the Administration of Justice* (New York: Twentieth Century Fund, 1967).

5. William S. Paley, "New Realities of Radio," Address to Ninth Annual Convention, CBS Radio Affiliates Association, New York, September 13, 1962. Brochure (13 pp.) distributed by CBS, p. 12.

6. John Daly, "The News—Broadcasting's First Responsibility (John Daly speaks out on Canon 35)," National Association of Broadcasters, 1957, p. 16. Brochure (16 pp.)

7. *Radio, Television and the Administration of Justice,* p. 203.

8. *Ibid.,* pp. 227-31.

9. *Ibid.,* p. 217.

10. Yosal Rogat, "The Eichmann Trial and the Rule of Law." Brochure, Center for the Study of Democratic Institutions (New York: Fund for the Republic, 1961), pp. 34-35.

11. A. J. Liebling, *The Press* (New York: Ballantine Books, 1961), pp. 158-59.

12. Rogat, *op. cit.,* p. 33.

13. National Association of Broadcasters, "Broadcasting Public Proceedings: Coverage Guide-Posts" (Washington, D.C.: The Association, April 1962), Preface, p. 2. Brochure (16 pp.)

14. American Bar Association, *Special Committee on Proposed Revision of Judicial Canon 35: Interim Report and Recommendations* (Chicago: American Bar Center, July 23, 1963). (Hereafter referred to as ABA Report). The case of *United Press Associations* v. *Valente,* 120, N.Y.S. 174, is quoted on pp. 85-86.

15. Quoted in ABA *Report,* pp. 86-87.

16. Quoted, *ibid.,* p. 88.

17. Daly, *op. cit.,* p. 14.

18. *Ibid.*

19. *Radio, Television and the Administration of Justice,* p. 103.

20. *Ibid.,* p. 76.

21. *Ibid.,* p. 71.

22. *Ibid.,* p. 72.

23. *Ibid.,* pp. 90-91.

24. *Ibid.,* p. 306.

25. *Ibid.,* p. 88.

26. *Ibid.,* p. 93.

27. Quoted in ABA *Report,* p. 79.

28. Donald Gillmor, "Free Press versus Fair Trial: A New Era?" *Journalism Quarterly,* 41, No. 1 (Winter 1964), 30.

29. Melvin Martin, "Did the Press Kill Caryl Chessman?" *The Progressive,* December, 1960, pp. 12-17

30. *Radio, Television and the Administration of Justice,* p. 97.

31. *Ibid.,* p. 89.

32. *Ibid.,* pp. 316-17.

33. ABA *Report,* p. 18.

34. *Ibid.,* p. 55.

35. *Radio, Television and the Administration of Justice,* p. 209.

36. NAB, *op. cit.,* p. 11.

37. Quoted in ABA *Report,* p. 89; from Mr. Williams' book, *One Man's Freedom* (New York: Atheneum, 1962), pp. 230-31.

38. ABA *Report,* p. 45.

39. *Ibid.,* p. 39.

40. *Ibid.,* p. 47

41. Frank Stanton, "The Right of Radio to Editorialize," Statement Before the Federal Communications Commission, March 1, 1948, p. 20. Brochure (22 unnumbered pp.)

42. Per Holting, "Where Does Friction Develop for TV News Directors?" *Journalism Quarterly,* 34, No. 3 (Summer 1957), 355-59.

43. Gregory James Liptak, "Influences on News Broadcasting in the State of Illinois," University of Illinois, Urbana, December 1963. (mimeographed, 26 pp.)

44. Harold Salzman, Illinois News Broadcasters Association *Bulletin,* January 4, 1960

45. Frank Stanton, "CBS Editorial," An Expression of Editorial Opinion, delivered over CBS Television and CBS Radio from New York, August 26, 1954, p. 4. Brochure (9 unnumbered pp.)

46. *Radio, Television and the Administration of Justice,* p. 281.

47. *Ibid.,* p. 317.

48. Erwin N. Griswold, "The Standards of the Legal Profession: Canon 35 Should Not be Surrendered," *American Bar Association Journal,* 48, No. 7 (July 1962), 618.

49. Fran Elkin, "Trial by Newspaper: A Transcontinental Tale of Two Judges," *News Workshop* (New York University), May 1960, p. 2.

50. Gillmor, *op. cit.,* p. 32.

51. *Ibid.,* p. 34.

52. John H. Colburn, "The Newspaperman Attitudes: Pre-Verdict Publicity Dialogue," Freedom of Information Center Publication No. 124 (Columbia, Mo.: School of Journalism, University of Missouri, June 1964), pp. 4-6.

53. ABA *Report,* p. 48.

54. Gillmor, *op. cit.,* p. 37.

55. "Bar-Press 'Guidelines' Discussion Widening," *The Quill,* March 1965, p. 12.

56. *Radio, Television and the Administration of Justice,* p. 203.

57. *Ibid.,* p. 224.

Toward Professionalism:
Some Needed Changes

If the ideal situation prevailed in television and radio news in the United States today:

1. We would have only qualified, trained journalists who are fully aware of the effects of their efforts.
2. They would be allowed the time, staff, budget, and freedom (from interference of superiors or sponsors as well as interrupting commercials) necessary to report and interpret what they consider news.
3. Their salaries and job security would be appropriate to their importance as professionals.
4. News would regularly be broadcast in prime time, evidencing broadcast management's recognition that news deserves time periods as valuable as those allocated to comedy, Westerns, and other entertainment programs.

Unfortunately, these conditions prevail among all too few of America's broadcast stations and newsmen, which are our special concern.

In his 1963 study for the Ford Foundation, the late David Boroff reported that both journalism and journalism education in the United States are far short of the quality the nation needs. Technological developments, he found, are outstripping human factors and training, and the gap is widening annually. Anti-professionalism and non-professional practices are on the rise. Journalism education, like the mass media in general, is in urgent need of reappraisal and redirection.

In an article on this problem in 1965, John Tebbel wrote:

A revolution is impending in the communications business that is going to change it perhaps beyond recognition. Journalism education ought to be in the front ranks of that revolution. At the moment it is somewhere near the rear guard.[1]

One of the principal causes of this pending revolution is television. Regardless of where readers may stand on polls purporting to show which medium is best for which kinds of news, there should be little quarrel over the fact that television is more rapid than any medium except radio and has many other advantages—and dangers—when compared with other press media. On television as it is now developing, the journalist does not merely say things. In all he does he is constantly *demonstrating* something to the people who view him. A Chicago newsman in the late summer of 1966 showed his audience how Molotov cocktails were made of coke bottles and gasoline. Next day the news media were able to report that over a hundred had *been* made and used in civil rights violence in the intervening twenty-four hours.

In view of the growth of many dangerous practices, and the increasing recriminations between the electronic and the print media, a sense of real urgency does prevail. Something must be done. Dean Edward W. Barrett of the Columbia Graduate School of Journalism wrote in 1965: "It is high time for the leaders in journalism and journalism education to be less tolerant toward the really shabby and the meretricious in American journalism."[2]

Referring to the chaos which prevailed at the time Oswald was shot, with TV lights blinding police and Oswald alike, newsmen disrupting police communications by hiding telephones for their own use, and so on, a distinguished radio and television commentator, quoted earlier, asked the crucial question: ". . . How do we bring some order and responsibility out of chaos?"[3] For chaos all too often prevails wherever TV coverage is present.

In how many true professions would the chaos and disorder which have so often prevailed where newsmen meet and compete (conventions, Khrushchev's visit to the United States, civil rights coverage) be conceivable? Certainly it would not long be tolerated.

Too many of the practices condemned by Boroff, Tebbel, Barrett, and outstanding newsmen themselves, are to be found more in *broadcast* journalism, as some like to call it, than in any other type.

Unfortunately, the words "broadcast journalism" carry with them very little specific meaning in professional terms. Like the word broadcaster itself, they do not represent any specific nationally or internationally recognized training, ability, integrity, discipline, or proof of qualification. This is in sharp contrast with a word like "physician" which, all over the civilized world at least, has a specific meaning in terms of both qualification and function.

Although broadcasting is one of the most powerful forces shaping social values and behavior, broadcast staffs and management in the United States generally have no specific professional standards to meet, other than the very general financial, legal, and character qualifications required of the licensee and the technical license which must be held by a station's transmitter engineers before the station can operate. It is as if, at drug stores, the delivery boy, or person responsible for transportation of the product, were licensed, but the pharmacist (in broadcasting: the writer, producer, or newsman) who puts up the prescriptions, needs to meet no specific standards. The need for steps to correct this weakness is becoming critical.

In news and public affairs, particularly, the fact that there is no national academic standard prerequisite to practice, and that neither the names of the schools from which newsmen graduate, nor their diplomas or degrees—if indeed they are even considered necessary to employment—represent any definitive standard of intellectual accomplishment, morality, character qualification, or even technical skill, is disturbing if not shocking.

Under the concept of free speech which we have held, it has all too frequently been considered inappropriate or somehow unconstitutional to require such qualifications. This may well be a valid consideration for preserving access to the media for the people as public: A citizen should not be barred from free speech by lack of specific education. It would seem to be overdue for reconsideration when staff qualifications are concerned, however. Why should newsmen be allowed to "practice" without proof of qualification any more than a physician, attorney, teacher, or nurse? As will be noted later, we are not talking about *government* control here. What is needed and preferable, if broadcast news is to be professionalized, is the establishment by practitioners themselves of qualification criteria. These might appropriately be established by a national standards committee selected by broadcast newsmen themselves from among their peers as a step toward professionalization. Such a step is needed in the desperate effort that will be required if the human factors involved are to catch up with recent technological developments in news and public affairs reporting by electronic means.

The concern examined here is not felt in the United States only. At the Eighth International Seminar of the Strasbourg Center for Higher Education in Journalism in 1964, distinguished speakers from many nations repeatedly called for an effective and binding international code of ethics among newsmen. The representatives of many new African nations repeatedly made clear that as they are called upon to devise news services for their new nations, as they get television, they will more often avoid than imitate United States practices. Jean Bikanda, former General Commissioner for Information in the Federal Republic of the Cameroons, pointedly criticized our television, which "makes of indiscretion a dogma of which it is a slave," while "the masses, docile, pleased with their easy lives, purr and are well content with what they have."[4]

"For the understanding necessary between our two worlds," he warned the "developed" Western nations, "there is more to be done than interesting the reader (or viewer) by means of original photos and catchy titles."[5]

As commercial factors and values have come to dominate U.S. broadcasting more and more, the status of the few professionals who still find careers in broadcasting has been reduced. Through the years, personality considerations have increasingly replaced substantial disciplines as qualifications. "Weather girls," disc jockeys, and other "personalities" have increasingly taken over from meteorologists, trained journalists, and qualified specialists. Through the years, also, the ratio of technical, sales, management, accounting, and other *administrative* personnel to creative, professional *program* personnel has risen. Today probably less than five per cent of the non-technical employees in United States broadcasting are engaged in program, news, or creative activities.

Numerous studies have been prompted by the high personnel turnover in radio and TV in the United States, and the difficulty of getting good personnel. Of the more than 101,000 persons now working directly in broadcasting in the United States, according to President Roy E. Morgan of the Association for Professional Broadcast Education, there is an annual turnover of 33 per cent in radio and 28 per cent in television each year. Of these, Morgan declared in 1966, "a growing number are moving out of the broadcast field and into other areas of employment."[6] Part of the reason is undoubtedly the low salaries paid in radio and television as compared to other news and advertising fields. The 1965 report on journalism graduates by the Newspaper

Fund of the *Wall Street Journal* noted that television salaries had dropped from fourth to eighth place during the past year, to $90.67 average weekly starting salary, as compared to salaries paid in the daily or weekly newspaper field, advertising, public relations, magazines, and even teaching. This was somewhat surprising since profits in television were higher than those in any of the other fields, and had in the previous year reached the highest level in the nation's history.

Though salary, job turnover, and lack of tenure are important reasons for the difficulties television and radio have in securing outstanding employees, departure interviews and other studies have indicated that the most frequent complaint, in the program and news areas—where turnover is highest and salaries lowest—is being over-ruled or having one's "professional" work vetoed or meddled with by management and sales personnel. One might conclude from the high departure rates from TV in these departments especially, that most who leave do so because they would "rather switch than fight," to paraphrase a familiar slogan.

For many years both the broadcast industry generally and newsmen in particular have used the term "profession" to refer to themselves. But when common broadcast and news practices or even "codes" are measured against those of real professions, it appears that they fall far short. This is especially regrettable in the news area.

In a recent study entitled "Professionalization Among Newsmen," Jack N. McLeod and Searle E. Hawley, Jr. concluded that: "If any sort of agreement exists, it is probably that journalism is partly professionalized but that it presently lacks some important ingredients of a fine profession."

Among the criteria to be met before an occupation becomes a profession, McLeod and Hawley list eight that meet with general agreement. They are:

1. It must perform a unique and essential service.
2. It must emphasize intellectual techniques.
3. It must have a long period of specialized training to acquire a systematic body of knowledge based on research.
4. It must be given a broad range of autonomy.
5. Its practitioners must accept broad personal responsibility for judgments and actions.
6. It must place greater emphasis on service than on private economic gain.

7. It must develop a comprehensive self-governing organization.
8. It must have a code of ethics which has been clarified and interpreted by concrete cases.[7]

Because the problem of professionalization is at the very heart of what is wrong with broadcasting as news and public affairs media, let us look more closely at other fields in which a profession has been created from within by an occupational group.

In the examples which follow, it should be noted how traditionally professions are characterized by "peer control"—control by professionals themselves. Professionals traditionally set their own standards and discipline their own kind. As another important characteristic: there are many specific things that professionals agree they *will not do for money* or for other personal or promotional advantage.

Of all the true professions surviving today, medicine is certainly the oldest. For over 2,500 years, medicine has had a code of medical ethics, capsulized today in the Hippocratic Oath. The Principles of Medical Ethics of the American Medical Association have been revised several times and were considerably rewritten in December, 1953. This document, consisting of eight chapters, each with several sections, could be studied with profit by broadcasters.[8] One of the principal strengths of this code lies in its enforcement provisions. It provides for barring from practice any member of the profession found, by committees of his peers, to be guilty of malpractice as defined in the Principles of Medical Ethics.

Less well known, perhaps, are the provisions of the Codes of Ethics of the American Bar Association. The principles of legal ethics and etiquette originated in England during the twelfth and thirteenth centuries. Their enforcement, too, is dependent in large part on the power of the Association, representing the profession and the peers of the attorney member, to censure, suspend, or disbar lawyers for violations of professional ethics and standards of conduct specifically set forth. A lawyer whose behavior as a member of the profession would cast serious reflection on the dignity of the courts, in which he practices, or on the reputation of the profession as a whole, may be disbarred from practice. The codes of the bar association cover the obligations of the attorney to the public, the courts, clients, and other lawyers. They also contain a statement of the lawyer's "cardinal loyalties," similar in many respects to the medical profession's Hippocratic Oath. One canon of the Code of Ethics, Canon 35, has been examined in earlier pages in connection with the discussion of television in the courtroom.

The American Institute of Accountants since 1917 has had a code which forbids the falsifying of facts, preparing reports subordinating the accountant's professional judgment to the desires of a client, or engaging in various occupations or practices which are specifically listed as unacceptable as conflicts of interest. In the field of accounting, state boards have the right to suspend or revoke the certificates of Certified Public Accountants for violations, following appropriate hearings. Members may also be admonished, suspended, or expelled from the association, with appropriate publicity, for violations of the Rules of Professional Conduct, which list sixteen types of behavior or practice which are not acceptable for accountants.

Perhaps more interesting to broadcasters are the Canons of Ethics for Engineers. These were originally formulated by the Engineer's Council for Professional Development. They are perhaps more relevant since engineers are not thought of generally as being members of a "learned" profession, and are perhaps closer to broadcasting in emphasis on the practical. It is notable that, since broadcast engineers are covered by these Canons, we find this one area in broadcast employment in which professionalism does already exist. It might serve as a useful starting point for similar codes in other departments of broadcasting, leading eventually, one would hope, to an over-all code, departmentalized as needed for specialized areas.

Like broadcasting, engineering is divided into several sub-areas or fields. The sub-groupings of the American Society of Civil Engineers, the American Society of Mechanical Engineers, and the American Institute of Electrical Engineers, all of which are represented in the American Association of Engineers, illustrates how newsmen, writers, producers, announcers, and other personnel in broadcasting might be organized as "broadcasters" in an over-all umbrella structure for professional advancement of all broadcasting. All might well have their own standards, which no owner or manager could force them to violate, any more than licensed broadcast engineers may today be forced to do certain things forbidden by their code or license, no matter what their boss orders them to do.

Like broadcasting, teaching has not yet reached the full status of a profession. Over one hundred years ago De Tocqueville spoke of teaching in the United States as an occupational group so open that "a multitude of people are constantly embracing it and abandoning it."

No group can be considered a true profession in which so large a number of practitioners leave and re-enter it each year, or practice it to earn pin-money as some wives and mothers do before marriage, between babies, or after raising a family. Since the turnover in broadcast staffs is even higher than in teaching and since salaries are now also generally lower, it would appear, however, that broadcasting has considerably farther to go than teaching, to achieve professionalism. At the college and university level, especially, solid gains in progress toward professionalization have been made.

Of the nation's half-million college and university teachers, a fairly large number belong to the American Association of University Professors (AAUP). In early April of 1966 the Association's Council approved a Statement on Professional Ethics which later that same month was adopted at the AAUP annual meeting in Atlanta, Georgia. A few quotations from this statement are relevant here because, unlike private practitioners in law and medicine, both teachers and broadcasters work for others.

> In the enforcement of ethical standards, the academic profession differs from those of law and medicine, whose associations act to assure the integrity of members engaged in private practice. In the academic profession the individual institution of higher learning provides this assurance and so should normally handle questions concerning propriety of conduct within its own framework by reference to a faculty group.

"The Association supports such local action," the Statement continues, but "stands ready . . . to inquire into complaints when local consideration is impossible or inappropriate."[9]

Several other provisions of this statement should be suitable for virtual adoption, as is, by newsmen. The professor's

> . . . primary responsibility to his subject is to seek and to state the truth as he sees it. . . . He practices intellectual honesty. . . . Although he observes the stated regulations of the institution (his employer), *provided they do not contravene academic freedom,* he maintains his right to criticize and to seek revision.[10]

What is most relevant about the AAUP, however, is that the national association, from time to time, "censures" the administration (or management) of member universities and colleges upon demonstrated proof of their having violated the academic or professional freedom and rights of individual members of the Association in the institution's employ. Unlike the situation in news broadcasting, a member of the AAUP has a large and powerful "professional" Association to turn to for defense if he is dismissed in violation of his contract, tenure, or academic freedom, or for other reasons comparable to those for which newsmen and other broadcast employees have often been summarily over-ruled, dismissed, or blacklisted. It would seem that newsmen and other groups may have to create and adopt similar structures and practices if their complaints of recent years are to be replaced by more effective measures. That sanctions or other organized forms of resistance by newsmen have not been more widely used, in view of the pressures to which they have been subjected, is surprising indeed.

The codes and standards of other groups also provide useful examples. Both the Mandatory Standards and the Obligations of Good Practice for architects, for example, illustrate specific approaches and statements of the type broadcasting would need to take if it were to professionalize itself. Others which might be consulted are the Codes of the American Rabbinate, the Code of the Catholic Clergy, the Code of Ethics of the National Education Association, and standards developed for dentistry, veterinary medicine, and theology.

There have been many claims that public relations is an occupation in which the practitioners will do anything for money. And there may be some justification for this opinion. There are many members of this group, however, who realize the need to correct this situation. Their efforts deserve note here.

The Code of the Public Relations Society of America, adopted in 1959 and amended in 1963, also contrasts markedly and favorably with the Code of the National Association of Broadcasters. Members *"shall"* observe, disclose, etc. and "shall not" rather than "should not" do certain things. Such examples suggest what the broadcast industry might develop, fairly specifically, to replace the present radio and television codes. The terminology of the radio and TV codes of the NAB clearly and uniquely illustrates unenforceably weak, ambiguous, evasive, and permissive language.

A distinguished jurist and attorney, acquainted with real professional codes, FCC Commissioner Lee Loevinger, in October 1966 told regional NAB conferences in both Dallas and Denver of his skepticism regarding broadcasting's claimed professional status. He urged that "The Radio and TV codes should be scrapped and new ones written which set forth truly professional standards."[11]

Even a fairly casual glance at the Television Code of the NAB (and the language of the Radio Code is similar) illustrates the reason for Judge Loevinger's remarks. The great majority of provisions begin with such words as: "The broadcaster should. . . ." Or such and such a practice "*should* be avoided." The language generally seems more permissive than restrictive. Rather than banning cigarette, toilet paper, or deodorant advertising, the code seems rather to tell operators how to carry such advertising and get by.

Where the words "shall" or "shall not" are used, they rarely seem to *prevent* the practice denounced. Such violations make a mockery of the code. Perhaps this is why such prohibitions are used so rarely, or are made so vague as to be ambiguous. Examples are: "The presentation of murder or revenge as a motive for murder shall not be presented as justifiable."[12] What is the meaning of this? Is revenge *not* the most used motive for most of the murders and attempted murders in Westerns and detective stories? Or are we merely "seeing things"?

"Drunkenness should never be presented as desirable or prevalent." In view of the frequency with which many characters make clear that "I really needed that drink," and the socially acceptable way in which drinking is presented, the same question might be in order.

"The use of horror for its own sake will be eliminated. . . ." As one of several hundred examples, it appears that ABC-TV *declined* to eliminate "horror for its own sake," as several NAB representatives labeled it, from various episodes of *The Untouchables*. It even denied NAB the right to preview these episodes. Since so many programs seem to contain such elements, what is the meaning or use of this provision?

> Advertising should offer a product or service on its own merits and refrain by identification or other means from discrediting, disparaging or unfairly attacking competitors. . . .

Except for razor blades, sleeping pills, bleaches, hair preparations, soaps and detergents, aspirin versus Anacin versus Bufferin, cold remedies, etc., etc., etc. perhaps?

> Stationary backdrops or properties in television presentations showing the sponsor's name or product, the name of his product, his trade-mark or slogan may be used only incidentally . . . "On camera shots" of such

materials should be fleeting, not too frequent [!] and mindful of the need of maintaining a proper program balance.

Does "just leaving it on" avoid the definition of "too frequent"? On news programs, especially, which already use up the full code quota allowed for length and frequency of commercials, how do we decide whether or not to complain about the additional ten minutes when the newscaster sits for his entire news presentation cramped behind cartons of Pepsi or under twenty-foot banners for Chevrolet?

In outdoor advertising do those who pay for billboard space not consider such visuals advertising? Do these code-displaying stations and newsmen really consider this professional or honorable behavior?

Products for the treatment of hemorrhoids and for use in connection with feminine hygiene are not acceptable (under the above-stated language).

The "above-stated language" refers to "particularly intimate products." How do you answer the question of university broadcasting students, looking forward hopefully to careers in this field, who, code in hand, find Preparation H advertised on powerful stations within an hour or two of the time when these stations proudly display the NAB Television Code Seal of Good Practice?*

Such would seem to be some of the reasons why the present NAB codes would have to be discarded, and new ones developed, before radio and television could expect their claims to professionalism to be taken seriously. A document so vaguely worded, so defensive, and so flagrantly violated, can hardly be seriously considered a real code of either ethics or practices. Certainly as a badge or banner of professionalism it is both flimsy and tattered.

The Code of Broadcast News Ethics of the Radio-Television News Directors Association, adopted January 2, 1966, goes about as far as any employee group can go, operating as it does under management which believes that nothing stronger or more specific than the NAB codes are needed. It excludes "sensationalism" as well as "undue use of sound and visual effects" and requires members to "avoid practices which would tend to interfere with the right of an individual to a fair trial." It is to be hoped that this fine group will be able to make such provisions "stick" against the all too frequent pressures of management and sales superiors. One respect in which this code represents a step in the needed direction is found in its frequent and insistent use

* The NAB Code now permits advertising Preparation H.

of "shall" and "shall not" as contrasted with the more permissive NAB code terminology as noted above.

In view of the number of years that newsmen and other groups have undergone blacklisting and have seen the last vestiges of professional standards and freedom crushed beneath purely commercial practices, it appears strange that they have not resisted more effectively and professionally. The recent network newsmen's strike, and questions raised at that time by Chet Huntley, suggest that this situation may be changing.

Would measures comparable to those of the AAUP, or other types of sanctions or organized resistance, not be effective? Might professional newsmen not decline to work for certain managements which, after documented review, are proved to have violated certain practices? Would such steps not be more effective, and more in line with progress toward professionalism, than most of the resolutions or codes so far developed? Are these codes not impossible of enforcement until the over-all (NAB) umbrella code establishes the professional environment and standards necessary for enforcement and survival of professionalism?

And before the all-important replacement of the present industry-management code takes place, some clarification of goals at various levels is necessary.

Robert Manning, representing the United States at the 1964 Strasbourg seminar, clearly stated the problem as it refers to the communications role of radio and television:

> . . . It is enough to say here that unless there prevails in journalism some central agreement on what is meant by "responsibility" of the mass communication media—responsibility of what sort, to whom and to what—there cannot be much precise agreement on the way that journalists can promote international understanding.[13]

Are peaceful or warlike values to be promoted? Is misunderstanding or understanding on a world-wide as well as a domestic scale to have priority? What is to be the extent, and nature, of the freedom of the professional from two equally unacceptable tyrants: business and government? Only after non-professional pressures limiting truth and freedom are definitely rendered impossible for broadcasting generally can effective *news* codes be assured of success. Then TV and radio newsmen in turn must make up *their* minds: are they to cover every fire, car accident, burglary, and murder, or must not other criteria of significance be adopted?

During the past several years Professor Alvin E. Austin of the University of North Dakota has collected and published most of the existing *Codes, Documents, and Declarations Affecting the Press*.[14] A number of these are useful in clarifying the function of the press in a democracy. In TV, with the all-engulfing environment and values which surround news, "docile masses" are, indeed, likely to be produced, if great care is not exercised. What kind of precautions will newsmen take? The duty to awaken, to satisfy the right to know, to recognize that the newsman or editor is essentially a social scientist, "as a physician is a medical scientist," to quote from the Code of the Colorado Press Association,[15] must be recognized and asserted if broadcast news is to be a profession. Truly effective safeguards against sales and management meddling, as well as government management, must be erected. Among the Seven Conditions to be Fulfilled, if freedom of the press is to be achieved, is the statement of Dr. Vincent Naeser of the *Berlingske Tidende* of Copenhagen that: "Guarantees must be created against government, political parties, proprietors and financiers meddling with the daily editorial work."[16] Broadcast newsmen, please copy! Two additional viewpoints on the sanctity and role of the journalist in broadcasting deserve quotation. Norman Swallow of the BBC has said:

> Television organisations should be careful to appoint the proper people as reporters and producers and then, having appointed them, allow them to get on with it.
> . . . I believe it would be a pity if the independence of the foreign correspondents of television were to be whittled away simply because distances have become meaningless and television executives increasingly powerful. The reporter is too valuable a part of television's public integrity for him to be demoted into a mere stooge.[17]

And France's Pierre Archambault told his colleagues at the Strasbourg seminar in 1964:

> . . . today's journalist fulfills the same function as the look-out of former times who was posted on a hill to scan the horizon and to signal—which is a means of informing—that an enemy tribe or a herd of wild beasts was appearing in the distance. I imagine that the job of look-out was not entrusted to just anyone, and that the man appointed had to

have, as well as certain qualities of observation and interpretation, an irreproachable character, making the tribe secure from betrayals. In the same way the journalist must have a permanent double preoccupation with truth and the general interest.[18]

Certainly, after nearly fifty years, broadcasting should be able to develop standards which will enable it to become a proud profession. Medicine, law, and the other professions provide specific services to the public. Broadcasting provides the equally indispensable service of communication. In each profession, vague generalities, and admonitions without rigid and sometimes painful enforcement provisions, have proved valueless. All genuine professions have established means for disciplining their own members for infractions of certain canons, without requiring government help. Broadcasting should be able to establish equally effective measures. The voluntary development of such standards, codes, and penalties would, in fact, go far toward lessening the need for government regulation. Only if voluntary steps are not taken by the industry itself, would there appear to be any need for having certain minimal standards of responsibility imposed by government, much as has been done in the food and drug businesses, in aviation, and in other transportation and industrial activities affected with the public interest.

Ads for newsmen in the trade press seem rarely to offer the salary or require the qualifications that will upgrade news as a profession. More often what is wanted is a disc jockey "who can also do news," or a newsman who is willing to do hard-sell commercials of all types. And this situation seems to be getting worse.

Many thoughtful newsmen, critics, and scholars have suggested steps for improvement. Some of the principal suggestions are:

1. Codes need to be developed and enforced. These would replace the present NAB Codes and expand and strengthen the Code of the Radio-Television News Directors Association to make it a thorough news and public affairs code. Recognition and observance of the latter, representing professional or academic freedom, would be one of the most important provisions of the former (the all-industry, management-level code). Another might be provision for the amount and kind of news and public affairs programming to be presented in prime time instead of at the "off hours" which are virtually the only times now available ex-

cept for occasional specials. However fine documentaries are, placing them on week-ends or in second-rate periods relegates news to an inferior position.

The news and public affairs code of the broadcast industry would need to include both a general over-all section, devoted to general principles and definitions, and several later chapters or sections devoted to specific problems such as covering trials, disasters, demonstrations, and so on.

The general section would need to examine the role of the news department. This would be aimed at freeing news departments from concern with programs in such fields as music, education, science, and other non-news areas.

Many broadcast systems, far less wealthy than our own, employ from several hundred to several thousand specialists in the various fields of human activity. These people are organized not under the news department but into music, art and architecture, drama, literature, and similar departments. The BBC, for example, and even the commercial TV companies in England, have their own full-scale natural history departments, on the assumption that producers or cameramen who are not trained in anthropology are not qualified to know what pictures to take. There are separate departments for music and other fields also. Once selected, these professional specialists, like newsmen, are left free to cover *their* fields, reporting and interpreting truth and developments, however palatable or unpalatable they may be to broadcast management, agencies, sponsors, or pressure groups. They must be protected in these freedoms just as doctors must be protected in their freedoms to practice their professions with no limitations except those of their own genius and ability.

2. Once the definitions and functions of news departments are spelled out, qualifications, responsibilities, and freedoms from interference would have to be spelled out and guaranteed. Consideration of the stages through which teachers and doctors have passed on their way to professional status, even though teachers

at all levels have not fully attained professionalism, should be useful in this connection.

Professionals, of course, traditionally were originally self-employed. The first teachers were individual tutors, like Socrates. The pressures of progress "organized" them into schools, and they now work for large and small institutions, as broadcasters and newsmen do. They sacrificed something, and there are still problems today. But academic freedom is growing, strengthened by such procedures as "censuring" administrations or employers for malpractices. And standards are fairly high and getting higher. Doctors and dentists, feeling the pressures of specialization, have also been affected. Many now work in clinics and hospitals. It would, however, be unthinkable for hospital or clinic directors or owners to tell them how much time they may have for given surgery, which cases they may accept, or how to do their jobs.

To spread the designation *newsmen* to cover people who do documentaries on music, the arts, education, or auto safety is as fatal to professionalism as including disc jockeys or sports announcers because they occasionally read a bulletin.

3. It must be recognized that news, like medicine or education, is too important to be entrusted to people without proper qualifications. Those who provide the news service the nation needs must be journalists with training and background in history, political science, economics, languages and culture, philosophy, and other "expensive" disciplines, and with the highest demonstrated standards of ethics, integrity, truthfulness, and autonomy. As the richest medium in the United States, television can well afford such people. The salaries paid and people employed for this service now are a disgrace. Good journalists, like seismologists, are *trained observers*. They are not merely men who have been given microphones or cameras. To deprive them of the right to interpret, by forcing them to report only the "facts," and not the meaning of the facts, deprives the nation of the unique contributions they should be making to national awareness and understanding. Norman Swallow notes the need to cor-

rect the present situation under which, all too often, newsmen are condemned to "handle news like eunuchs."

4. The general section of the News Code would also erect safeguards against such things as:
   —Staging events to liven up on-the-spot reporting, as has happened all too often.
   —Selection of materials for visual or shock value as opposed to significance.
   —*Firstness,* as opposed to caution and double-checking, to prevent the broadcasting of false reports, which have also, all too often, been part of the past record.
   —Overbalancing news in the direction of accidents and violence as opposed to peaceful developments such as research.
   —The use of warlike, violent, or inflammatory, stereotyped, pejorative language, so characteristic of American broadcasting and denounced by international bodies as conducive to diminishing peace and understanding.
   —The use of public relations releases as news.
   —Misapplying definitions of "objectivity." The careful balancing out and cancellation of one fact or bit of evidence by another today often results only in confusion and reduction of all such evidence to meaninglessness.

In general, provisions are needed to correct the present situation in which, all too often, badly arranged gluts of occurrences, reported without criteria, standards, understanding, or organization, merely clog the doors of perception and make what should be marvelous communication media not merely non-communicative but anti-communicative.

Following such general provisions should be specific sections, spelling out conditions of coverage of courtroom trials, hearings, disasters, etc.

A sample of one type of section or chapter that might be developed is suggested by the *Suggestions for Reporting of Civil Disorders,* distributed by Dr. Kenneth Harwood, formerly of the University of Southern California and now Dean of Communications at Temple University. The six suggestions, omitting the fuller explanations for reasons of space, are:

a. Avoid emphasizing stories on public tensions while the tensions of a particular incident are developing.

b. Public reports should not state exact location, intersection, street name or number, until authorities have sufficient personnel on hand to maintain control.

c. Immediate or direct reporting should minimize interpretation, eliminate airing of rumors, and avoid unverified statements.

d. Avoid the reporting of trivial incidents.

e. Because inexpert use of cameras, bright lights, or microphones may stir exhibitionism of some people, great care should be exercised by crews at scenes of public disorders. . . . Unmarked vehicles should be used for initial evaluation of events of this nature.

f. Cruising in an area of potential crisis may invite trouble. It is suggested that reporters make full use of the law enforcement headquarters nearest such an area until a newsworthy event occurs.

Similar sub-codes or sections for the covering of other events (war, natural disasters, fires, auto accidents, etc.) would also be desirable. But one of the most important steps is to recognize in the over-all industry code the need for special provisions, dispensations, and protections of the news and information functions of broadcasting.

However, professionalization requires more than the development of codes and penalties strong enough to serve as real deterrents. It also requires the development of certain traditions and practices. Professions depend upon accumulated bodies of specialized knowledge. Toward this end, broadcasters must develop programs of basic media and communications *research* as a prerequisite to meeting the conditions and practices which characterize a profession.

One of the cardinal rules of real research is that it cannot be mixed or combined with public relations. Wherever this occurs, the purity of research disappears. Research is intended to reveal; public relations is more often intended to conceal, revealing only selectively. Honest research frequently produces unexpected or distressing results. But it also is indispensable to survival, and to a profession. Broadcasting can no more exist without real research than medicine or science can.

Millions of dollars have been spent in the United States on research into "market" effects of the mass media. But little has been done to develop significant research by the broadcast industry into learning theory, and the many kinds of effects which broadcasting has on different kinds of individuals, under different circumstances. A great profession would conduct such research, and would develop information theorists who would guide operators of these media in their wisest and soundest uses.

Certainly the hit-and-miss and frequently irresponsible uses now being made of the broadcast media need to be replaced by more valid ones. New and better uses of these media need to be developed, guided by sound principles, empirically based, and tested by experimentation. Present research, dedicated to finding ways to by-pass man's rationality, in order to get him to buy what he does not really need, or to do what a manipulator would have him do, needs to be replaced by research into human and social impacts related to the nation's physical, mental, and emotional health. Broadcasting should help man find fulfillment in life, rather than merely create a desire for more and more material possessions.

Better criteria for the measurement of broadcasting effects need to be developed, so broadcasters may know how viewers and listeners are really affected by them, emotionally and subconsciously, rather than merely in their purchasing habits. How may better feedback be secured from the people of America, so broadcasters may capitalize on needs not now met, and latent cultural and educational tastes, waiting only to be awakened? Such are some of the problems to which a profession, as contrasted with a business, would devote research.

Another step is needed if broadcasting is to become a profession. That is the replacement of the sometimes cynical concept of these media—in which many of its managers will not allow their own children to view some of the objectionable programs—by an idealistic concept which would allow nothing for which one has no respect, oneself, to be broadcast. Financial profitability must not be allowed to justify any practice, however brutal or inhuman. Intellectual, spiritual, and democratic values must somehow be lifted to a point where they are again respected. One should no longer have to be defensive about being honest or idealistic.

Fashionable as it may be to speak only in terms of practical values, as broadcasters today normally do, a true profession has a moral quality. It must unashamedly recognize that altruistic services to the public and clients are not to be laughed at as soft, and that learning and intellectuals, and old-fashioned virtues, are to be respected. Without altruism, integrity, intellectual and artistic independence, self-discipline, the courage to resist outside pressures, dedication to worthwhile human rather than financial goals—admittedly all high-sounding qualities—there can be no great profession.

Habib Boulares, former Director-General of the Tunisian Radio and Television Network, has invited his colleagues in every land to help wipe out poverty, misery, war, and disease. In an impassioned appeal to journalists everywhere, he has said:

> If all information media devoted a part of their potentialities—immense, despite everything, it must be recognised—to knowledge of the world, to education in its broadest sense, perhaps in time we should reach the stage of raising bridges between peoples and communities, and of opening a sure way to understanding.

> . . . a little saving would be enough to banish hunger, epidemics and analphabetism from the world, if the money spent on armaments, and especially on research into new arms, were reduced.

> Would it be, despite everything, like believing in Santa Claus to say: journalists can be the missionaries of this hope?[19]

Another objective which broadcasting must achieve is the integrity and courage to stand for what is right, regardless of such (usually financial) outside pressures as the threat of boycott or other types of business "retaliation." Advertisers need television and radio at least as much as broadcasting needs advertisers. Just as broadcasters should not presume to tell the manufacturers of automobiles, soap, cigarettes, and other products and services how to conduct their business or profession, so broadcasting should achieve that status in which it will not yield to pressures from such groups to determine what *it* may not do, or may do, or how.

The claim that broadcasting is, or must be, primarily an entertainment medium, must be challenged. All such concepts and limitations on the freedom of broadcasting to develop as a separate and independent social force must be rejected if broadcasting is to be a profession, rather than a patchwork of incongruous and incompatible practices and standards, borrowed from public relations, mercantile traditions, and show business. The situation today, in which salesmen have been given a monopoly over some of the most powerful, dangerous, and yet magical instruments of our age, is incompatible with democracy. To attack these individuals for their mistakes, or shortcomings, however, is to fail to attack the problem at its roots. These men are not dishonest or malicious by business standards. They are only the wrong individuals, with the wrong standards and values, for managing such powerful and yet delicate instruments. These instruments should be entrusted only to professionals, who study their effects as carefully as new drug manufacturers are expected to test new drugs before putting them on the market.

If broadcasting is to achieve professionalism, its position on education and its relationship to it must also be altered. Not only must education's rights to frequencies, access to satellites, and so on be recognized, but broadcasting's lessons must somehow be made compatible with those of our nation's educational system.

In many ways, commercial broadcasting contradicts and subverts the lessons of education. Spending is taught rather than saving; waste rather than conservation; show people rather than scientists, educators, or artists are shown as heroes to be imitated; emotional rather than rational bases of decisions are urged; violence and do-it-yourself justice is shown as faster and frequently preferable to due process in solving problems. Must society not make sure that broadcasters *support* rather than undercut the efforts of education and our other public, social, and political institutions? What, in this sense, *is* operation in the public interest? Should it be any more permissible to ridicule education, educators, or intellectuals than it is for one company to ridicule or deprecate the products of another, which is frowned on in the NAB Codes?

At a time when our greatest weapon is not military defense, but strong universities, strong public schools, and pride in intellectual accomplishment, to have education ridiculed in the media or to have our educational system opposed by broadcast operators in its pressure for access to the electronic media is no more satisfactory than to have a second-rate national defense system. Broadcast leaders seem to have provided less real help for correcting this situation than one would hope.

In many countries there is greater respect for education, intellectuals, artists, and professionals, generally, than there is in the United States. Educators, doctors, editors, lawyers, sociologists, novelists, historians, and poets are frequently members of broadcasting control boards in Britain, Italy, Germany, Holland, France, Japan, and scores of other countries. Few such people are found at the council tables of RCA, NBC, CBS, and ABC. Many of the leaders in various broadcasting systems in many countries are former members of Parliament, linguists, or former statesmen or ambassadors. More such people need to be involved in policy-making in United States broadcasting in order to counterbalance sales and materialistic orientations, which have gotten out of hand.

The time is ripe for the creation by American broadcasters of an Academy of Broadcasting, devoted to the development of the kinds of basic research, training, personnel, and traditions of service that would make broadcasting great and noble and respected instead of merely popular and commercially effective.

Such a national center might well include among its functions the continuing examination of such problems as are listed above. For example, broadcast control structures in a democracy should be democratic instead of totalitarian. Rather than having a broadcasting service run by decisions from the top down, however often its managers may cite "what the people want" as the basis of their policy-making, the nation needs a service run by democratic *procedures,* in which the public and the various professions participate.

In his powerful study of the problems of the communications media in Great Britain, Raymond Williams has said:

> Where the means of communication cannot be personally owned, because of their expense and size, it is the duty of society to hold these means in trust for the actual contributors, who for all practical purposes will control their use.[20]

Great strides toward the establishment of professional standards can be made by publicly owned non-commercial stations which are already beginning to provide carefully designed job or position descriptions, with specified educational and other qualifications, de-emphasizing personality, which so completely over-rides qualification in commercial broadcasting. Progress toward the establishment of a profession of educational broadcasters has already been made in educational and instructional broadcasting as a result of the overlap with educational traditions and qualifications for staff and teaching positions. With educational broadcasting as an entering wedge, this tendency is beginning to be seen even in other countries. In its 1965 Report, the Canadian Committee on Broadcasting declared: ". . . For scholastic broadcasting it is essential for CBC educational staff to have academic and pedagogical qualifications."[21] Educational television recognizes that television is always teaching, whether it does so intentionally or wisely or not. The yardstick functions which public agencies, other professions, education, and government can provide in the establishment of a profession in this respect must not be overlooked.

Several years ago, a bill was introduced into the California legislature which would disbar from the practice of advertising anyone who helps to prepare or present false or deceptive advertising. The practice of advertising would be licensed, subject to the meeting of specified qualifications of education, experience, and demonstrated professional competence. The licensing and policing program would be administered by a six-member board of qualified advertising counselors. Although this approach has its dangers, it reveals the concern that is beginning to manifest itself. It also suggests some steps which may be taken, if the industry itself does not act soon. Similar efforts might be initiated by the broadcast industry, in cooperative efforts involving both management and newsmen, for example, before the public finds it necessary to take appropriate action through government.

Julian Huxley used to say that every individual in the modern world may have to recast his ideas once or more during his working life. The same could be said for institutions and professions. Surely when such organizations of journalists as Sigma Delta Chi declare that "freedom of information is currently at its lowest ebb in history," as it did through its Freedom of Information Committee in 1963, the need for a change in all the news media is obvious.

In informational broadcasting, which is the particular province of this book, concern is high. Speaking to his colleagues in the electronic media in 1961, Wilbur Elston, editor of the editorial page of the Minneapolis *Star and Tribune* declared:

> It seems to me that radio and TV cannot claim to be major news media until they have the quality and quantity of newsmen needed to report and edit the news and then are willing to devote sufficient time in their programming to their news reports. . . . I am not talking here about coverage of accidents and fires that get so much attention on television.[22]

As long as newsmen, artists, and writers are subject to the kinds of vetoes and censorship noted in earlier chapters, there will be no real professionalism in broadcasting. As long as newsmen accept and broadcast, as news, public relations handouts and advertising "plants," professionalism is out of the question. Surely the present situation, in which so-called professionals and professional standards are made subservient to financial, sales, public relations, and management considerations is professionally intolerable and dangerous in a democracy.

It is to be hoped that broadcasters will themselves develop the necessary procedures to correct the growing de-professionalization of all broadcasting, but especially in the news field. Such a step would greatly reduce the type of outside or government regulatory control likely to be needed. For institutions operated by high-level professionals, with proud traditions of integrity and public service, traditionally require little or no outside or governmental supervision.

NOTES

1. John Tebbel, "Journalism Education: Myth and Reality." *Saturday Review*, November 13, 1965, p. 95.
2. Edward W. Barrett, "It's High Time," *The Quill*, October 1965, p. 32.
3. Quoted from *Radio, Television and the Administration of Justice: A Documented Survey of Materials* by the Special Committee on Radio and Television of the Association of the Bar of the City of New York. (New York and London: Columbia University Press, 1965), p. 93.
4. Jean Bikanda, "International Fund for the Development of Mass Media," *Journalism* (University of Strasbourg), 22 (Fall 1964), 46.
5. *Ibid.*, p. 47.
6. Reported in National Association of Broadcasters, *Highlights,* October 24, 1966, p. 4.
7. Jack M. McLeod and Searle E. Hawley, Jr., "Professionalization Among Newsmen," 1965. (Copy kindly provided by the authors) (Mimeographed)
8. An excellent history of professional standards and codes of ethics, "Ethical Standards and Professional Conduct," edited by Dr. Benson Landis, and published as the January 1955 issue (Volume 297) of *The Annals of the American Academy of Political and Social Science* is highly recommended to broadcasters and public interested in this problem.
The author is indebted to this fine collection as well as to the executives of such groups as the Public Relations Society of America and the Radio-Television News Directors Association for providing copies of their codes and many of the historical and analytical facts used in this discussion.
9. "Statement on Professional Ethics," American Association of University Professors *Bulletin* (Autumn 1966), p. 290.
10 *Ibid.*, pp. 290-91.
11. NAB *Highlights,* October 24, 1966, p. 2.
12. All quotations are from *The Television Code,* National Association of Broadcasters, 11th ed., August, 1966.
13. *Journalism* (University of Strasbourg), 22 (Fall 1964), 14.
14. Alvin E. Austin, *Codes, Documents, Declarations Affecting the Press* (Department of Journalism, University of North Dakota, August 1964). (Mimeographed)
15. Cited in Austin, *op. cit.*, p. 4.
16. *Ibid.*, p. 35.
17. Norman Swallow, *Factual Television* (New York: Hastings House, 1966), pp. 108, 113.

18. Pierre Archambault, "A French Point of View," *Journalism* (University of Strasbourg), 22 (Fall 1964), 23-24.

19. Habib Boulares, "Introduction" (Keynote Address to Strasbourg Seminar), *Journalism* (University of Strasbourg), 22 (Fall 1964), 9.

20. Raymond Williams, *Britain in the Sixties: Communications.* (Baltimore; Penguin Books, 1962), p. 122.

21. *Report of the Committee on Broadcasting* (Ottawa, Canada: Queen's Printer, 1965), p. 280.

22. Wilbur Elston, "A Newspaperman Speaks to His Electronic Colleagues," *Static,* February 15, 1961, p. 3.

Index